TEARS OF RAGE

Southern Literary Studies
Fred Hobson, Series Editor

SHELLY BRIVIC

TEARS OF RAGE

The Racial Interface of
Modern American Fiction

FAULKNER

WRIGHT

PYNCHON

MORRISON

Louisiana State University Press)|(*Baton Rouge*

PUBLISHED BY LOUISIANA STATE UNIVERSITY PRESS
Copyright © 2008 by Louisiana State University Press
Manufactured in the United States of America
First printing

Designer: Michelle A. Neustrom
Typefaces: Trade Gothic, Arno Pro
Typesetter: J. Jarrett Engineering, Inc.
Printer and binder: Thomson-Shore, Inc.

LIBRARY OF CONGRESS CATALOGING-IN-PUBLICATION DATA

Brivic, Sheldon, 1943–
    Tears of rage : the racial interface of modern American fiction : Faulkner,
Wright, Pynchon, Morrison / Shelly Brivic.
       p. cm. — (Southern literary studies)
    Includes bibliographical references and index.
    ISBN 978-0-8071-3354-5 (cloth : alk. paper) 1. American fiction—20th
century—History and criticism. 2. Race in literature. 3. Literature and society—
United States—History—20th century. 4. Race relations in literature.
5. Identity (Philosophical concept) in literature. I. Title.
    PS374.R32B75 2008
    810.9'355—dc22

                               2008008712

The paper in this book meets the guidelines for permanence and durability of
the Committee on Production Guidelines for Book Longevity of the Council on
Library Resources. ♾

For Barbara, t.o.l.

CONTENTS

PREFACE

My first plans for this book were made in 1971, when I conceived it as a study of the literary treatment of the Third World. Early in the 1970s, I wrote articles for it on Wright, Borges, and Faulkner, the first two of which were published. Then I put the idea aside to concentrate on my main interest, James Joyce, but as the decades went by and I discovered Pynchon in the 1970s and Morrison in the 1980s, my thoughts often returned to this project as something I'd love to do. When I got to teach American literature courses, I felt better able to relate to my black students than I had with Joyce, and courses on the books I discuss here went well. On publishing my fourth book on Joyce in 1995, I decided to return to this project, and it has generally been my main focus since then. I believe that I have learned about it in almost all of the thirty-five years since the project was conceived.

Morrison takes two opposed positions in *Playing in the Dark*. On one hand, she argues that images that white Americans have of black ones are inevitably distorted by a set of stereotypes she calls "the Africanist persona" (5–8). She also realizes that blacks misunderstand whites, as we see, for example, when Sethe attacks Mr. Bodwin in *Beloved* (309). On the other hand, she sees it as imperative that the literary imagination reaches across boundaries in a "racialized society" to allow "response-ability" (xi): "for me, imagining is not merely looking or looking at; nor is it taking oneself intact into the other. It is, for the purposes of the work, *becoming*" (4; italics in original). The boundary that must be crossed here has to be racial, and Morrison examines whites. So it is impossible for people of one "race" to understand the other, yet the two "races" must get through to each other if there is to be progress. We have here what Lyotard calls a *differend* (dispute): for every significant intellectual point, there are always two opposed positions that cannot be reconciled. The two statements must be kept in mind at once, for only by realizing that it is impossible for me to understand the other side of "race" can I have a chance of approaching the difficulty of perceiving that side apart from my projection.

Another major point of Morrison's is less basic and more opinionated. In her book on white writers, the ones she finds of value are those who confront the race issue, while she condemns those who avoid it, regardless of whether they are liberal. For example, she writes, "No early American writer is more important to the concept of American Africanism than Poe" (32). Now, Poe was an awful racist, but he made a valuable contribution by mapping out racial fantasies so that we could see the structure of American civilization, including the psychic dependence of white people on black ones. The writers she finds most harmful are the ones who pretend that racism does not exist. Perhaps the core doctrine of racism is that there is no racism. Morrison says, "A criticism that needs to insist that literature is not only 'universal' but also 'race free' risks lobotomizing that literature . . ." (12). She also says, "The act of enforcing racelessness in literary discourse is itself a racial act" (46). Here we have another *differend,* for our aim should always be to eliminate "race," but not by pretending that it is not there. We must look this monstrous fantasm in its bloodshot eye.

One of my regrets is that I had no time to consider other minorities, such as Latinos, the largest one in America today. I console myself by imagining that if I can find some way to alleviate prejudice in one of its most appalling roots, my message may apply to its branches. I was involved in the civil rights movement in a modest way during the 1960s. Two important events of my undergrad years were indelible lectures by Herbert Aptheker and Malcolm X. As I get on in years, it makes me feel young to think of the incredible march toward freedom.

The three people who helped me most with this book were Barbara Brivic, Lynda Hill, and Carolyn Karcher. Others who were very helpful were David Bloom and Namorah Byrd. I also owe thanks to Joyce Joyce, Marc Schuster, David Bradley, Sue Wells, Shelley Fisher Fishkin, Leiza Brown, Patrick

McGee, Margo Crawford, Jane Tompkins, Robert Newman, Robert Caserio, Chip Delany, Suzanne Gauch, Jeremy Brivic, Roland Williams, Eliot White, Josh Lukin, Muffy Siegel, and Paula Robison. Miles Orvell and Frances Restuccia helped me to stick to my title. Joanne Stearns, who helped me with a number of points in the book, also indexed it.

I am grateful to Temple University for giving me a study leave to work on the project and another in which I finished this book and wrote most of one on Joyce. I thank *Novel* for permission to quote much of my 1974 article on Wright, which is considerably changed here. John Easterly of LSU Press has been an empathetic editor and Susan Brady was an outstanding copy editor.

ABBREVIATIONS

Full titles and bibliographic data are listed in Works Cited.

AA	William Faulkner, *Absalom, Absalom!*
B	Toni Morrison, *Beloved*
BE	Toni Morrison, *The Bluest Eye*
C&R	P. H. Coetzee and A.P.J. Roux, eds., *The African Philosophy Reader*
D	Jean François Lyotard, *The Differend*
GR	Thomas Pynchon, *Gravity's Rainbow*
HF	Mark Twain, *Huckleberry Finn*
LiA	William Faulkner, *Light in August*
MJ	Ishmael Reed, *Mumbo Jumbo*
NS	Richard Wright, *Native Son*
PD	Toni Morrison, *Playing in the Dark*
PE	Max Weber, *The Protestant Ethic and the Spirit of Capitalism*
PM	Jean François Lyotard, *The Postmodern Condition*
S&F	William Faulkner, *The Sound and the Fury*
SE	Sigmund Freud, *The Standard Edition*
SL	Thomas Pynchon, *Slow Learner*

TEARS OF RAGE

The Fictional Interface

CULTURE TO CULTURE

Most histories of the modern American novel have followed lines of development grounded in its European aspect, giving subordinate positions to African American authors—even when such studies were as concerned with racial issues as Leslie Fiedler's *Love and Death in the American Novel* (1960).[1] One exception is the chapter in Alfred Kazin's *Bright Book of Life* (1973) titled "The Absurd as Contemporary Style" (245–81). Here Kazin credits Ralph Ellison's *Invisible Man* (1952) with presenting a view of the irrationality of existence that is powerful because of Ellison's racial position as an outsider, and that influences absurdist writers such as William Burroughs and Thomas Pynchon.

More recently, black critics have worked to situate African American novelists within their own traditions. This is necessary to give these writers proper credit and to hear perceptively whatever voices they transform from Africa.[2] Neither African nor European culture passes into American literature without being Americanized, but African influences have to be seen beside the European ones, and this is one of my aims. American culture has been designed to valorize the civilizations of Europe and to denigrate those of Africa, and all Americans have been deprived by the negation of their African components.

I argue that most Americans combine black attitudes that tend to be turned against Eurocentric authority with white ones inclined to support the estab-

lished order. African Americans are usually oriented mainly toward the oppositional side, and European Americans toward the dominant one, so it is
practical to recognize people and discourse as mainly on one side or the other.
Many African Americans have conservative values, and they may be called
middle-class, with the likely implication that they tend to seem white. Similarly, whites who are rebellious may appear to have African American sympathies. Moreover, it is possible to see a black writer moving toward the white
side, as Richard Wright did by cultivating French existentialism from 1947 to
1953—or to see a white one moving toward the black side, as Faulkner did
when he took up the "race" issue in the 1930s.[3]

The polarities of black and white are abstractions that rarely match actual
people fully. The "races" are sets of stereotypes that people share to varying
degrees, not terms that sum up what individuals are. Each American contains
more than one "race" in changing proportions. The mixing of such racial attitudes in everyone shows that these attitudes are partial patterns rather than
independent truths. While they are created by history rather than genes, they
are like the respiratory system and the circulatory one in that they cannot exist without each other. An individual's racial mix is changed continually by
factors such as local culture and social history. Yet the imaginary system of
racial abstractions operates tenaciously in our society, so they must be projected in reified form to see their powers both for destruction and for creative
exchange. The periods in which they fuse and black and white are indistinguishable should be enjoyed; but these fusions need to be seen in the double
context that feeds them. Thus we can comprehend the activity of fusion, and
beware of our tendency to evade its conflictive reality. Without these conflicts, we are immobilized in the ethnic dimension.

"Race" is a destructive delusion, but it may be more harmful to ignore it
than to confront it. Henry Louis Gates begins "Writing 'Race' and the Difference It Makes" by saying that the concept of "race" is dangerous because
it assumes that difference is natural when it is fictional ("Race" 4–5). But he
ends the fifth section of this essay by saying, "We must . . . analyze the ways
in which writing relates to race, how attitudes toward racial differences generate and structure literary texts by us *and* about us" (15). So racial difference
remains the object of his work, but he studies its operation critically, as a historical illusion. Even Paul Gilroy, in his forward-looking *Against Race: Imagining Political Culture beyond the Color Line* (2000), says that while scientists

increasingly see racial features as randomly distributed and not separable into groups, this "[s]adly" does not mean that "ideas of 'race' based upon immediate appearance have become instantly redundant, . . . residual" (21). He adds that glamorous images of African Americans that pervade the media "do nothing to change the everyday forms of racial hierarchy" and feed "lack of confidence in the power of the body to hold the boundaries of racial difference in place" (22). This uncertainty "creates anxiety about the older racial hierarchies" and "requires us to forget the political movement" behind the assertion of blackness (22). So "new hatreds are created not by the ruthless enforcement of stable racial categories but from a disturbing inability to maintain them" (22). This suggests that the best way to diminish the significance of "race" is not to pretend that it is not there, but to attend carefully to its effects: exposing stereotypes and their social causality may be the best way to undermine them.

Of value here are the views set forth in *Critical Race Theory* (1995). The editors—Kimberle Crenshaw and three other lawyers—argue that the equation of racism with awareness of "race" has been used to construe racial consciousness in African Americans as racism. The notion that the oppressed are engaging in racism results in "exclusion of virtually the entire domain of progressive thinking about race within colored communities" (xiv). At the same time, the legal definition of racism may be limited to definite decisions to exclude people of color, so that the de facto segregation of schools, jobs, and housing would not be detectable. Therefore it "would remain the same. Having rejected race-consciousness in toto, there was no conceptual basis . . . to identify the cultural and ethnic character of mainstream American institutions; they were thus deemed to be racially and culturally neutral" (Crenshaw et al. xvi). The power of this formation to protect actual racial privilege is invulnerable because it is invisible. To see institutions as neutral is to conceal their white foundations, and denying racial consciousness is so germane to the dominant system that from some excluded black points of view, it is the bulwark of the system.

On the other hand, the danger of focusing on cultural differences at the expense of political practice is developed in Madhu Dubey's *Signs and Cities: Black Literary Postmodernism* (2003). She claims that the promotion of black culture enshrines sociopathic features of an "underclass" instead of attending to how such differences are aggravated by government policies favoring business over the poor (8–12). Dubey may lean too much on views of black culture as a pathology created by deprivation, undermining its ability to counteract the dominant white structure. She critiques the authenticity of the black cultural heritage in the light of postmodern skepticism (76). Awareness of the illusions and obstacles in the transmission of African culture can help us to define how it mixes into American hybridity. What appears among modern African Americans is not African culture, but a diaspora culture with African roots. Yet a critique that cuts off these African roots leaves only European elements active, eradicating black interaction.

My book will examine the interface between white and black cultures, seeing it as central to the development of the American novel throughout the century. I am less interested in tracing direct influences than in the ways in which writers on both sides partake of a system whereby each side shapes and activates the other. The racialization of society obliges individuals to take sides that correspond to their biological "race" to varying degrees at different times. The ethnic traditions that circulate among people must be studied in action in order to delineate the levels on which they combine. As Eric J. Sundquist puts it, "I would like to keep alive the necessary contradiction that the two traditions can be seen as both one and separate" (*To Wake* 22). Neither side should be obliterated, for the activity of both feeds the actuality of the mainstream.

I aim to present the history of the twentieth-century American novel as a continuous narrative dialogue between white and black voices.[4] This involves me in perplexities that intervene in contact between the two sides. For example, Morrison argues in *Playing in the Dark* that until recently, American fiction was understood to be addressed to white audiences (xii). So white writers were speaking to their people, while black ones had to address the other side. The steps necessary to promote communication, then, would include white writers gaining awareness of the kinds of thinking on the black side. African Americans, on the other hand, need to be less preoccupied with the white side and to speak more to themselves; thus they can contribute cultural positions of their own to generate dialogue.

For years, common assumptions ran against African Americans *having* cultural positions of their own, and ideological forces still work against those views. Yet I hope to demonstrate progress toward consciousness that is both American and African, and that has been of value to both "races." The influence of white writers on black ones, which has been obvious and extensive, is of less interest to me than the influence of African American writers on European American ones, which is newly emerging because it has been denied. Yet the active but neglected role of black language in shaping white modernism is examined by Michael North in *The Dialect of Modernism* (1994). American awareness of African-derived culture emerges increasingly during the last century among writers of both "races."

Homi K. Bhabha says, "it is the 'inter'—the cutting edge of translation and negotiation, the *in between* space—that carries the burden of the meaning of culture" (38). Thus active cultural development takes place in dialogic interplay between cultures. Such interplay may take place within an individual, who generally contains both sides. Each culture forms itself constantly by reaction to its other, and it is a chimera to posit any isolated culture prior to such reaction. Gilroy, speaking in *The Black Atlantic* of how African and European cultures interact, insists that it is unrealistic to imagine "fully formed and mutually exclusive cultural communities" (7). But the hybridity of culture in America was recognized long ago by such African American thinkers as W.E.B. Du Bois and Zora Neale Hurston.

In "Characteristics of Negro Expression" (1934), Hurston envisions an African American civilization produced by social mixing. She defends her people here against the charge that they lack originality and can only imitate Europeans, a charge that results from the denial of African culture. Hurston's defense emphasizes that while the Negro "lives and moves in the midst of a white civilization, everything that he touches is re-interpreted for his own use" (*Sanctified* 58). Moreover, she realizes that white people imitate African Americans, and she uses the quintessential American art form of jazz to suggest how many folds of mimicry may combine: "Paul Whiteman is giving an imitation of a Negro orchestra making use of white-invented musical instruments in a Negro way. Thus has arisen a new art . . . , and thus has our so-called civilization come. The exchange and re-exchange of ideas between groups" (59). Eric Lott describes a parallel layering for Elvis Presley: "his hair pomaded in imitation of blacks' putative imitation of whites" ("White Like Me," in Kaplan and Pease 484). In these cases of multiplied levels, no original with integrity can be recovered, only an interplay. And Hurston implies that imperial cultural dominance may be such that the subordinate group must express itself by reinterpreting material from the dominant one.

Yet African American interpretation of European material admixes something based on African input. And the difficulty of recovering what is really black or African in American culture sent Hurston on an anthropological quest to disinter buried levels of folk consciousness. She vivified African elements in African American life in such nonfiction works as *Mules and Men* and *The Sanctified Church,* celebrating voodoo conjurers and modified African divinities such as "High John de Conquer" (*Sanctified* 69–78). As Lerone Bennett Jr. says in *Before the Mayflower,* "the slaves reinterpreted white patterns, weaving a whole new universe around biblical images and giving a new meaning and new dimension to Christianity" (99) as part of "a complex world view that included spirits that were not visible to white Christians" (102). It is mainly because black Americans combine African elements with European ones that Hurston can say that they transform whatever they touch. Moreover, the Africanization of European culture greatly influenced white people, so that when Hurston refers to "our so-called civilization" above, she means not just a Negro one (which would not be called "civilization" in the racist context of her time), but a biracial American one. Out of a shared body of material that is interpreted in different ways by the two "races," a new civilization has been built that consists of continuing exchange. Hurston here prefigures the decentering effects of deconstruction in seeing that a culture cannot exist outside interchange with its other, and she mentions too that it is virtually impossible to recover the true original. She is able to prefigure Derrida here partly because she picked up Nietzschean ideas at Barnard (Plant 52–60), but mainly because she has the viewpoint of those who are excluded. The most advanced thinkers of the West and the most rebellious of the colonized world meet at this focus on the limits of the Western effort to unite all thought in a synthesis of linear rationality.

I will delineate the interaction described by Hurston and Bhabha by going back and forth from examining European American novels to examining African American ones—from Faulkner's *Absalom, Absalom!* (1936) to Richard Wright's *Native Son* (1940) to Thomas Pynchon's *V.* (1963) to Toni Morrison's *Beloved* (1987). Each of these works expresses a transformation in American fiction: Faulkner's modernism, the social activism of the 1930s in Wright, Pynchon's postmodernism, and Morrison's multiculturalism. I argue that as we move from each of these works to the next, the conception of liberation for minorities grows more advanced, the language shifts from Standard English toward Black English, and the philosophical outlook grows increasingly non-Western. My alternation of perspectives with these books will follow the footprints of a cultural progression that moves through both sides, though in different forms.

This back-and-forth organization is similar to that of Sundquist's monumental *To Wake the Nations: Race in the Making of American Literature* (1993). But while Sundquist develops a wide-ranging historical survey, I concentrate on four of the most important American novels of the century, and read them as following the displacements of a cultural opposition. Sundquist's account leaves off in 1930, and my focus on a more recent period may be one reason why I tend to see more active conflict between the two sides. Such conflict may be productive. Ultimately, I will show that the interface between these novels shifts from side to side while striding ahead toward the two-sided goal of racial justice. As it does so, it unfolds a new vision of American reality and consciousness.

Phillip M. Weinstein's *What Else But Love? The Ordeal of Race in Faulkner and Morrison* (1996) is incisive on the perspective each race has of the other (161–66, 179–83); yet it does not say much about interchange between the positions of the two authors he treats, and it may underestimate the revolutionary impulses in Faulkner. A similar limitation is found in Patricia McKee's *Producing American Races: Henry James, William Faulkner, Toni Morrison* (1999). McKee perceptively maps out cultural constellations in which her authors are suspended, arguing that white culture is visual, while black culture is aural; but she sees Faulkner as devoted to reproducing white values, so she does not notice the force of dark rebellion in his works. Nor does she recognize his attack on the basis of white southern society, which Edouard Glissant defines sharply in *Faulkner, Mississippi* (20–21). Cyrus R. K. Patell, in *Negative Liberties: Morrison, Pynchon, and the Problem of Liberal Ideology* (2001), sees philosophical parallels in the views of two novelists who insistently critique the tradition of American liberal individualism. He shows a common cause between Morrison and Pynchon, yet many criticisms that he indicates appear already in Faulkner and Wright, in the pathological individualisms of Thomas Sutpen and Bigger Thomas.

My perspective is that fictional texts by white or black authors that consider the range of social realities in twentieth-century America are always addressed both to white audiences and to black ones, though many levels of this speech have been submerged—in particular, the addresses of texts by both black and white writers to black readers. Virtually every significant sentence of all of these works may be read on a white level and a black one. And the ways in which the two levels interact in each sentence are parallel to ways in which black and white cultures interact within the work. No racial identity ever exists except as a dialogue with its opposite. In this dialogue, incomprehensible communication, being unclear but significant, suggests the other side, enabling those who hear it to loosen their frames of reference, an operation shared by both "races." The interaction of racial constructions should allow one side to be translated into the other, but a translator must know both languages. And because the white system has dominated the black one, the black side must be revealed. To distinguish the two sides is difficult because they continually change and slide into each other. It is also dangerous because Americans have often tended to see differing linguistic systems as naturally or biologically defined, when in fact they are constituted by historical situations.

What we need may be a theory that sees cultural systems as arbitrary linguistic patterns produced by circumstances. Such a theory would focus on the points of maximum difference between linguistic systems where the greatest possibility of beneficial transformation appears as an urgent need shaped by the difference between cultures. This translation is made possible by an awareness that one is in neither one culture nor the other, but between them. The functioning of such a suspension is defined by the sharpness of one's awareness of differences between racial codes.

THE *DIFFEREND*

To delineate the conflictual interplay between the two cultures, I'll move from an anecdote to a theory. In 1962, as a student in New York City, I attended a lecture by Malcolm X, who declared that slavery had never really been abolished in the United States. I reacted with shock and thought that X was exaggerating the problem, was unrealistic to ignore advances that had been made by what I then called Negroes. Yet on another level, I suspected a deep truth in what he was saying, that he was right to claim to speak for the way most black people really felt. In succeeding decades, the validity of his statement grew on me. Though progress was made in civil rights, it brought to light the original calamity and its reverberations. A century after emancipation, the horror of slavery and its aftermath had not been confronted so as to bring closure to a cultural and political bondage that afflicted all Americans. Now I write to show that the greatest works of our modern fiction have advanced this confrontation; and that it has revealed new ways to constitute reality while relieving the bondage by revealing its concealment.

X was communicating through anger, a mode that may be unclear and have delayed effects, but can say a lot to illuminate the distance between his viewpoint and mine. There is a theory to describe the operation of such distance as what Jean François Lyotard calls the *differend* (difference, quarrel, dispute): "The differend is the unstable state and instant of language wherein something which must be able to be put into phrases cannot yet be. This state includes silence, which is a negative phrase, but it also calls upon phrases which are in principle possible. This state is signaled by what one ordinarily calls a feeling: 'One cannot find the words,' etc." (*D* 13). X's terms confronted me with incomprehension and doubt that would later speak differently as the margin between us shifted in his direction. At the *differend,* phrases are not possible at the moment, but there is an urgent demand that they become possible: "In the differend, something 'asks' to be put into phrases, and suffers from the wrong of not being able to be put into phrases right away" (13). This matches Morrison's claim that the writer seeks "the words to say it" (*PD* xiii).[5]

The *differend* is a space between two systems of language that points to what is beyond language. These systems keep shifting, but in America, they have often traditionally aligned themselves around language structures designated as white and powerful on one hand and others designated as black and excluded from power. The white code has usually been able to fix its names on things, but has been haunted by a doubt that it is founded on an illusion. This doubt has been shaped by the black vision, which is suffused with authenticity, but hounded by an inability—enforced by the white system—to make its words effective. Each side seeks reality outside its own language through conflict with the other. So the ultimate reality for each is beyond its own code, an illusion it projects on the Other.

Jacques Lacan refers to what is beyond language as the Real, "*that which has not yet been symbolized*" (Fink 25; italics in original).[6] I capitalize the *Real* to distinguish his term from the ordinary word *real.* We always try to reach the Real insofar as we aim to tell the real or objective truth, but we can never get beyond the misrepresentations framed by particular languages. Because the Real cannot appear in language, it can only be manifested when language turns inadequate. So one cannot live in the Real; instead, one lives over it by concealing it with language to form what one sees as reality. The *differend* expresses the Real as the creative conflict that makes one think of a new phrase, the onset of the awareness of the inadequacy of one's language. It is both terrible and beautiful, what Yeats, in "Easter 1916," calls "a terrible beauty." Thus the clash of black and white meanings betokens a new order that will result from both.

The racial construct operates in such a way that white language typically fails because the established forms it systematically controls leave out physical or psychic reality. Black language tends to be in touch with omitted reality, but has difficulty developing a consistent system because it lacks the power to claim totality. The division of the two cultures as systematic and particular respectively, or monistic and pluralistic, defines why one cannot exist without the other, why all Americans combine both—though the racial situation usually conditions a person to emphasize one side or the other.

McKee resists the current tendency to deny characteristics of "racial and cultural identity" so that "the power and reach" of black and white culture are obliterated (3). While there is a danger that the predisposed will see ethnic patterns of perception as inherent no matter how one insists that they are historically constructed, there is also a danger in pretending that there are no differences in thinking between racial orientations. For this drags us back into the tradition of a single, universal way of seeing things. *Uni-versal* means "turned one way," and this mentality, which Lyotard calls totalitarian, has invariably been posited as white. Of course, reality has actually been mixed, but the only way to recognize its heterogeneous elements is to focus on difference. Patell critiques the deceptive American idea of universal liberty that has only applied in practice to white males with property, and at times he parallels Malcolm X: "At the turn of the twenty-first century, the ostensible universality of the nation's founding principles serves to prolong the nation's inability to recover fully from the evils of slavery" (25).

The racial system must be seen as an abstract code that classifies people without fitting them—but it must be *seen* to alleviate it. McKee says that whites project a field of representations that are abstract and interchangeable, and that this visual field constructs European Americans as subjects and African Americans as objects, whites as abstract and blacks as concrete (4–6).

Most people escape this system much of the time, but it surrounds them with language. To adopt terms from Lyotard for the racial system, white language, in claiming expertise, features cognitive (knowing) phrases, while black language features ostensive (showing) ones. Each kind of phrase needs to be validated by the other to claim reality, for any presentation of reality includes both cognitive and ostensive phrases. In "there is a blue flower," the cognitive phrases use categorical definitions, such as "blue is a range of wave lengths," or "flower is a kind of organism." The ostensive phrase presents the example: "Here it is." To have reality, a category must be presented as an example, and the example must fit the category (*D* 29, 41). Yet the two kinds of phrases are not commensurate, and can only join in a term that contradicts itself: blue is both there (as a particular color) and not there (as the concept of blue outside any specific color). The latter corresponds to abstract visualizations that McKee sees whites projecting to make up the field of whiteness (4–6). The idea of a reality that combines both opposed registers ("that blue flower"), which we depend on, can never stop contravening itself (*D* 42–43). It is a reality that exists only through the sufferance and credence of each other side.

Gates, in speaking of the confrontation between "two parallel" white and black "discursive universes," emphasizes different modes of signification (*Signifying* 45): in the standard white mode, a signifier or word is linked to a definite signified equal to a concept. But in black Signification (capitalized as a different process), the signifier is linked to a rhetorical structure derived from African modes of interpretation (48–49). His focus on rhetoric indicates that the ostensive mode is far from simple. Rather than presenting cognitive material as fact, it raises the question of how the "fact" (meaning "made") is fabricated, a question that extends into different registers of language and society and their complex interplay.

Gates's account of ethnic ways of thinking is, like some of my formulations, subject to the charge of essentialism. If this term means that people are born with the values of their group, I oppose it completely. But I reject the use of *essentialism* to condemn any indication that people can think in ways that are not European. Edward W. Said is right to critique Orientalism for its "absolute demarcation between East and West" (39). Yet this denial of essentialism may work better for Asians—who are supposed to be steeped in traditional ways—than for African Americans, who have had their culture suppressed. If black people have had a hostile culture imposed on them, then the

recovery of their own ways of thinking can serve to liberate them from identity formations that condemn them as a group. The most absolute essentialism is the assumption that the white order is not essentialist because it is objectively true. So a user of European logic has no construction imposed on
him: he is merely observing reality. But any thinking that does not follow European rules is essentialist or a false order imposed on people who should be
seen objectively as thinking logically, like white people, in European ways.[7]

Dwight A. McBride, in "Speaking the Unspeakable: On Toni Morrison, African American Intellectuals, and the Uses of Essentialist Rhetoric"
(1993), claims that Morrison's essay "Unspeakable Thoughts Unspoken" uses
essentialism—and that such use is problematic, but necessary. McBride grants
that essentialist labels such as "the black community" deny heterogeneity
and promote stereotypes (139). But he sees Morrison as justified in using the
first-person plural to speak of black experience because human suffering is
involved. If African Americans cannot speak of themselves as a group, they
cannot testify against injustices. Therefore "a strategic essentialism becomes
an almost indispensable tool" (150) in the struggle against the pretense that
there is no racism. And if essentialism must be used, it should be handled so
as to make its illusory construction obvious.

My analysis shows the artificiality of essentialism because the language
patterns that I distinguish cannot be exclusive to a group. Everyone abounds
with both cognitive and ostensive phrases, so it will not be easy to show that
the two categories express social positions claimed by two ethnic configurations. Yet I can indicate how the concentration of language at either extreme tends to characterize each group. European Americans, insofar as they
hold authority, cultivate the cognitive activity of making precise distinctions
among categories, and a word for prejudice is *discrimination.* The main device
for making precise distinctions in our day is the computer, and the disparity
between the percentages of whites and of minorities who are wired grew rap-
idly during the 1990s.[8]

The appropriateness of the ostensive mode to African Americans may be
expressed by the phrase "telling it like it is." This means using words to fit what
is actually there rather than using them correctly: the word *like* is intentionally misused to signify that correct usage falsifies the actuality that Black English claims. In *Native Son,* the white Jan Erlone tries to capture the black ostensive: "'You got something there,' Jan said, looking at Bigger, 'Did I get that

right, Bigger?'" (*NS* 73). Here "something" works as a signifier without a signified.

Jan presents an example of a line addressed to both "races" on different levels. It allows black readers to be amused at white imitators, and allows white supporters of Negroes to see how foolish their appropriative effort can seem to African Americans. It is ironic and pathetic, for Jan is an offensive fool in this context, particularly as he is seen by black readers, or by whites imagining their views. Yet readers of both "races" may well realize that Jan is an enlightened person trying to help, and he will eventually forgive terrible injuries that Bigger does to him. So readers may finally pity and admire Jan, and white ones may be inspired to follow his brave, progressive path. The levels addressed to the two ethnic groups multiply richly, as they do on most pages of these novels.

In contrast to Jan's line, language based on white principles tends to posit the signified without the signifier by defining things so clearly and correctly that the signifier is transparent. While Wright uses Jan to mock a stereotype, the connection of a word to what it means in Black English tends to be not as firm as it is in the King's, or Standard, English. The ability to attach signified to signifier is a function of the political power to make your word the law or science that rules. Legal or scientific language makes the word equal to the thing itself, primarily by imposing a fiat. In contrast, the position of "telling it like it is," which combines black culture and political protest, insists on the conflict between the signifier and the signified; and the creative function of changing categories or authorities is on the black side of the code. Black language is deconstructive in that it tells us by its parodic vigor that the ruling white language is a false construction.

Linguist Geneva Smitherman says, "Black Semantics is highly context-bound," that is, the meaning of a word in the "black lexicon" depends on its situation. She cites the word *bad,* which can mean not only its standard meaning, but "pretty" for a dress, "tough" about a man, telling the truth for Angela Davis, and so on (*Talkin* 59). Smitherman finds a source for this use of *bad* in a phrase of the Mandinka language of West Africa "which means, literally, 'it is good badly,' . . . so good that it's bad!" (*Black* 20). The change of the word's meaning by situation reflects the drive of African American discourse to insist on actuality as against the official framework or meaning. The ostensive impulse rearranges conventional perspectives and definitions so as to bring out an oppositional view of "where it's at": not where it's supposed to be, but where it's opposed to be.

The central reality in America tends to be suspended between black and white phrase universes, each defined or articulated by its anticipation of the other, its anxiety toward an opposed reality incomprehensible to it. The white system maintains an order designed to make everything comprehensible, while black discourse insists that it is denied comprehension, invisible. Both excluded realities, the comprehensive and the particular, are apprehended by Lacan's Real, which he describes in terms that resemble Lyotard's *differend* when he says that the Real is what anxiety (fear without a definite threat) is about. Anxiety is generated when there is something one cannot explain, something outside one's system. This is why Lacan says that "among all the signals, anxiety is the one which does not deceive" (*Anxiety* 142). So the anxiety each "race" feels for the other is a prime source of new truth. Slavoj Žižek, though he holds that the Real is on the side of fantasy, describes it as a "spectral traumatic event" that, in the words of Lacan, "doesn't stop . . . *not* being written" (*Fragile* 64, 67; Lacan, *Encore* 59).

In the history of "race" in America, the Real that cannot be expressed is what stirs anxiety from either other side. And the ultimate root generating anxiety, the worst aspect of the crime, is the injury of slavery and the submerged infection of its aftermath. This is true of both racial groups, but especially of African Americans. One of its worst features is the intensity with which it cannot be expressed. The most eloquent testimonies about slavery come from exceptions such as Olaudah Equiano, Frederick Douglass, and Harriet Ann Jacobs, who were much more successful than most in denying their legal status—they all escaped. Even they encountered levels beyond expression. Jacobs says, "as for the colored race, it needs an abler pen than mine to describe the extremity of their sufferings, the depth of their degradation" (798). Morrison's re-creation of the inner life of slavery in *Beloved* was motivated by a sense that the original witnesses could not bear to dwell on its psychological extremities (Taylor-Guthrie 247), and was a flight of genius over an abyss of history.[9] But if slavery is expressed better from a distance, this obstructs its being expressed accurately.

Christine van Boheemen-Saaf says of traumatic experiences that although they repeat themselves obsessively in thought, they cannot be remembered clearly because they were not really experienced. Traumatic events are by definition beyond what the mind can take in or express, and for this reason, van Boheemen-Saaf equates them with the Real (19–20). This pattern appears in *Beloved* when Sethe walks in a circle around a traumatic subject that she cannot identify (*B* 189). Van Boheemen-Saaf says that for the Irish, being forced to speak English was a traumatic "loss of a natural relationship to language" (2). Most African Americans do not even know *which* language was taken from them. Gurleen Grewal quotes Cathy Caruth, who says, "To be traumatized is precisely to be possessed by an image or event" (98). Therefore Africans who saw their American experiences in African terms as possession anticipated psychology. Their myths allowed them to see that their minds were invaded by an alien force that deprived them of self-possession, a language from elsewhere. Lyotard sees a *differend* as a loss of language, for it attempts to express a wrong, which is a damage "accompanied by the loss of the means to prove the damage." If the victim succeeds in testifying effectively, then it is merely a damage that can be litigated (*D* 5). This defines the imperative for expression.

The experience of slavery, however, is a negation of humanity that can never be expressed—only approached through reverberations and ghosts. Žižek speaks of "ghosts which are not to be simply dismissed as fantasmatic, since they haunt us on account of their very excessive, unbearable *reality*, like the holocaust" (*Fragile* 69). The novels that I treat move windingly closer to the inexpressible nightmare, approaching it within each book and between them in sequence. None of them portrays slavery in the present, but three of the four show it re-created by characters from later perspectives; and the fourth, *Native Son*, portrays a man who is legally supposed to be free, but whose mind is rarely under his control. Abdul R. JanMohamed sees him as bound to the psychological state of slavery (*Death-Bound* 77).

The stature of these novels suggests that racism was the main issue in American fiction from 1930 to 1990: Faulkner, Pynchon, and Morrison may be our greatest novelists of the century, and Wright's masterpiece is the novel that had the greatest impact on "race" relations since *Uncle Tom's Cabin*. The novels I treat are the best by all of these writers but Pynchon, whose *Gravity's Rainbow* is too vast to fit into the course I map out.

All of these books are witnesses finding words. By seeing the depth of injustice, we can measure the human potential that has been denied. When what could not be spoken is put into words, people can stop being ashamed of it and recognize it as a product of historical circumstances; and to see history in depth, it must be seen from both sides. Morrison's focus in *Playing in the Dark* on the effects of racism on its perpetrators (11–28) indicates that this disease afflicts racists as well as their victims. Moreover, by exploring what has been most completely denied, one can discover the most powerful source of new understanding, so the "race" issue turns out to be a great source of visionary creative innovation for our fiction.

HEARING DIFFERENCE

Of works by black writers who attacked racism before Faulkner did, such as Douglass, Du Bois, and Charles Chesnutt, the likeliest to influence him was probably Jean Toomer's novel *Cane* (1923). Sherwood Anderson was a mentor to Toomer in 1922 (*Cane* 148–50), and to Faulkner in 1925 (Blotner 400–418); and *Cane* was published by Boni and Liveright, Faulkner's publisher from 1925 to 1927. *Cane* portrays the terrifying effects of racism and lynching and the struggle of African Americans to find ways to assert their own culture and to resist oppression. Faulkner is not known to have read *Cane,* but I will later note a possible reference to it in *Absalom*.

Two writers admired by Faulkner who protested against the southern system were Theodore Dreiser and H. L. Mencken. In *Black Boy,* Wright tells how Mencken's denunciations of the South first inspired him to use words as weapons (293). Joseph Blotner's *Faulkner* repeatedly indicates that Faulkner thought highly of the radical Dreiser (500, 1056, 1313, 1351), whom Wright put at the top of American literature (Kinnamon and Fabre 163). On 13 November 1931, Faulkner wrote from New York to his wife, Estelle, that he seemed to be "the most important figure in American letters," for Dreiser and Mencken had arranged to see him (Blotner 737).

Dreiser's story "Nigger Jeff"—first published in 1901 and included, in 1918, in Dreiser's *Free and Other Stories* (published by Boni and Liveright)—is a horrified account of a lynching. Faulkner's knowledge of the evils of racism, however, must have come primarily from his life, and he could hardly have failed to notice evidence of many lynchings over the years. Joel Williamson reports in *William Faulkner and Southern History* that a lynching took place a thousand yards from where Faulkner lived when he was ten, the victim's bullet-riddled body having been left hanging naked from a telephone pole as a lesson (159). Such experience must have been behind the terrible castration in *Light in August* (1932), compared to which Dreiser's depiction is decorous.

Faulkner must have been struck by signs of black resistance through a series of discords in his relations with African Americans. In *The Sound and the Fury,* black people disturb Quentin Compson as he senses the unfairness of their lives. Between *Flags in the Dust* (published as *Sartoris* in January 1929) and *The Sound* (October 1929), there is a marked increase both in questioning the racist order and in modernist technique, suggesting that the technique served to question the order. Quentin remembers a black man on a mule whom he passed and felt impelled to give a quarter so as to feel at home by patronizing blackness (*S&F* 55–56). But Quentin noticed his dependence on the stereotype here, and had a sense of black people's "tolerance for white-folks' vagaries"—their irony toward the weaknesses whites exposed to them. Here Quentin enters the point of view of a black man to whom a white spontaneously offers enough money for five loaves of bread (*S&F* 80)—exposing guilt. Quentin links this scene to the ironic tone that a black man called the Deacon insisted on in exchanges with him (*S&F* 62–64). Quentin is haunted by uneasy intimations of a destabilizing reality behind the stereotype—a hidden racial dimension that emerges in *Absalom.* The realities Faulkner could sense under the surface in his youth, as well as the actual horrors he witnessed, planted the seeds for his implacable demolition of Jim Crow during the 1930s.

Walter Benn Michaels, in his influential *Our America* (1995), sees Quentin and Faulkner as supporting racism in that no one can escape from it in *The Sound and Fury;* but this ignores Faulkner's tragic opposition to the world of bigotry he portrays. When, for example, Quentin refers to America as "Land of the kike home of the wop" (*S&F* 79), he is not complaining that there are too many immigrants, as Michaels maintains (2–3). Here Quentin is with an appealing Italian child, and he is bitterly ironic about all of the prejudices in America, which are among the traditional views by which he feels trapped. Michaels sees Faulkner, Hemingway, and Fitzgerald as enthusiastic racists, whereas they were all trying to attack racism, with varying degrees of success. He sees Faulkner as supporting Jason's xenophobia and Fitzgerald as affirming Tom Buchanan's white supremacy in *The Great Gatsby* (7); yet most readers find Jason and Tom loathsome. If Faulkner were to approach Michaels's definition of nativism (quoted from John Higham) as "intense opposition to an internal minority" (2), he would be driven to eliminate African Americans. But Faulkner saw such Americans as central to his own culture, and he repeatedly insisted that they would outlast the white people (*S&F* 215; *AA* 302; *Go* 294). Michaels can imagine Faulkner's support for white power only by ignoring his blistering assault on racism in *Light in August, Absalom,* and *Go Down, Moses.*

Faulkner's attacks on racism helped to open up a literary space in which Wright could launch *Native Son* to expose the situation of the African American masses as an appalling, virtually incurable crisis, and as a paradigm of modern alienation. After this point, it became unreal for fifty years for intellectuals to conceive of American culture as a valid unity; so that the only tenable progressive positions became the opposing minority positions of postmodernism—a condition in which all groups are minorities and there is no possibility of finding a single correct position.[10] This plurality, now endangered by the threat of terrorism, has had the virtue of allowing oppressed groups to be heard.

During the 1950s, Ellison's *Invisible Man* presented a sophisticated and influential elaboration of the alienation that Wright had revealed.[11] And from 1959 to 1964, the affliction of racial injustice was the primary problem that alienated the young people, whose viewpoints received their greatest expression in the postmodern novels of Pynchon. Dubey speaks of "the enabling centrality of African-American culture and politics to the emergence of postmodernism" (19–20). Pynchon's deconstructions of Western reality decentered traditional authority so radically as to lay a negative foundation for the substantiality of a world outside the white one, as the 1960s led to Black Power. One of the writers who has given most substance to this world is Morrison. Her cultivation of the folk consciousness of her people raises spirits descended from Africa who speak for an alternative realm of psychic and cultural experience, a developing world of possibility that can revitalize Pynchon's exhausted world of control.

The African-influenced consciousness that has emerged in our literature since the 1960s may serve as a healing force, but insofar as such consciousness remains attached to Western racialism, it may promote splitting. The idea of Afrocentrism has great value in recovering Africana that has been suppressed, but is dangerous if it leads to black chauvinism. Molefi Kete Asante's *The Afrocentric Idea* strives to avoid intolerance in its thoughtful effort to posit "Africans as subjects rather than as objects," but it has limits related to its centripetal structure and its need to be "perfectly valid" (xiii).

In any case, a development that had passed through my other three novels is completed when Morrison embodies a new Africanized perception of American reality. I have touched on just a few of many lines of connection, but they sketch the continuity between these novels in a progressive revealing of concealed forces that work for and against racism—yet the books engage this continuous exposure from two different sides. Often where one gives, the other takes. Like parties around a *differend,* they speak incommensurable languages, and they can meet more accurately by realizing this.

The concentration on difference in language that separates racial constructions is upheld so insistently because there is no essential biological difference. Kwame Anthony Appiah, in his essay "Race," sums up the contemporary scientific conclusion that the term "race" does not refer to significant genetic differences between people (277). *Absalom* presents the argument that the reason the slavers insist so much on their dissimilarity to the slaves is that in the rough Mississippi of the 1840s, their lives are not really so different: "only in the surface matter of food and clothing and daily occupation any different from the negro slaves who supported them—the same sweat . . . ; the same pleasures" (*AA* 78). This does not mean that "race" is not important: history has given it a powerful role. White people may ignore it for the wrong reasons, to avoid guilt or to deny the underpinnings of privilege. Faulkner's observations on the similarities of whites and blacks overlook how African Americans have been forced to see the importance of "race." Awareness of how "race" has been imposed by history is a necessary step toward shedding its control in all four novels. Whether we are white or black, we must overcome the tendency, built into our perceptions through language, to see alternative models of knowledge as inferior, faulty versions of Western thinking. Only by doing so can we allow non-Western people sources of intellectual substance that do not consist of imitating Europeans, of partaking of a system designed to deny their consciousness.

INEQUALITY AND THE SHIFT

To be receptive to the movement of culture across the interface, we must sustain a two-sided perspective, and focus on how white and black cultural positions give each other existence. The term *symbiosis,* used by Gates (*Sig-*

nifying 50), may help to suggest how the two sides activate each other, provided that this interactivity is recognized as perhaps more conflictual than harmonious. When one side is oppressing the other, harmony may turn discordant. If two people stand in five feet of water, one standing on the other's shoulders, it is not fitting to say that they should both get along equally. In fact, from a point of view that includes the black perspective, there was from 1930 to 1990 a shift across the racial interface by which the main center of creative cultural activity passed from a European context toward a projected African or non-Western one. Bhabha suggests that the dislocations of modernism, its questioning of established truths, can be seen as serving a purpose by disintegrating the Western worldview in order to open up the perception of non-Western realities (31–39). These realities insist further in the irreparable disruptions of postmodernism. Patrick McGee says that narrative that ceases to reproduce the established order of value comes from "the Other, the intersubject, the true subject" (12). The intersubject is the true one because the subject can exist only as a relation to the Other. The foundation of racism is the claim that Western reality is independently true, while other outlooks are essentialist or invalid.

Traditional, Eurocentric definitions of modernism tend to indicate where it was coming from, whereas the multicultural view (which includes feminism) shows where it was headed. Conrad, for example, was a refined stylist who supported the British Empire while criticizing it; but he was also an outsider to Western Europe from the colonized Poland; and he developed by confronting African perspectives in *The Nigger of the Narcissus* (1897) and *Heart of Darkness* (1899) (North 37–58). The defamiliarizations of modernism jolt Western consciousness out of its established, authoritative, self-enclosed perspective. But then it has always been in keeping with the sharpest aspect of Western rationalism to question itself, and to do so by trying to understand the viewpoints of those outside the West.

In the history of fiction, one of the first important novels in English was *Oroonoko, or, The Royal Slave* (1688), by Aphra Behn. While this original version of the Noble Savage is often Eurocentric, it does portray with sympathy a rebellion of black slaves against their European masters. It has been called the most realistic novel up to its time (Day 48). Two other pioneering works in the use of realistic framework were Defoe's *Robinson Crusoe* (1719) and Swift's *Gulliver's Travels* (1726). To give their fantastic scenes verisimilitude, both writers calculate physical details on levels that were unprecedented in fiction. They summon realism to confront otherness, and like *Oroonoko,* they project voices from the Third World, suggesting that viewpoints outside Western mythology may have been crucial to the development of realism in the novel. Realism began as a critique of myth with Cervantes' *Don Quixote* (1615)—a satire of the abstract transcendence of Western chivalry from a country that had been under African control for centuries. In fact, Cervantes claims that the story of the Don follows a Moorish author, Cide Hamete Benegeli (67–68, 151; see Presberg 175–92). In the American novel, the focus on minorities is more pervasive than in Europe, as is shown by such nineteenth-century figures as Cooper, Melville, Stowe, and Twain. These writers discover the nature of America partly by seeing it reflected in American natives and African Americans. The two greatest American novelists who avoided writing about nonwhites, James and Wharton, ended up settling in Europe.

David Minter says in *A Cultural History of the American Novel* that a key feature of American modernism is "opening literature to new sounds . . . in the environment" (131). The first strong example of this pattern that he cites is Gertrude Stein's *Three Lives* (1909), most of which is taken up by its best section, "Melanctha: Each One as She May," a stereotyped but deeply imagined immersion in the life of a working-class black woman. North shows how Stein used dialect to develop modernism as an interplay of voices in "Melanctha" (70–75). Levels of influence may interlaminate, so Stein's dialect ends up playing a role in the development of African American fiction with Wright's first attempts to write a novel in 1928: "Under the influence of Stein's *Three Lives,* I spent hours and days pounding out disconnected sentences for the sheer love of words" (*Black Boy* 330). The discontinuity that Wright derives from "Melanctha" involves inability to resolve contradictions. For example, Jeff Campbell says of Melanctha Herbert, "I ain't got any way ever to find out if she is real and true now always to me" (Stein 413). Suspension in doubt, as the subaltern situation in the grip of forces that one cannot control, is a key to *Native Son.* Stein seemed to derive this uncertainty from observing black people.

Obviously, African American writers have addressed "race" issues, but most of the best white novelists in our century have also been seriously engaged with "race." Morrison discusses three works by Hemingway in *Playing:* "The Battler" (1924), *To Have and Have Not* (1937), and the posthumous *The*

Garden of Eden (1986).[12] Other writers are James Agee (*A Death in the Family,*
1957), Robert Penn Warren (*All The King's Men,* 1947), Saul Bellow (*Henderson the Rain King,* 1959), William Styron (*Confessions of Nat Turner,* 1967),
Joyce Carol Oates (*Because It Is Bitter and Because It Is My Heart,* 1990), and
Philip Roth (*The Human Stain,* 2000). Unfortunately, many fine writers have
exhibited racism. The end of book 1 of Fitzgerald's *Tender Is the Night* (1934)
can be read this way,[13] and the charge has been leveled at Thomas Wolfe (*Look
Homeward, Angel,* 1929).[14]

As the disturbing reflection of the West by its cultural Other grows more
acute with the decline of colonialism through the twentieth century, the voices
of the people on the other end are heard more and more. The novels that I
use are daring works that confront racial themes in strong terms, and even
create such terms. So they trace this trajectory away from the West with special force, yet they trace it from opposite sides. In many ways, white and black
Americans are on different sides of a mirror, so that even when both sides
agree on goals, the motive of each may reverse the other's. In the radical tradition that my four writers follow, both races can agree that social structures
or discourses based on racism should be criticized and dismantled, and possibilities for nonracist structures, developed. In such procedures, however,
white writers use critique on the framework that defines them as whites, while
black ones use it against a system that excludes them. And insofar as whites
aim at building a nonracist society, they step outside their privileged identities, possibly becoming what Norman Mailer called "White Negroes," and
increasing their alienation. On the other hand, African Americans who build
a social context free from racism are asserting their identities and decreasing
their alienation.

There are many variations, such as white or black people who are conservative or who do not want to identify with "races." Rarely does an individual fit a social category exactly, and African Americans increasingly claim
the right not to be limited to the "race" issue. Yet as Claudia Tate puts it, the
"race" line has not been eliminated: it has just been complicated (11). There is
a systematic antithesis whereby the moral imperatives of white people tend
to focus on deconstructing themselves, while those of black ones—who have
been denied their own subjecthood—tend toward self-construction. While
perceptive people on both sides may agree on what should be taken apart and

put together, they can understand each other better if they are aware of the submerged *differend* between their orientations. The deconstruction of the European American system feeds the construction of the African American one. The two actions are contained in the same displacement of traditional meaning as seen from different sides.

In *Playing,* Morrison refers to these internalized codes with opposed directions by contrasting herself with white writers: "My vulnerability would lie in romanticizing blackness rather than demonizing it; vilifying whiteness rather than reifying it" (*PD* xi). Positing blackness and whiteness as coherent systems of value and perception, she knows that she must be clear about what whiteness and blackness are if she is to stop her blackness from being swallowed by whiteness. She does not, however, see anyone's adherence to the "race" one belongs to as simply a matter of the self-interest of the group. Rather she sees the two ethnic configurations as intertwined. I call them configurations because they extend across groups, both being parts of every American. The statement sees Morrison engaged in a conflict: she is tempted to press her side, but this may make her vulnerable by weakening the truth of what she says. For defensive reasons alone, she has to see her white opposition as ongoing and intelligent, a vital part of her to which she must be fair. On the other side, white writers resist the temptation of self-interest by seeing the value of blackness, and they show vulnerability by demonizing it. They express generosity by attacking whiteness and weakness by extolling it. So if both races read the same phrase by, say, a white writer, the white reader would be kind to focus on the negative aspect of the phrase, while the black one would be unkind. Generosity and urbanity become possible once the two sides are clearly distinguished.

In this context, the same reaction to the same word has opposed meanings for the two readers. By perceiving through different linguistic systems, they see the same field as different fields. In Lyotard's terms, if two parties agree on the same phrase through opposed frames, the phrase is not the same: the *differend* is submerged in the underlying codes. Americans who agree that they want "equality" may be for or against affirmative action. Indeed, the same feelings or impulses have different charges on the two sides. Because the whites have been the oppressors, it may be noble for white people to be generous, but a weakness for black ones. Yet ongoing awareness of the other generates exceptions to the rule of self-interest. Morrison's quote strengthens her claim for her side by being generous. The *differend* allows her to say something new by considering both of the sides to which American discourse is addressed. ·

African Americans have been forced to speak with and against the white Other, and Gates examines their strategies for this interlanguage. Derived from African traditions, the techniques of Signifying use a series of tropes to play with words so as to undermine white language and transform it into black (*Signifying* 74–88). The usages of *bad* cited above are examples, and Gates signifies by spelling the term "Signifyin(g)." The blackness of such discourse lies in its displacement from Standard English, and Signifying runs through variations. Gates argues that blackness, as a signifier without a signified, derives its spiritual force from being excluded from definite meaning (233), and he traces the liberating power of the indefinable back to Africa. Gates derives the Signifying tradition from Esu Elegbara, a divine trickster of Yoruba mythology whose rituals spread from Africa to much of the Western hemisphere. As a mediator between gods and humans, Esu is concerned with interpretation and with language that works on two levels. He is a god of indeterminacy (*Signifying* 11), so the techniques of conflicting discourse that he provides may be used for criticism and analysis. By turning English into black discourse, Signifying has rebellious overtones, for as Gilroy observes, black "expressive culture" speaks for "emancipation" (*Black* 56–57). This god of ambiguity suggests levels on which African cultures may have intellectual advantages over European ones, as well as being situated in an ethically strong position of resistance. Gates recounts a Yoruba creation myth in which Esu, here called Edju, is told by Orungan as representative of the sixteen gods that he should gather sixteen palm nuts and learn their meaning if he wants to earn the goodwill of mankind. Then the monkeys tell him to "go round the world and ask for their meaning everywhere. You will hear sixteen sayings in each of the sixteen places" (*Signifying* 14). As a result of gathering these different interpretations, Edju wins favor with the gods and is able to convey their knowledge.

Here the greatest diversity of interpretation is the highest knowledge. In its recognition of the play of multiple meanings, this is a more advanced way of thinking than concurrent Western Enlightenment philosophies. I will return to the ways in which multiple deities encourage tolerance. From many African points of view, the transformation of European language into African

Signifying is an expansion into a wider, more complex system of interpretation. After centuries of seeing African culture as mumbo jumbo or gibberish, America has begun to move toward seeing its intellectual and cultural strengths, which we have been using all along. That there has been turmoil in parts of Africa, usually as a result of the effects of colonization, should not serve as an excuse to condemn African civilizations any more than the World Wars convict European ones. I will argue that the organization of Western languages is limiting and oppressive—and that African elements in Black English indicate important philosophical realizations that English is designed to exclude. All four of my novelists move toward such realization by making the voices of blackness heard.

Lyotard speaks of a point in Plato's *Laws* when a participant in the dialogue goes from listening to asking a question as a metalepsis, and cites Gérard Genette's definition of this term as the crossing of a "shifting but sacred frontier between two worlds, the world in which one tells, the world of which one tells" (*D* 25). The shift I am discussing is a metalepsis—the substitution of one figuration for another—by which the black world goes from being the world *of* which one tells to being the world *in* which one tells by playing an active role in our world. Gates says that metalepsis is only one figure involved in Signifying, but that as the reversing of tropes, it tends to stand for the whole range of signification as a process of change from one level to another (*Signifying* 52). This shift does not maintain a straight line: it may advance in some areas and retreat in others, but through this shift America has often been most creative. White writers have used black dialect to expand rebellious alternatives, while black ones have increasingly put excluded feelings into literary words that matter to America. Both sides extend the ambiguity of double consciousness.

Because African Americans are on the side of the unknown, movement toward them heads for what is new; and insofar as it aims at progress, or revealing what has been suppressed, the center of cultural gravity shifts toward the African orientation. So if the two linguistic systems were envisioned as interlocking circles, the overlapping area—a great part of the diagram—would be filled with conflict, including both hate and love; and the darker circle, initially smaller, would be growing, expanding the realm of the black Symbolic, or articulated language. Both "races" need to grow more aware of realities outside the white sphere, and in all four of my novelists, the growth of

the dark circle gives voice to the underprivileged, expressing the need for social change by bringing to life the consciousness that has been denied, a child
that has been lost.

THE LOST CHILD

Perhaps the most vital image of excluded alternative views of reality—and
of social injustice as the cutting off of possibilities—is that of the lost child.
All four of my novels focus on children who are cast out by their families or
the order of civilization, so these works follow the century's growing crisis
of neglected children. *Absalom* and *V.,* by Caucasians, take viewpoints that
are mainly within the social order that tends to exclude children who do not
meet standards of whiteness—children like Charles Bon, who is rejected by
his father, Thomas Sutpen, in *Absalom* because Bon's mother is partly black,
and *V.,* who seems to be cast off for not following Anglo-Saxon propriety.
The African American novels, however, *Native Son* and *Beloved,* are trans-
fixed by the viewpoints of the excluded children that their titles refer to. These
young people—turned by racism into spiritual orphans whose lives are over
before they are lived—dominate the books that they appear in, and references to dark outcast youngsters appear in other titles by Wright and Morrison, *Black Boy* and *Tar Baby.* Perhaps what bothered African Americans most
as the twentieth century ended was what bothered Baby Suggs after sixty
years of slavery in *Beloved:* losing children. Houston A. Baker Jr. says that the
nineteenth-century motif of the "daughter's departure" can still clarify our
situation today (*Workings* 19). The motif refers primarily to leaving the South
for the North, but it also refers to leaving one's family to make a new one. It
is like a child divorcing irresponsible parents, a rupture of family tradition
that abrogates the old order, starting a new one. The central figures of my first
three novels are divorced children: Thomas Sutpen, Henry Sutpen, Charles
Bon, Bigger Thomas, and V. all repudiate their families. Beloved is also sev-
ered from her family, and insofar as her motive is revenge, she is alienated
from Sethe.

Ultimately, images of the lost child can be illuminated by dividing the
novels by generations. In the first two, *Absalom* and *Native Son,* the lost children are sons, Charles Bon and Bigger Thomas. In the modernist framework
of these books, the son seeks a legitimacy that he can never attain because he
is black and the family is built on racist principles. The effort to carry on the

black heritage (which is based on Africa) is doomed and tragic. In the later novels, *V.* and *Beloved,* the lost child is a daughter who is recovered through another daughter: V. returns as Paola Maijstral, and Beloved returns as Denver. While the sons try to claim dominant identities, the surviving daughter stands for the passing on of a diaspora culture that is mixed and recessive, capable of working, but only indirectly. If the modernist family is an impossible certainty, the postmodern one is an uncertainty that is possible.

The lack of family stability that has often characterized American fiction may involve a sense of not feeling at home in America, and none of the novelists I focus on can accept the nation as parent. This politically orphaned state leads the white writers to project alienated pessimism and the black ones to seek synthetic families. For Wright, the projected family involves an idealistic conception combining Marxism, nationalism, and existentialism. For Morrison, it is a visionary family that draws its strength from African retentions—elements of African culture that survived the harrowing passage through slavery. His family is more politically efficacious, while hers is more humanly conceivable. Both reshape the problematic of family radically, and Dubey favors the assembly of postmodern familial groups out of discordant parts (65–68).

Both of these imaginary families are extensions of the impulse of black nationalism, the need of African Americans to develop a social structure of their own that will support them rather than destroying them. I will show that in both *Native Son* and *Beloved,* the acting out of the separatist impulse may lead toward reconciliation with America based on newfound self-respect. As Wright recognizes in "Blueprint for Negro Writing" (1937), the black separatist position is faulty, but necessary for an oppressed people. It must be kept in perspective as one area of life (*Reader* 42). Nationalism is not a substitute for democracy or socialism; it is rather something that democracy must allow to exist. In modern or postmodern American society, it should be clear that there is no one position that can encompass truth. No American has a singular cultural identity. Mikhail Bakhtin's dialogic principle indicates that modern man constantly shifts through a range of dialects and ideologies (*Dialogic* 295–300). We pass through different political and cultural positions every day. Nationalists believe that one is either one or the other and that the Other must be denied; yet the more they strive to eliminate the Other, the more it infects them, so that black nationalists may resemble white racists.

In *We Who Are Dark* (2005), Tommie Shelby presents an ideal version of black nationalism that would be free of identity because blacks would be bound together by a shared sense of injustice rather than ethnicity. The contradiction of a nationalism without nationalism may be no more impossible than the *differend,* and Shelby's miracle is worth aiming at insofar as it promises solidarity without essentialism. But Shelby asks black Americans to react to their oppression as white ones would, and at the end of the book he speaks of passing beyond nationalism into full democracy (255); so his program turns out to be one of assimilation. Shelby is a cogent thinker, and his amelioration of nationalism is sensible, but one problem is that he assumes that black people can give up their identities for a race-free discourse. There is no such language; they can turn only to a white racist language named after England. To move toward nonracist discourse, they must recover the African culture that was torn away from them by English culture. I show that serious steps toward this recovery have proceeded with the effective cooperation of both "races." So to use Shelby's logic, African Americans may be giving up more than they have to by accepting the position that African culture is not really needed (252).

Neither African American nor European American culture could approach its present form without the other to react against. Du Bois recognized that they have much to offer each other, and that it will serve the "ideals of the American republic . . . that some day on American soil two world-races may give to each other those characteristics both so sadly lack" (220). The mode of relation by which people can further this aim by feeding each other information takes place when people realize that they speak in several voices.[15] So multiculturalism, as the ability of people to recognize that each combines many cultures, is the cement that holds our society together. People who see conflicts between categories can avoid them by shifting to other levels that allow understanding. This shift between categories is promoted by double-consciousness, so it is linked to African Americans. Gates, developing Esu as a spirit of critical thought, sees him as a god of crossroads, the power to switch paths (*Signifying* 41–42).

Black double-consciousness is analogous to the American philosophy of pragmatism in combining different systems according to what works. Our idea of choosing between multiple possibilities was influenced by our cultural polyphony. In his essay "The One and the Many" (1907), William James questions whether the world can be put together as a unified system. Instead he argues for a pluralism that allows for "alternative universes" and the "free play of parts" (39–42). This resembles the earlier Yoruba system described by Gates. Of course, Du Bois' double-consciousness is imposed by history, while pragmatism emphasizes choice. Yet there is often a level on which Americans can choose between supporting the system or rebelling against it, though the choice is harder for the oppressed. Shelby's argument for "pragmatic" nationalism (28, 254) assumes that pragmatism is characteristic of black people because they have had to make choices without frameworks.

Among the possibilities to be considered for different situations, that of liberation for the oppressed has the advantage of leading to departure from the status quo. It is our best guide to the active part of what has been silenced. Whatever our ancestry, we tend to be black when we associate with resistance and white when we feel threatened by it. So while blackness can be forced on people, it can also involve choice. Steve Biko says, "Merely by describing yourself as black you have started on a road towards emancipation, you have committed yourself to fight against all forces that seek to use your blackness as a stamp that marks you out as a subservient being" (C&R 360). Suppression has made blackness a symbol of freedom, and here is the basis of the strength of Shelby's argument.

Yet it is a disturbing symbol for both "races." In *Native Son,* except for a walk-on figure named Jim (*NS* 250–52), every Negro is threatened by Bigger because they feel it is unsafe not to comply with the white order. Wright here asserts the black voice by pointing out how African Americans are controlled by the white one. Likewise, Morrison's Beloved, an African spirit of protest, is rejected by the black community of Cincinnati. The European codes that rule our society are partial and need to engage in exchange with what they exclude. Only if nonwhite voices are heard can such a dialogue take place, and this is the best way to prevent the breakup of the uneasy American family. Real coherence is promoted not by pretending that things are fine and no action is needed, but by striving for the toughest criticism of our situation. How the racial interface progresses will depend on history, but much indication of how it developed will be found in the novels I treat, all of which speak in multiple voices whose interchange breaks down racial distinctions. It may help to guide us toward right conclusions if we see how intensely the modern American novel, at its most insightful, has fought against the racial system.

Another polarity extends in the present: some evidence suggests that the situation of African Americans has improved considerably in the last half century—such as civil rights laws and the growth of the black middle class. Yet other evidence indicates that things are not better, such as the growth of hate groups and the increasing percentage of African Americans attached to the penal system.[16] Moreover, school segregation proliferated during the 1990s (Mezzacappa), and in June 2007 the Supreme Court declared the active integration of schools to be illegal on the basis of the principle that people should not be distinguished by "race." We're back to "separate but equal."

To focus on the evidence that racial problems have been solved would have conservative effects, whereas to focus on continuing difficulties will serve to promote change. Insofar as the racial situation is better, which is the prevalent outlook today, the novels that I examine present vital steps in a process of regeneration through growing awareness. Yet insofar as this situation is not better, the grievances of these books are still aimed at live targets. My feeling that it is morally safer to emphasize ongoing conflicts corresponds to the spirit that animates all of these novels. By insisting that the race problem is worse than people think, the books share a common vision that expands humanity. This vision of a new world beyond European conventions has the potential to transform reality in its basic principles in order to accomplish a re-formation that will not just substitute one version of domination for another.

1

Absalom, Absalom!
and the Tragedy of "Race"

THE FIELD OF BLOOD

Absalom, Absalom! and *Native Son* are racial tragedies—caused by the impossibility of "race." They are also, like *Hamlet,* about sons unable to claim their patrimony or controlling position in the social family. "Race" parallels patriarchy as an inheritance that warps human life by claiming an absolute identity that no one can fill. This can destroy one whether one is trapped by patrimony, like Thomas Sutpen, or excluded from it, like Bigger Thomas. The name of St. Thomas, the doubter of faith, is chosen for Sutpen, but attached to Bigger. Mr. Compson tells his son Quentin that they are talking about a time when people were "victims . . . who had the gift of loving once or dying once instead of being diffused and scattered" (*AA* 71). That is, while we now have many identities, nineteenth-century people could only have one "uncomplex" one, and this was their doom.

Absalom begins with a series of ominous, inexplicable mysteries, especially how Sutpen's children could be doomed from birth to destroy themselves. Other puzzles are posed, such as how Judith Sutpen could have been a widow without being a bride, but the children's self-destruction—referred to five times in chapter 1 (*AA* 5, 15, 17, 18, 19)—is the chief mystery. As James A. Snead points out, the information that is withheld throughout *Absalom* has as its "central reference point, the black" (118), so that once the racial truth is revealed at the end, the mysteries become explicable. Here Lyotard's *differend* leads to a darkness that has been excluded; but because the darkness continues to be denied, the novel's quest for truth has to lead to destruction. This darkness is linked to Africa because the negation of Africa is fundamental to the ruling white ideology.

Faulkner first wrote the Sutpen saga as the story "Evangeline" in 1931, but it was rejected and was published only posthumously.[1] While much of the story of Sutpen's children is presented in "Evangeline," Quentin Compson, who receives all of the narratives in *Absalom,* is not in this story told from the point of view of an unnamed, undistinguished white male first-person narrator. Faulkner decided to bring Quentin back to reverberate with the Sutpen story so as to focus on a deeper level of racial motivation behind Quentin's suicide.

In *The Sound and the Fury,* Quentin commits suicide mainly because of his obsession with his sister Candace's lost purity; but her purity is related to his sense of what his father, speaking about the high quality of his male line of descent, calls "racial superiority" (*S&F* 28). In fact, Quentin bitterly blames his sister for behaving "*like nigger women do in the pasture*" (*S&F* 59). So his disturbance at his sister's sexuality is parallel to his aching uneasiness at the shadowy presence of the African American, whom he recognizes as an "obverse reflection of the white people he lives among" (*S&F* 55).[2] Racism here colors all values.

In 1956, Faulkner told Jean Stein van den Heuvel that he first tried to tell the story of *The Sound and the Fury*—initially based on the image of Candace climbing a tree—from the point of view of her brother Benjy, but he felt that the story was not told, so he wrote it again from Quentin's viewpoint; yet it still was not told, so he tried again twice (*S&F* 233). It seems significant that the fourth attempt to tell the Compson story, the Dilsey section of "April 8, 1928," is told from the point of view of African Americans and is largely about them (*S&F* 165–99). In line with the metalepsis I discussed in the introduction, as we approach the truth of the Compson story, we enter a black world. *Absalom* continues the movement in this direction as a further attempt, or series of attempts, to tell the Compson story through Quentin. Here his story is more rooted in history than in the earlier novel so as to constitute a tragedy of the racial unconscious. The idea of social protest reaches more deeply into tragedy than is usually realized.

While comedy indicates that society may not be so bad by setting things right at the end, tragedy usually envisions society as terribly maladjusted by showing a noble hero destroyed. (S)he is always destroyed by the social order, though that order may change or appear as theology. Lacan sees *Antigone* as a turning point in the field of ethics because it questioned society's law (*Ethics* 243). Joyce Ann Joyce, in her book on *Native Son* as tragedy, derives from Richard B. Sewall a view of the tragic hero as involved in a struggle for the improvement of mankind (23).[3] Terry Eagleton describes tragedy as a revolutionary force that can represent "political hope" by focusing on who is responsible for suffering (*Sweet* 27–29). Therefore tragedy may be the strongest form for presenting social protest, and in *Native Son* and *Absalom,* tragedy is caused by "race."

Glissant points out that Faulkner's writings put the institution of southern society "at risk": "He questioned its very legitimacy, its original establishment" (21). Tragedy generally questions the legitimacy of the social order it presents: the *Oresteia* questions the justice of the gods, *Oedipus* questions the incest prohibition, and in *Hamlet,* the king is a criminal. But tragedy also reveals an elitist side by its links to tradition and by its hero's nobility or exaltation above ordinary humanity. Faulkner, whose greatest works are tragic, displays tragedy's ideological ambivalence. Having been raised in a world of extreme racism, he set about questioning racist ideology in *The Sound and the Fury* (1929), and tore it apart in *Light in August* (1932) and in *Absalom.* But his strenuous critique of the racism he grew up with could not yield a vision free from bias. So even while he dismembers racism, he slips into its assumptions, as when he grants more than human powers to Col. Sutpen, who can never be defeated until he is sixty and in despair. Yet Sutpen, the progenitor of a racist dynasty that destroys itself, is also a demon, and Faulkner's interior knowledge of white supremacy made his attack on it devastating.

Before turning to this attack, I will observe how the novel can reveal submerged racism even in its liberal gestures. We are told that Sutpen "never raised his voice" to his slaves: "instead he led them, caught them at the psychological instant by example, by some ascendancy of forbearance rather than by brute fear" (*AA* 27). Such claims lead Dirk Kuyk Jr. to say that among the uncertainties surrounding Sutpen, we cannot "be sure that he was exploiting Negroes" (102). Kuyk's point is valid in that it matches a Faulknerian intention. Yet the idea that by treating slaves well one does not exploit them is an extension of racism: it justifies slavery, kidnapping, terrorizing, and dehumanizing people. Being nice is a luxury in this system, which uses tokens of generosity to inspire itself. We should stay aware that while Sutpen's portrayal is designed to attack racism, the attraction of superiority still clings to him. In this respect he resembles Faulkner's America.

Tragedy delineates the human image for the culture it springs from, and Sutpen stands for a cultural complex that reaches deep into both southern and American civilizations. In strict historical terms, of course, he represents only a certain kind of landowner in a part of Mississippi in the mid-nineteenth century. The plantation owners worked quickly, with cotton tending to replace wilderness throughout the state, mostly in the single decade, the 1830s, in which Sutpen arrives (Parker 5). The chief distinction between Sutpen and the other Yoknapatawpha aristocrats, the Compsons and the Sartorises, is that Sutpen is an *arriviste*. Coming later and starting with less status, he has to be more ruthless, so he represents the cutting edge of white power. Morrison parallels him to William Dunbar, an actual plantation owner who exemplifies the "new white man" who attained unprecedented freedom and enlightenment by controlling slaves (*Playing* 40–45).

Sutpen's power clearly derives from his ability to subdue Africans, both in Haiti, where he gains his fortune by facing a mob of black rebels, and in Mississippi, where he uses slaves to build and work his plantation. His success rests on an ability to intuit African viewpoints that are outside of polite civilization. By 1840, African Americans formed a majority of the population of Mississippi. They were controlled best through the skill at which Sutpen is a virtuoso. In this system, the leaders can avoid racism, which need only be directly applied by poor whites. Faulkner reproduces this ideology by having Sutpen rule through bravery and nobility; yet Faulkner reveals evil behind this nobility. Through this system that separates the leader from ostensible bigotry, racism has been preserved in Mississippi and the United States. In fact, Sutpen is shown defying at some risk an early version of the Klan when they insist that he ride with them (*AA* 130): so he holds himself clear of the racism on which his fortune rests. Indeed, slavery on Sutpen's plantation is largely invisible. One reason is that Faulkner's ancestors were not planters, but businessmen. Col. William Falkner, the main model for Sutpen, had only a few slaves (Williamson 24). The brutal plantation world of field slaves and overseers never appears in *Absalom,* and such erasure is part of "the disease" that *Absalom* sees as maintaining its grip in the twentieth century (*AA* 7). While he needed to make Sutpen a lord of the land to attack the system,

Faulkner may also express a wish that his people had been big landowners, for he bought a plantation and liked to pose as an aristocrat.

Though Sutpen fits the local model most closely, his further extensions are powerful. Eagleton states that strict historicism may work against radical politics (*Sweet* xi), and in this case, historicism occludes the progressive value of the text, for Faulkner keeps indicating that Sutpen's world is the United States. For example, Quentin at Harvard during the twentieth century says that it took "*Sutpen to make all of us*" (*AA* 210). The strongest statement that Sutpen represents America appears in Hortense J. Spiller's "Who Cuts the Border," her contribution to her collection *Comparative American Identities* (13–16). It is easier to see Sutpen as long ago and far away than to accept Faulkner's insistence that he is disseminated all over America in a continuing now.

Sutpen as the South and America is divided by struggle against forces in himself that his civilization opposes, and the parts of himself that he denies appear in his children, especially the dark ones. Qualities that make Sutpen a leader in a society built on white male values also make him destroy his children. His main tragic analogue, Agamemnon, has to sacrifice his daughter Iphigenia in order to sail for Troy, and Faulkner implies that for thousands of years, the leader who wants to rise high will have to destroy his feminine side.

Warwick Wadlington's study of Faulknerian tragedy observes that while Sutpen is the main tragic figure in *Absalom,* his children, like Agamemnon's, are also tragic, including Charles Bon. Wadlington speaks of "this tragedy of the unrecognized, marginal son who must be purged" (180). In fact, Bon and his brother, Henry Sutpen, though less central than Thomas, may be the strongest tragic figures in *Absalom,* just as Brutus is the tragic hero of Shakespeare's *Julius Caesar.* Like Brutus, Sutpen's sons gain nobility by being idealistic. David Paul Ragan sees Quentin as *Absalom*'s tragic hero (15–18). The weakness of this view is that Quentin is largely a listener in *Absalom* and does not act.

The most complete tragic subject in the Sutpen story may well be a combination of Sutpen's two sons, repeatedly described as fused by "the heart and blood of youth" (*AA* 236). Their potential to join together in brotherhood is the noblest thing about them, and is precisely what is doomed by "race." Of these two, it is Bon who plays the leading role: he initiates the crisis by appearing in Henry's stabilized world, and he makes the final decision that destroys them. The only action that Henry can take is either to follow Bon or to give in to his father. The latter course that he chooses does not involve enough volition for tragedy.

The tragic hero is a sacrificial figure, and Bon fulfills this role far better than Sutpen. For while Sutpen's innocence generates some compassion for him, he remains remote and unpleasant, unable as he is to admit weakness. Thadious M. Davis says that Sutpen is not tragic but pathetic because he denies himself to imitate an unwholesome system (186). And because this system dehumanizes Sutpen, few readers are sorry for him when Wash Jones kills him. He is a little like Richard III, whose evil is so untragic that we are glad when he gets what he deserves. Sutpen's efforts to have sound motives are too spurious to be moving. In Bon's case, however, we feel his sensitivity and suffering when we read his poignant letter and more and more as we approach the end of the book. But if Bon is the real tragic hero of *Absalom,* his story springs from Sutpen's, so to encompass it we must first understand his father's fate.

Absalom's form—with its back-and-forth jumps in time and various levels of narrators whose stories span the continent from Canada to Haiti—yields swarms of indirect perspectives. Sutpen's story is thus rendered mythic: its distant, far-ranging abstraction leads us to see in it the soul of a culture, or group of cultures. As Faulkner said, Sutpen is so big that none of those who speak of him can see more than a part (Gwynn and Blotner 274). And while contradictions exist between various interpretations of the evidence, every speculation in the book contributes to the composite Sutpen myth. The cubist fragmentation of the novel, in fact, not only calls the basis of historical truth into question, but represents structurally a divided world of clashing realities separated by differences between value systems inherent in southern and American society.[4]

Judith Sutpen describes her world as an assemblage of people caught up in an incomprehensible tangle of motivations and connections: "having to, move your arms and legs with strings only the same strings are hitched to all the other arms and legs and the others all trying and they dont know why either except that the strings are all in one another's way like five or six people all trying to make a rug on the same loom only each wants to weave his own pattern" (*AA* 100–101). Judith recognizes a multiplicity of codes, each claiming to be exclusive. Opposed conceptions regulated by "race," gender, religion, and class cause the threads to impact against each other and snarl.

Faulkner starts the story of how this hurtful confusion was perpetrated with a version of the myth of the American Adam, the idea that the New World was free of the sins of the old one (R. Lewis 5). Sutpen, like Mississippi, went from wilderness to plantation within a decade. He was born in an area without clashing patterns, the wilds of what was to be West Virginia.[5] Here "he didn't even know there was a country all divided . . . with a people living on it all divided . . . because of what color their skins happened to be and what they happened to own" (*AA* 179). The last thirteen words show that Faulkner's critique of society during the 1930s joined race and class, bound together by the radicalism of this decade. Noel Polk reports that while it was rare for Faulkner to part with manuscripts of his mature work, he "donated" the manuscript of *Absalom* in the 1930s "to support the freedom fighters of the Spanish Civil War" (x).

The Marxist Wright saw Faulkner's works as strongly progressive. In a 1938 radio interview, Wright said, "the two writers whose work I like most today are André Malraux and William Faulkner. . . .[B]oth . . . are saying important things." After calling Faulkner the only white writer "in Mississippi who is trying to tell the truth in fiction," Wright says, "What Faulkner is to a small area, Malraux is to the progressive movement all over the world. . . . Faulkner shows how human beings are stunted and degraded in Mississippi, while Malraux shows how millions all over the world are trying to rise above a degraded status" (Kinnamon and Fabre 10). The parallel is meaningful because Malraux was at the time a revolutionary Marxist.

Faulkner said in 1957 that Sutpen initially sets out to establish that a man "cannot be inferior to another man through artificial standards or circumstances" (Gwynn and Blotner 35). But Sutpen is sidetracked by his lack of social perspective, a tragic flaw linked to the wilderness: "innocence" as a lack of the accumulated insight of group experience. After the death of Sutpen's mother, "a fine wearying woman" whose enterprise "had got his father even that far West" (*AA* 180), the Sutpens descend from the wild mountain to the plain seeking "ease." The mother who moved the Sutpens into the wilderness indicates his dark side as a member of an oppressed minority: "a mountain woman, a Scottish woman who . . . never did quite learn to speak English" (*AA* 195). In early nineteenth-century America, Scots were seen as inferior, dark, violent people.[6]

Sutpen's father, however, represents his white aspect and fits into the social system by regularly beating black people to assert status: "We whupped one of Pettibone's niggers tonight" (*AA* 187). He and Wash Jones—the other poor white male in the novel, who constantly hears African Americans jeering him (226)—fester with resentment because they are certain that slaves not only have more job security than they have, but live under many better conditions: "better found and housed and even clothed" (226).[7] Whites felt that blacks had too many advantages, even during slavery.

When young Tom is turned from a rich man's door, he is shocked to realize that some men have the right to say that because of what they own, they are superior (*AA* 185), an insight that could lead to the left. But perceiving that poor whites are treated "as cattle ... brutely evacuated [defecated] into a world without hope or purpose for them" (190), Sutpen decides that the only way to avoid a meaningless, subhuman life is to make a fortune and assume a privileged position in the system: "to combat them you have got to have what they have" (192). Though he chooses to support a system that oppresses him, the decision is from his limited perspective the only viable alternative to oppression that he can conceive. He commits his life on the basis of the innocence that is both his strength and his doom, not realizing what his choice means in terms of values. As Judith says, "You get born and you try this and you dont know why only you keep on trying it" (100).[8]

Hearing of a place where a fortune can be made quickly, Sutpen goes to Haiti, "the halfway point between what we call the jungle and what we call civilization" (*AA* 202), and gains wealth by confronting the terrible energy of a mob of black rebels. One can only transform one's status outside existing boundaries, so Sutpen must develop his power outside "civilization" by contact with the nonwhite side to which his supposed inferiority links him. Here he gains the godlike ability to create an entire world, as indicated by the stark power with which he methodically imposes order on chaos stage by stage (like the six days of Creation) in chapter 2, which resembles Genesis: "the *Be Sutpen's Hundred* like the oldentime *Be Light*" (4).

Sutpen embodies the force that builds America, and the book describes him "as if he were run by electricity" (*AA* 31, 218), with the implication that his is the "*electric furious immobile urgency*" (129) that powers the bulbs wherever his story is told: the dim bulb on Mr. Compson's porch (71, 101), the one Rosa Coldfield (rejecting Sutpen) refuses to light (70), the one in Quentin's room at Harvard (288), and Quentin himself when he feels "exactly like an electric bulb" (143). If Sutpen is identified with electric energy, then the Harvard bulb is one of many indications that his kind of power extends throughout the United States.

The bulb image could be influenced by Toomer's *Cane.* In the "Bona and Paul" section, the African American Paul sees his blond and energetic roommate Art in these terms: "He is like the electric light which he snaps on" (*Cane* 74). Faulkner may refer to this passage, unless there was a prior pattern of calling white people incandescent. In any case, this image of whiteness in Faulkner seems to take up a black point of view.

Sutpen's power rests on his ability to span both the "civilized" and "uncivilized" sides of life. He makes light from darkness by harnessing the primitive energy of peasant rebellion to a meticulous observation of the system of power. And he builds an empire not only by observing the rules, but by being able to violate them: "that was where his power lay . . . that anyone could look at him and say, *Given the occasion and the need, this man can and will do anything*" (*AA* 35). Early in *Absalom,* Sutpen is seen covered with mud, indistinguishable from his slaves (28, 16); and he reaffirms his contact with the lower side of life by engaging in periodic fights with them even after he becomes the richest landowner in the county. He speaks the language of the Haitians, "the only men on whom he could depend" (43). In fact, as his wealth multiplies, neighbors believe that he uses his slaves to "actually conjure more cotton per acre from the soil" (57)—that is, to employ African religion. They see him as in league with the Africans. Moreover, Quentin speculates that Sutpen's French architect, who was close to him, ran away partly because he feared that if food ran out, he might get eaten by the slaves "(and maybe Colonel Sutpen too)" (177).

This is bigoted slander, but the presence of African spirits in the Sutpen household is suggested by *Revolt in the Earth,* the unproduced screenplay that Faulkner based on *Absalom* in 1942. Bruce F. Kawin says that the script is very weak and entirely different in plot from the novel, but its characters are the Sutpens; and Kawin thinks that Faulkner "did all of the writing." The "main concern" of the script "is with voodoo," and the curse on the family here derives from what the screenplay refers to as "witch doctors one jump from Africa" who are linked to Sutpen's mulatto daughter Clytemnestra (Kawin 31–32). These facts prove nothing about *Absalom,* but they indicate ideas Faulkner associated with the novel.

Whites on plantations frequently were outnumbered many times over by African Americans, as Sutpen is at the start and his family evidently remains. Such whites must often have absorbed African cultural material, but they had to deny African influences on their lives in order to maintain their purity and to insist that African culture was of no value. Barbara Ladd's "The Direction of the Howling: Nationalism and the Color Line in *Absalom, Absalom!*" says that after the Civil War, there was a "suspicion that the former slaveholder was . . . tragically compromised—morally if not genetically—by his intimacy with the savage" (Hobson 229). A major aim of segregation was to prevent the pollution of white people by African civilizations, and the influx of African lore was heavily obliterated. Scholars are now unearthing concealed African elements in southern culture. Judith A. Carney shows that the Carolina rice industry was built on African technology. And the banjo, thought of as a white instrument, is "indisputably" African: Samuel Charters calls the Appalachian banjo playing of country music, "likely the most authentically African music in the United States."[9] Another example of white absorption of African culture is the Uncle Remus stories of Joel Chandler Harris (1840–1908), a white man who heard folk tales from slaves in childhood. It was claimed that they had European sources (Sundquist, *To Wake* 348–49).

The Caribbean Glissant speaks of Faulkner's "almost instinctive association and use of African customs and models: the extended family, the difficult-to-measure network of 'family relations,' the mystique of twins, the supposedly magical knowledge of animals—especially dogs and horses—and the important roles of uncles." Here "African tradition asserts its inextricability . . . in the rigid patrician" (133). What the impressions of those neighbors in *Absalom* may indicate is that the dependence of Sutpen's strength upon his African connection is not merely a physical matter of slaves working for him, but something that operates on a mental level. He gains energy and comprehension not only by opposing Africanism, but by partaking of it.

If, as Morrison observes, the psychological use of slaves generated a "new white man" in America with unprecedented freedom and authority (*Playing* 15, 39–44), then his strength depended on justifying his dominance. It was crucial to his sense of self-value to avoid the lurking suspicion that he was only taking advantage. In relation to Hegel's notion that the slave is the truth of the master (Hegel 117), Sutpen can only keep his consciousness vital by recognizing those of his bondmen, maintaining maximum awareness of their thinking. But he denies his need to do this and strives to avoid the uncouth (what the polite do not know) as he settles into hegemony. When, in an effort to purify himself, he rejects the son who embodies the vitalizing African connection, it inevitably leads to his downfall. The lower-class obscurity or darkness upon which Sutpen's claim to patrician whiteness is built means that the African Haitians are the only people he can trust because they are on the level of his reality; so he can never trust his legitimate children. It is precisely because he wants to make them purely white that Henry and Judith as well as Bon are bound to betray him.

ILLUSIONS HE BEGOT

Unlike Sutpen, his children do not combine both sides: they embody an extreme division reflecting Sutpen's cultivation of the divided values of the society that he forces his way into. He marries his first wife, Eulalia Bon, in Haiti mainly because she is brave enough to take many of the same risks that he takes (*AA* 204). He does not check her pedigree, but he later finds that his first son, Charles Bon, is part black.[10] Being on the wrong side of the deepest chasm in the book's social order, Bon must be denied by his father, thrust into a cultural wilderness, and seen as less than human. Having rejected the wife and son who combine both sides (and are most like him), Sutpen selects a new wife who is immaculate, Ellen Coldfield, who is so sheltered that she has scarcely any contact with the reality of life.

Rosa Coldfield wonders how such a ruthless man as Sutpen could have become linked to Goodhue Coldfield, pious father of herself and Ellen: "what there could have been between a man like that and papa—a Methodist steward" (*AA* 13). But the mysterious bond between ruthlessness that needs respectability and piety that needs power is the fusion at the core of American society—a society that justified the extermination of Native Americans and the enslavement of Africans as serving a higher cause.[11]

The southern combi-nation of pseudo-aristocracy and Puritanism was only a local variant of the prevailing national pattern. I call it *pseudo* because the serfs were mostly imported and barred from rising, but Faulkner implies through Sutpen that aristocracy is generally based on pretense. Daniel Aaron says that self-made men like Sutpen created the myth of a Cavalier aristocracy in the Low Church context of the South; and W. J. Cash, in *The Mind of the South*, traces the process by which settlers who often came to America as criminals used slavery and land seized from Indians to make themselves aristocratic in decades (3–21). Faulkner says that the first Sutpen "probably" came to America from "the Old Bailey" prison (*AA* 180).

Henry and Charles are *"just illusions that he* [Sutpen] *begot"* (*AA* 277), as Henry realizes, because as polarized aspects of the order Sutpen must exaggerate to lead, they are extensions of their father: the side he strives to cultivate exclusively and the side he wants to obliterate. Sutpen's judgment worked when he was able to operate between his white and black sides. Lyotard sees judgment as combining cognitive and ethical genres, two incommensurate discourses (*D* 150). When Sutpen casts off his dark (and ethical?) side, he may lose his ability to judge soundly.

If society motivates African Americans to cultivate their black sides, and European Americans, their white ones, an individual may well feel the need to go against stereotypes. So Bon goes against his suspicion that he is black (he may not *know* it until he has to admit that Sutpen has rejected him) by becoming a refined law student. Similarly, Henry goes against his ruling principle of purity by attaching himself to Bon and his world of pleasure. Their inclinations toward each as other might lead to progress, understanding, and reconciliation; but since we know that Henry will kill Bon, this beautiful hope never has a chance.

The relation of Henry to Bon emerges as a portentous mystery that starts the text throbbing in the fourth chapter: "Because Henry loved Bon. He repudiated blood birthright and material security for his sake ..." (*AA* 71). Why should Henry, on meeting Bon at the University of Mississippi, come to love him so that, forced by Sutpen to decide, he immediately chooses Bon, "where honor and love lay," over his father, "where blood and profit ran" (72)? This love is not adequately explained by the fact that the two men (though Henry does not know it) are half-brothers, or by the role of Judith as the prize they both covet.[12] It is a love rooted in adulation, for Henry is "seduced" (76) by the star Bon when Henry is one of the university students "who aped his clothing and manner and ... looked upon Bon as though he were a hero out of some adolescent Arabian Nights who" could "pass from the scene of one scarce imaginable delight to the next one without interval or pause or satiety" (76). Their latent homosexual desperation is generated by Bon's "tangible effluvium of knowledge, surfeit: of actions done and satiations plumbed and pleasures exhausted" (76).

Werner Sollors observes in *Neither Black Nor White Yet Both* that Mr. Compson, who narrates this section, avoids the idea that Bon could be black (326), yet Bon's "effluvium" is an aura that makes him exotic. Sollors points out that it is the later generation of Quentin and Shreve that adds Bon's blackness (329); but this need not invalidate their insight. Later generations could see elements that were submerged in slavery, and Faulkner ratifies Bon's blackness in his appendix (305).[13] One ultimate truth in *Absalom* is not a cognitive one, but an ostensive one, *a black truth of historical vision that overwhelms every generation* "like it is." The novel has a white intention that denies Bon's negritude and another that insists on that blackness to give the book its greatest power.

For the youths, Bon occupies the position of a white Negro because he breaks the rules. That he is Catholic and Latin is a step in the direction of blackness because prejudice against Catholics was strong in the South at this time. Sundquist tells how eleven Italians were lynched in a single incident in New Orleans in 1891 (*To Wake* 261–62). As for Henry, he may well start to suspect (or deny) that Bon is black as soon as he suspects that Bon is a concealed brother. That the final revelation of Bon's blackness is insinuated throughout the book is linked to the form of the novel on two levels. It fits a high modernist tradition in which novels by writers like Joyce and Woolf are read repeatedly and most readers know the book's subject matter before they begin. It also follows the pattern of Greek tragedy, in which the audience knows the story and senses on a deep level what will be revealed. With *Absalom* as with the *Agamemnon,* tremendous suspense is generated by *knowing* what is going to happen, which is announced or hinted from the start. Bon's power to move people is connected to uncanny senses that readers get of acute repressed racial concerns.

THE ADORATION OF BON

Faulkner conceives of Henry and his classmates as unconsciously sensing that Bon is black, though they are not aware of it. Bon's role as a star for young white people is filled today by such racially ambiguous figures as the singers Michael Jackson and Prince. The mulatto is a sublime object of ideology in our society, partly because people of both races need to see the racial interface as permeable or negotiable. Sollors, after reviewing the dangers of the "tragic mulatto" stereotype, ends up defending the potential of the mulatto for challenging the division of black and white (240–42). Žižek says that the sublime object is based on negation, something that the skull has in common with the sex organ (*Sublime* 6–7, 16–22). What we believe in always rests on suspicion that what it affirms is not possible, with religion and love as key models. Love between white people and black ones attracts idealists because it aims at a world where race does not exist. This ideal of interracial love helps make the first two acts of *Othello* sublimely romantic. But a realistic basis for such love must be built on recognizing difference.

Racially mixed people may be idealized, but they are also seen negatively by racism as sites of corruption. If they are not good at playing their mixed deal by compromising, their lives of responding to white fantasies to promote themselves can be torture. Witness the thirty-three years of Joe Christmas— and the youth of Malcolm X, who was in the process of getting crucified when he extricated himself from the penal machine by finding a black myth to believe.

The combination of idealization and torment visited on the mulatto reflects a wider pattern. People usually worship what they torture, just as the Inca sacrifice became a god. In the Middle Ages, when religion dominated Europe, people were often tortured in public while images of tortured people (Jesus and his saints) were worshiped. Freud argues in *Totem and Taboo* (1913) that in early hunting communities, the animal the tribe hunts and butchers is what it worships. He sees this as a formative stage in all religions that remains embedded in them.[14] This theory is often discredited, but Freud's theories were current among modernists, and *Totem* has an influence, for example, on Joyce's *Finnegans Wake* (1939).[15]

In any case, we have a powerful portrayal of a tribe that worships the animal it hunts in "The Bear," one of the best things Faulkner wrote after *Absalom*. The killing of Ben the bear leads to Ike McCaslin's realization of the seriousness of the crime against African Americans. Both work together to make him give up his patrimony, so they are in effect the same, and Davis argues that Ben represents the Negro as abstraction (244–46). The African American often served as the totem animal that the white tribe hunted and worshiped. Joel Williamson reports that before the Civil War, all white males in Mississippi were supposed to participate in patrols that hunted for slaves after dark, and tortured those found breaking the curfew (29).

René Girard emphasizes that what is sacrificed is sacred (1), and white

America has often depended emotionally on the sacrifice of African Americans. Cleanth Brooks says that Faulkner may be called a "primitivist" insofar as he admires the spiritual qualities of nonwhite people, Native- and African Americans (37). This suggests a disturbing charge: that Faulkner used minority difference for uplift while derogating them to essentialist inferiority. As I said, the level on which Faulkner is caught in racist ideology must always be watched for. The inadequate answer to the charge may begin with the question, "Where else could Faulkner take inspiration?" He not only found African Americans morally superior to European Americans, but he derived from them ideas that were intellectually advanced, he used his sense of their perspective to criticize white society devastatingly, and he insisted on the fury of their rebellion as had hardly any twentieth-century novelist before him. Where else indeed could he derive his program of mental action? To delineate what is true in Faulkner's vision, we must be aware of the submerged myths that impinged on and shaped this vision.

The most intense and positive religious feelings in Faulkner's works are directed at African American objects. Conventional white Christianity in the novels is generally dismal and oppressive—as it is for the Coldfields and for the Burdens of *Light in August* (listen to those names)—or self-righteous, as it is for Cora Tull in *As I Lay Dying* (1930).[16] This religion is infused with racialized notions of righteous purity, while black religion is charged with the drive toward freedom. Faulkner's most vivid portrayal of the spiritual power of black people is the stupendous revival meeting in the last part of *The Sound and the Fury* (182–85), but the pattern is also active with Joe Christmas and Bon, and it reaches its final climax with Nancy Mannigoe in *Requiem for a Nun*. The main white characters in this 1951 novel all desperately ask the black ex-prostitute Nancy what they should believe in—just before they cannot stop her from being executed at the end (233–43). Glissant points out that as a "Negro," she is expected to sacrifice herself for the spiritual development of white characters (93).

Yet in line with the dual intentions that *Absalom* introduces through "two separate Quentins" (*AA* 4–5), Faulkner is a critical observer of this worship as well as a participant in it. Modernist use of mythology often incorporates a sharp critique of religion, and there is something grotesque and unnatural about the worship of Bon, which implicates an impossible attempt to do penance for a racism that cannot be eliminated. The worship of the wilderness is practiced by those who are encroaching on it, and Bon is worshipped by Henry, who is in the process of murdering him from the day he meets him, as Ike is with Ben. Faulkner knows that they could not worship these divinities if they were not exterminating them. In fact, Christian doctrine holds that humanity continually crucifies God by being sinful: the sermons on hell in Joyce's *Portrait of the Artist* warn that "every impure thought" is a "lance transfixing" Jesus's heart (134).

Henry's dismal religion enhances the glamour in Bon that makes Henry idolize him. This is mapped out as we read of the trip they make to Bon's haunts in New Orleans. Bon is cautious in exposing the sensuous, cosmopolitan city to Henry, who comes from a world ruled by a fusion of Anglo-Saxon racism and Christianity: "imagine him, with his puritan heritage . . . of fierce proud mysticism and that ability to be ashamed of ignorance and inexperience, in that city . . . this grim humorless yokel out of a granite heritage where even the houses, let alone clothing and conduct, are built in the image of a jealous and sadistic Jehovah" (*AA* 86). This Jehovah is Sutpen, whose control over Henry can never be broken, and who allows Henry no erotic feelings that can approach enactment. One reason Henry is attracted to Bon is that Henry can never enjoy himself. The New Orleans sojourn accentuates the opposition between the brothers. The Puritan culture that encloses Henry sees what is physically attractive in the semi-tropical city as evil: "the architecture a little . . . femininely flamboyant and therefore to Henry opulent, sensuous, sinful" (87).

Confronted with this Latin sensuality, Henry falls back on his "puritan heritage which must show disapproval instead of surprise or even despair and nothing at all rather than have the disapprobation construed as surprise or despair" (*AA* 88). Surprise would reveal that he has physical feelings he cannot control, and this would compromise the pure white respectability for which Sutpen designs him. Paradoxically, Henry's inability to perceive emotions he cannot control leaves him bound by his system and entirely under the control of his emotions: "he never thought. He felt" (77), "with that puritan's humility toward anything which is a matter of sense rather than logic" (88). Despite Henry's endless, tortured rationalizing (both brothers are tormented by the system), his attempts to live within the bounds of logic and control appear to Charles, who concentrates on the other side of life (and achieves a real rationality by following his feelings), as "fetich-ridden moral blundering" (74). Ironically, he sees the "fetich-ridden" whites as primitives.

FLESH

French New Orleans is an extension of French Haiti, only somewhat more than halfway toward Anglo-Saxon civilization from the ancient values that Latin culture, as Faulkner sees it, preserves from the primitive. Like Bon, the courtesans of New Orleans strike "straight and true to some primary blind and mindless foundation of all young male living dream and hope" in Henry (*AA* 89). Because Henry is so restrained, the release Bon tempts him with stands for freedom. Even Mr. Compson—who tries to resist Puritanism and insists on positive values in Bon's outlook—is driven by his repressive world into cynical despair. In 1909, as *The Sound and the Fury* shows, his life and those of his best children are being wasted by an inhuman moral order of purity. Michaels is misguided to claim that Faulkner affirms this order, which he has Bon reveal as self-annihilating.

Bon's speech explaining his octoroon mistress to Henry presents his darkly ironic values. Bon says that his version of God must approve of the saving of one sparrow, the keeping of one concubine, because he was once young, and is human: "surely someone who has . . . looked at as much crude and promiscuous sinning without grace or restraint or decorum as He has had to, to contemplate at last . . . honor, decorum and gentleness applied to perfectly normal human instinct which you Anglo-Saxons insist upon calling lust and in whose service you revert . . . to . . . abasement and flagellation" (*AA* 92). Bon's deity is witty and sardonic, having seen it all; His morality is based on who gets hurt rather than on the Puritan emphasis on denying desire, and he does not demand monogamy. Accepting the weakness of the flesh as natural rather than damning, Bon is able to apply reason to central functions of life from which Henry is outcast because he cannot confront or acknowledge an area of darkness and physical passivity, of giving in to feeling. Bon eulogizes this area as

> a female principle which existed, queenly and complete, in the hot equa-
> torial groin of the world long before that white one of ours . . .—a prin-
> ciple apt docile and instinct with strange and ancient curious pleasures of

the flesh (which is all: there is nothing else) which her white sisters of a mushroom [upstart; see *Go* 114] yesterday flee from in moral and outraged horror—a principle which, where her white sister must needs try to make an economic matter of it . . . , reigns, wise supine and all-powerful, from the sunless and silken bed which is her throne. (92–93)

This female principle links women and Africans as people who express the desire denied by the repressive white male power structure. There is value in seeing how the two groups are subject to similar conditions by imperialism: it shows the seriousness of women's oppression and some of the emotions involved in racism. But the dangers of this analogy are great insofar as women may be seen as foreign or Africans as female. The problems are slightly relieved by seeing the wise woman in her bed/throne as Africa itself, often envisioned as a woman (Brivic, *Waking* 62–63).

The passage gives a grotesquely distorted view of Africa, which was all that was available on the public level in the nineteenth century. Off the record, many slaves held on to African roots, though they were punished for doing so. Marlene van Niekerk points out in "Understanding Trends in 'African Thinking'" that the prevailing theory in the West through most of the century was that of degeneracy—that Africans had been created by God as civilized and subsequently degenerated. A great improvement on this was E. B. Tylor's theory of animism in *Primitive Culture* (1871). This at least attempted to describe African religions, but it simplified them into one irrational pattern that should be eliminated (C&R 57). Despite Bon's limited conception of Africa, he clearly supports values linked to this continent, and the rest of the novel follows him. Bon's matriarchal vision is less like white views of Africa as barbarous than like black views that saw it as an ideal original state from which the West was a decline. A more informed version of Bon's female African principle is Beloved.

Bon's parenthetical remark that nothing exists except flesh or its pleasures represents his reaction against the world he finds. He continues to affirm the bodily values Henry is blind to in his letter to Judith of 1865, which describes the state of his confederates: "*hungry . . . . shoeless . . . grown accustomed to it, only, thank God (and this restores my faith . . . in man) that he really does not become inured to hardship and privation: it is only the mind, the gross omnivorous carrion-heavy soul which becomes inured; the body itself, thank God, never reconciled from the old soft feel* (*AA* 103). He argues that the mind, in effect, lusts after wild ideologies that violate nature, such as the rationales of war and slavery; but the body represents an absolute standard of morality because it never abandons the basic needs of reality. His formulation reverses traditional Christian morality such as Henry's, which elevates spirit to virtue and denies the body.

This reversal of moral values is echoed in a key speech by the very different Rosa Coldfield in the next chapter, who speaks of "*something in the touch of flesh with flesh which abrogates, cuts . . . across the devious intricate channels of decorous ordering, . . . not spirit, soul; the liquorish and engirdled mind is anyone's to take in any darkened hallway of this earthly tenement. But let flesh touch with flesh and watch the fall of all the eggshell shibboleth of cast and color too*" (*AA* 111–12).

Contrast between the touch of flesh and the "eggshell" social barriers that divide people reverberates through *Absalom*. Faulkner here anticipates a salient image that emerges in different forms from two black women writing separately in 1987. Spillers, in "Mama's Baby, Papa's Maybe: An American Grammar Book," speaks of the value of flesh before it has been transformed into the abstraction of an exchangeable body. She presents flesh as the "zero degree of social conceptualization" (*Black* 207). And Morrison's *Beloved* has the soulful lay preacher Baby Suggs exhort the community, telling them that they must love themselves as flesh (*B* 88). That Spillers and Morrison are influenced by Faulkner's Africanism suits Dubey's postmodern skepticism about authenticity, but to deny that any of them are connected to Africa cuts Americans off from the dark continent in a way that no one would dream of cutting us off from Europe. The image changes in its new contexts; for example, Faulkner has little sense of the value of flesh as something shared by the community. Yet much of the force of the later declarations is involved in *Absalom*'s emphasis on the power of "the touch of flesh" in opposition to racism, an opposition connected to Africa.

Rosa embodies or entombs the suppression of flesh as intensely as any figure in literature. In this scene, she knows that Clytie is doing her "more grace and respect than anyone else I knew" (*AA* 111); but Rosa cannot accept grace from a black woman, so she settles back on her side of the invisible wall, saying, "Take your hand off me, nigger!" (112). She is angry at Clytie here for calling her "Rosa" rather than "Miss Rosa," though this expresses love. The distance she maintains from her dark relative recoils on her in the last chapter, when Clytie needlessly destroys Sutpen's mansion and Henry because she misunderstands Rosa. During the war, Bon waits five years to *"just touch flesh"* with his father (255, 278), and destroys himself when that contact is irrevocably denied. And Sutpen says to the poor white Wash Jones, "Stand back, Wash. Dont you touch me" just before Wash says, "I'm going to tech you, Kernel" (229), and cuts his throat.[17]

Rosa's speech and Bon's letter are surprisingly parallel in their extreme reversal of the Western valuation of mind over body: both see the body as pure and the mind as a prostitute. Thus Bon contrasts *"the gross omnivorous carrion-heavy soul [,] which becomes inured"* to anything (*AA* 103), and the *"incorruptible fidelity"* of the body (104). Rosa clearly sees the mind as a whore: *"the liquorish and ungirdled mind is anyone's to take in any darkened hallway of this earthly tenement."* That two characters so far apart share such unusual views suggests that these attitudes fill the book; and it turns out that Sutpen's proper children, Judith and Henry, embrace the same views. Rosa shares with them the sense that Judith describes of being caught in a machine that violates their natures by inserting them into *"intricate channels"* (112) of stereotype.

Imposed on them from above is a racist polarity exemplified by the brothers in which Henry is linked to purity, enlightenment, and control, while Bon is supposed to embody darkness, the senses, and release. Both men are impelled to resist these crippling abstractions by their efforts to survive, and Faulkner continually shows that what they are supposed to be is crucially different from what they are, which consists of a series of reactions against these suppositions. Henry keeps grinding away at logical distinctions, but something—the concealed specter of "race"—keeps his logic from having the slightest validity. "Race" is the model for his distinctions that leave out actual beings. His arguments are suspended in air because he is alienated from his brother. Bon, who is presumed by the system to be unclean and intellectually weak, is decidedly cleaner, smarter, and better educated than Henry. As Snead observes, Faulkner keeps ironically indicating that people do not really fit their stereotypes (111–17).

Nevertheless, these are the codes of racism into which the characters are inserted, and they cannot escape from them in Faulkner's tragic world. An advantage of starting my study with *Absalom* is that the novel shows how the polarity of racial insignia has been historically manufactured by a series of crimes as an unnatural system that does not match the reality outside itself, which it conceals. The ugly stereotypical limits imposed on African Americans by this polarity underline the destructive effects of the system. Yet the polarity also delineates the margin on which creativity operates through the need of the two sides to recognize their extension into each other, to develop themselves by moving toward each other. This movement can take place within individuals as well as between them when we realize how stereotypes distort us. As we trace the separations between categories, we perceive their artificiality.

The crucial distinction has to do not with people's natures, but with how they are situated in relation to language: Henry is inside and Bon is outside of the Symbolic order, the system of language organized around the law of the Father. Henry, attached to the Father, has a center of meaning that ties everything together in the continuity that should allow control and logic. He believes in the exact meaning of every word he says, yet his thinking seems uncontrolled and illogical. In fact, the hidden, remorseless logic that he cannot escape leads to murder, and his efforts at denial only build toward it. When Henry says to Bon at the end, "*You are my brother*" (*AA* 286), this is a fact, but it is not (in Black English) what's happening. Bon replies climactically: "*No I'm not. I'm the nigger that's going to sleep with your sister.*" This is not a fact, for the *n* word, as a stereotypical label, hardly fits the elegant Bon, and he will not sleep with her. But on the level of feeling that the book tries to bring out, this is where it's at: not the facts, but what the system makes of them.

In contrast to Henry, Bon is exiled in a world of desire where every signifier slides away from the signified it aims at. Because he is absolutely barred from the authority of the father, no word he uses has any particular meaning. His letter, written in stove polish, gives the ghostly impression of being anti-written in water. What this letter announces doubtfully ("*I cannot say when to expect me*"; *AA* 104), that he will come for her, will never happen, as he suspects. Therefore his mode of Gates's Signifying frames every phrase as in quotes, unreal: "*you and I are, strangely enough, included among those who are doomed to live*" (105). He always knows better. Like that of the hipster Benny Profane in *V.* (but with refinement), Bon's speech is "made up of nothing but wrong words" (*V.* 144). There is no identity that Bon can claim, so he starts by saying that he will not claim "*to be a voice from the defeated,*" and then says, "*if I were a philosopher*" (*AA* 102). He shows class by using the subjunctive, the mood in which he lives. His cognitive definitions are usually hypothetical: *"sometimes I think it has never stopped"* (104). His descriptions of himself are submitted without authority: *"I wont say hungry. . . . And I wont say ragged or even shoeless. . . . So say we merely needed ammunition"* (103). He is glad that his strongest source of perception, his body, is *"still . . . bemused in recollections of old peace and contentment"* (104). The truth for Bon is in the body (the Real prior to language), but the body's concrete actuality is disallowed by the Sutpen/Coldfields, for whom he is a bodiless wraith.

PURITANISM

The scarcity of the touch of flesh between the two sides means that in this interface, the emphasis is not on constructive negotiation, but on destructive isolation. Though Henry and Bon are physically close to each other for years, they can't reach or change each other. One explanation for this failure of contact has to do with the male pride that Lee Jenkins emphasizes in Faulkner's novels (196). It may be that fear of homosexuality is a factor both in Rosa's recoil from Clytie and in the inability of Henry and Bon to get through to each other. The main historical explanation that I will give for the separation, however, involves Puritanism, which sees the rational Symbolic realm of control as the realm of the saved, and the irrational realm of release as that of the damned. Afflicted by this dichotomy, *Absalom* expresses grief for the lost touch of flesh and the suppression of the dark values of the body. Not that it argues that the Bon values are good and the Henry ones are bad; rather it deconstructs the dichotomy to show that while one side has been privileged, the other should be built up because they both need each other. Spirit and body cannot live without each other. Whatever virtue the Bon values have depends on their situation in a world run by the Henry ones.

Faulkner had already analyzed how the code of racial polarity controls people's lives in *Light in August* (1932), the novel that led to *Absalom*. Actually, Faulkner found it a strain to write *Absalom* and took a break from it to write *Pylon* (1935), a fine short novel that is not about "race." In *Light*, the biracial Joe Christmas runs from the "lightless hot wet primogenitive Female" life of blacks to the "cold hard air of white people" (115). The same pattern is referred to forty years later in Pynchon's *Gravity's Rainbow* when the African Enzian perceives that in Europe love essentially "had to do with masculine technologies," with systems won "away from the feminine darkness" (324). These polarities pervade our culture, so that it is hard to separate physical characteristics from moral associations or a sense that they are natural. This is why writers must use radical imagination to disassemble such polarities. One reason they are so pervasive is that they are linked to the major bases of Puritan judgment.

Max Weber, in his classic account of Puritanism, *The Protestant Ethic and the Spirit of Capitalism* (1920), notes that it has been powerful in America. Because Puritans believe that one is predestined either to be saved (among the Elect) or damned, they must constantly strive for proof of grace. This striving works through "systematic self-control which at every moment stands before the inexorable alternative, chosen or damned" (*PE* 115), and which involves a continuous effort to rationalize and control the world. Being convinced of the "depravity of the flesh" (131), and viewing feeling and emotion with suspicion, it has as its "most urgent task the destruction of spontaneous, impulsive enjoyment" (119).

Weber says that Methodism was "the last great revival of Puritan ideas in the eighteenth century" (*PE* 117). Faulkner, whose family was Methodist, portrays intense Puritanism in this group through the Coldfields. He also presents Puritanism in Yoknapatawpha County in a more standard form with the Presbyterians of *Light in August,* the Burdens and the Hightowers. Though southerners often associated Puritanism with Yankees, New England being its central seat, it was dominant in the South, and Faulkner sees it as controlling most white people's lives in his county. Rev. Gail Hightower, for example, reflects on his people: "Pleasure, ecstasy, they cannot seem to bear" (*LiA* 368). *Absalom* deploys Puritanism as a pervasive system dividing a rational realm of whiteness from a sensual one of blackness, with the word *puritan* used ten times in chapters 2 to 4 of the novel (32, 45, 54, 74, 86–87, 88, 89, 91). Cash says that southern Methodists were stricter than others (84), and emphasizes that in the decades before and after the Civil War, the "bitter fanaticism" of Puritanism in its "rigid narrowness" increasingly held "sway . . . over the whole mind of the South" (59), under a "Calvinized Jehovah" who was the "resistless orderer of all things" (135).

Because Puritan devaluation of physical life often led to distrust of one's neighbor, Weber sees each Puritan (who is a potential capitalist), in his anxiety to believe himself one of the Elect, as "divided from the eternally damned remainder of humanity by a . . . terrifying gulf . . . which penetrated all social relations with its sharp brutality" (*PE* 121–22). This impassable gulf corresponds to the barriers in *Absalom* that separate what should be one big family. Weber's critique of Puritanism, a critique associated with Pynchon, parallels the way an African might see European society. Steve Biko, for example, says in "Some African Cultural Concepts," "We regard our living together not as an unfortunate mishap warranting endless competition among us but as . . . a community of brothers and sisters" (C&R 27).

Faulkner recognizes linking skin color to morality as the essence of racism when he says that Bon's son, Charles Etienne Saint-Valery Bon, grew up where "pigmentation had no more moral value than the silk walls and the scent" (*AA* 161). In fact, one reason Etienne Bon is sundered from Yoknapatawpha County is that he was raised in a sensual world of Catholicism, but this is a less serious occasion of bigotry against him than his almost invisible trace of black blood. Etienne Bon is an extreme case of the destructive effect of prejudice. Having grown up like Sutpen in a place without "race," he is confronted by the fact that he "must be, a negro" (*AA* 161). Quentin imagines him showing his fixation on how he is reflected by staring at a mirror in grief (162). This corresponds to Lacan's theory of the mirror stage, which holds that one forms one's bodily image in infancy by being seen by others (*Écrits* 3–9). The racial definition of Etienne disintegrates his fundamental self-image. On seeing himself reflected as black by the social Other, he takes on the image of the accursed, assuming "the uniform—the tattered hat and overalls—of his ancient curse" (166). This corresponds to Frantz Fanon's traumatic realization of how he is seen as a Negro: "I become aware of my uniform" (*Black* 114).

The curse Etienne assumes is the endless servitude God imposed on the descendents of Ham (Gen. 9:25), which racists affixed to Africans.[18] Ham is punished for seeing the nakedness of his father, Noah, and telling Ham's brethren about it (9:22), while Bon shows the meanness and falseness of Sutpen. His advent indicates to Sutpen's other children that the clothing of whiteness is not on the emperor. Yet black and white moral polarity compels Etienne to take on the guise of the damned. He reacts with a defiance parallel to his grandfather Sutpen's when he was turned away from grace: "a furious and indomitable desperation which the demon himself might have shown" (164, also 168). Yet being on the wrong side of the divide, Etienne cannot conceal his demonism in a structure that shifts evil onto others: all he can accomplish with his defiance is to crucify himself (169).

Etienne's crucifixion implies a protest against injustice that ultimately works to promote the possibility of a more human social order. This shows the power of Christian patterns on the black side. Of course, Etienne appears to be deranged, but Christ seemed that way to all but his followers when he died. It took a century of interpretation to prepare his message for the world; and likewise Faulkner's novel is a step toward interpreting the deaths of people like Charles Bon and his son. To become visible, their meaning must appear on a field of racial polarities.

THE WHITE NEED

In portraying the polar stereotypes of racism as products of Sutpen, Faulkner shows how American society has sundered itself, intensifying traditional distinctions by importing a population to be racially marked off. The whites have distorted features of African behavior that struck them in order to form a mold into which they forced the blacks. Behind this distortion is projection: qualities condemned by the white system in its members are cast off from the whites and projected onto the African Americans. Men enact a similar process with women, and in a feminist context, Judith Butler says that Julia Kristeva's idea of the abject describes what one expels from one's own body to constitute the alien: "The construction of the not-me as the abject establishes the boundaries of the body which are also the first contours of the subject" (*Gender* 133).[19] Because the creation of the abject defines the subject's boundaries, Sutpen can never give up on the subordination of others (his children and victims), for if he did, his subject would disintegrate. His identity requires the existence of those into whom he discharges the feelings he is ashamed of. Butler says that the exclusion that forms the subject "requires the simultaneous production of a domain of abject beings." They fill "'uninhabitable' zones of social life which are nevertheless densely populated by those who do not enjoy the status of the subject, but whose living under the sign of the 'unlivable' is required to circumscribe the domain of the subject" (*Bodies* 3).

African Americans—and women, children, and the poor, as well as other sinners—are forced to live in and comprise the psychological refuse of Puritanism. One result is that insofar as they are persuaded, they feel incomplete and yearn for the pure values linked to the whites. This pattern is shown strongly by Pauline and Pecola Breedlove in Morrison's *The Bluest Eye.* And so Bon loves Henry too, longing for the stability and morality of Henry's world (*AA* 86, 259).

The result that concerns me most, however, is that having cast off the qualities they see negatively and imposed them on the blacks, the whites become themselves seriously lacking and dependent on their others. Many children of white America who sought wholeness have been attracted to black culture since the nineteenth century, particularly in music, which has been dominated by black influence in America since ragtime—and music provides the vitality that moves one through life. Moreover, young whites have often sided at least temporarily with blacks against their own people from the time of Huckleberry Finn, who uses black dialect and risks danger and damnation to protect his friend Jim. The black sector represents not only physical release but a moral issue, and a mode of existential freedom that attracts many white youths who imitate blacks as Henry aped Bon. They are called "hipsters" by Norman Mailer in "The White Negro" (1957), and Pynchon features them.

The white compulsion toward imagined African American points of view contributes not only to Faulkner's themes, but to his techniques, as Davis indicates in *Faulkner's "Negro"*: "For Faulkner, because he is a white Southerner and a sensitive artist, *Negro* generally suggests the possibility of wholeness, of establishing the missing parts of his world or vision. But the suggestion does not necessarily lead to a single, unified, or even constant vision, because *Negro* stands, as well, for the unresolved tensions of southern life. Thus emerge the prevalent fragmentation and the artistic counterpoint in Faulkner's fiction" (4). Davis effectively shows that Faulkner focuses on the Negro, a creation of the white imagination, rather than on the actuality of black people. She points out that in *Absalom* black people are always seen through white ones since all of the narrators are white (187–89). Because she focuses on the idea that Bon is more illusory than the other Sutpens, however, she does not consider that Bon's letter presents the discourse of an African American more directly than the words of any of the other Sutpens are presented. This indicates that the viewpoint of black resistance plays a more active role in *Absalom* than has been noticed, for the letter announces that Bon will break the white rules even if it should cost his life. This action makes Bon sacred so that Americans of both "races" have a moral obligation to imitate him.

Lott argues that the ability to imitate African American males is "part of most American white men's equipment for living" (Kaplan and Pease 480), and that it serves the white male's need to define himself against the other and to control the other (480, 482); but it also renders the color line open to transgression or disruption (481). Henry is not able to sustain his fantasy of going over to Bon's side, but his temporary rebellion allows Bon to penetrate the defenses of Sutpen's demesne. On an allegorical level, the resistance of white abolitionists helps make the Civil War possible, and therefore in effect speaks significantly for black liberation. Lott discusses a common pattern in which young white males dally with Africanism, then move on to settle into white identities (480). But Henry does not do so: the imprint of Bon's image holds him in its grasp. When he kills Bon, he completes the dreadful process of making Bon his god.

THE TRUTH OF BON

Faulkner always favored values of direct physical experience over those of mental abstraction in which he found himself enclosed, though he saw the need for both sides to balance each other. In fact, Spillers argues that *Absalom* often indicates that reality cannot be seen directly, but only from a distance (*Black* 352). The character most connected to immediate experience is Bon, and the immediacy he enacts represents the hope for release from social control. But he is an ungraspable phantom who can no more be seen directly than can reality. His immediacy, as Lacan's Real, can appear only as contradiction (*Encore* 93), and this contradiction expresses Bon's resistance to explanation and authority—a divine quality in every rebel without a cause.

In *Absalom,* Bon's Africanist affirmation of the flesh is situated as the most powerful impulse of goodness, though it is a goodness as bleak as a crucifixion. Rosa extends her weirdly ironic support for Bon's physical values after her speech on touch by saying that the senses are "*the substance of remembering—. . . not mind, not thought*" and that the brain transforms the reality of feeling into "*some trashy myth of reality's escape,*" "*figment-stuff warped out of all experience*" (115; italics in original). She reverses the Western assumption that rational reality is more real than sensory reality by saying that our ideas about what we feel are mere fantasies. Rosa's support for Bon's sensuality, like her adoration of him, is especially poignant because she appears virtually never to have had a sensual experience. She calls herself a "*warped . . . . root*" (115), and she is a *rose* planted in a *cold field* who spends her life in bitterness, and whose soaring, abstract poetry speaks for all the love that never came into being.[20] She ends her account of her vicarious love for Bon (117) by saying that she not only never saw him, but she could not even feel his weight in the coffin she bore (122).

That she could make no contact with Bon stands for his resistance to containment. Yet Shreve McCannon, the healthiest figure in *Absalom,* with his smooth, pink skin and his deep-breathing drill (*AA* 176) speaks for Bon in the final chapter of historical testimony. Even Henry solidifies his commitment to Bon's view during the war: he is ready to yield Judith until his ultimate limit is broached by the fact that it will be miscegenation, not just incest. Right before Sutpen tells him that Bon is black, Henry says to his father, "*nothing matters except that there is the old mindless meat that dont even care if it was defeat or victory*" (283). This is part of a nine-line speech in which Henry argues that he will let Bon marry Judith. This speech repeats almost word for word a longer speech that Bon made to Henry five pages earlier (278–79). It shows that Henry follows Bon's ideas slavishly, and that he is less educated, since Bon's language is more polished. Bon's devotion to the body is linked to an intellectual critique of prevailing destructive abstractions, whereas Henry's devotion is intellectually hollow, being based on Bon's.

Even Judith, the noblest figure in the book and the greatest lover of Sutpen, also loves Bon. In the first chapter, the six-year-old Judith screams because the carriage in which she raced to church with her father has been replaced by a phaeton driven by a servant (*AA* 17). Bouncing in that carriage with Sutpen may have been her most exciting experience. The figure to whom Judith corresponds in the *Oresteia* is Electra, and the only time she cries is when her father returns from the war, seven months after the death of Bon (128). She loves Bon because he resembles her father absolutely—loves her father's worst enemy, his youth. Like Lear's Cordelia in that her unselfish insistence on the truth seems to bring her little but suffering, Judith must get satisfaction by believing that she stands for love of the good (Bon). Though Rosa writes bitter words on her tombstone (171), Judith decides to transmit *Absalom.* She gives us the major historical document—Bon's epistle announcing his doctrine—and, through Quentin's grandmother and father, the major speech of the Sutpen saga. When she gives the letter to the grandmother, she says, "maybe if you could go to someone, the stranger the better, and give them something—a scrap of paper" (101). Judith says, "the stranger the better" because she realizes that the further apart people are, the more can be communicated. *Absalom* can be written only because she decides to convey the truth of her interracial love, the strongest love in the book. By doing so, she expresses a feminine ability to reach across boundaries.

Finally Rosa, who describes what she feels for the Bon unknown to her as "*more than even love*" (*AA* 117), also maintains that only the love that Bon disembodies could give meaning to the catastrophe of the family and the war: "*he was to die; I know that . . . else how to prove love's immortality? . . . love and faith at least above the murdering and the folly*" (120). All of the love in the book reaches to or from Bon—from Judith, Rosa, and Henry. And Judith remains true to Bon's principles, though her experience during the war with Clytie and Rosa suggests that life in a wilderness without social distinctions is not much better than animal life (124–27). She finally comes to throw her life away for Bon's principles and his son: "*But I was wrong. Nothing matters but breath, breathing, to know and be alive*" (168). This statement in which she decides to support Etienne Bon—a decision that causes her death—echoes the early Charles Bon: "there were three things and no more: breathing, pleasure, darkness" (240).

Judith follows the principles of one African American to give her life for another, and this suggests that *Absalom* is addressed to black readers— as Faulkner's novels generally are. American literature is usually addressed to both "races," among others, and to omit such address is like cutting off a speaker in a stereo. A fine example is the speech Judith makes on transmitting the letter from her black brother and lover that is the seed of the novel (*AA* 100–101). She states that people follow social customs without knowing why, and that these customs have nightmarish effects because people are unable to comprehend each other, being woven into different patterns. This parallels Lyotard's idea of incommensurate phrase genres, more than one of which makes up the *differend* in significant phrases (*D* 55–56). So a phrase addressed to multiple, opposed audiences would be typical in this system. One important meaning of Judith's phrase "the stranger the better" is that she would like to reach people who are outside the racist world she lives in, and there is no one for whom her explanation is more deeply meant than for African Americans. There is a convention in the blues of referring to African Americans as strangers, as in Jesse Fuller's "Stranger Blues" (1960). Of course, Judith has an ideologically distorted sense of what her black audience really thinks, and

Faulkner also has limitations in this area. Yet Judith has spent the war sleeping in the same room with her black sister Clytie (*AA* 126). She, Clytie, and Rosa shared the hardships of the war "*as though we were one being*" (125). Judith, however, could not talk to Clytie of her love for their black brother; speaking of the three women, she says, "*We were three strangers*" (126). Ironically, in trying to speak to a larger world beyond the social derangement that she describes, she is trying to say something to her half-sister that she could never say in person—her sister the stranger.

The intensity with which Faulkner is addressing African Americans is notable in the final section of *The Sound and the Fury*. It is impossible that he could present such a powerful version of a black church meeting without having a black audience in mind, though African Americans may be offended by his stereotypes. In fact, the main figure of this section is based on the black woman who raised Faulkner, Caroline Barr. She lived on Faulkner's land until her death at the age of eighty (Blotner 1034–35). She was not able to read the novel, but Faulkner later recorded the revival scene, so he may have read it aloud during her life. Any fictional portrayal of a real person is a communication with the person, especially when she is as vital as Dilsey. So one of the main addressees of this scene of the novel was black; and by the 1930s, Faulkner must have known that he had black admirers like Alain Locke, Sterling Brown, and Wright.

Even racists address African Americans, but what they say is, "Something is wrong with you." What Faulkner is saying is, "We white folks are responsible for your troubles, but look at how disturbed we are." Many typical rhetorical devices of *Absalom* can be seen as communicating to outside readers a sense of extreme anguish and confusion among white Mississippians that both resulted from and allowed the racist order. For example, there is negation: Rosa's "voice would not cease, it would just vanish" (*AA* 4); Quentin "was not a being, an entity, he was a commonwealth" (7). Such negations appear on most pages of the novel. One of their effects is to show that words do not mean what they seem to mean for these people who are so caught up in contradictory abstraction. Words cannot tell, can only suggest the intensity of the feelings that slave owners are subject to. The submerged burden is that the incredible turmoil of their feelings explained the awful things they did.

Such extenuations, while they speak to southerners, take much of their charge from being aimed at those who are outside the system, the northerner

Shreve and the independent black person Bon. Bon appears with most depth in the novel as the creation of Shreve, the resistance of the African American seen through the Canadian who is above the most oppressive racism. This is another way in which the novel's rhetoric is aimed at black people, and in fact the pattern of negation passes into Morrison, who also uses it to convey extreme mental states that explain terrible deeds: "The ice pick is not in her hand; it is her hand" (*B* 309). Other typical devices of *Absalom*—such as long sentences, oxymorons, and the shifting of temporal sequence—also serve to convey extreme mental states that explain the atrocious by enacting its inexplicableness. The grief and agitation of the Sutpen family has one of the main focuses of its upset discourse on the black people who infiltrate them: grief over, against, and for African Americans. And all of the unhappiness of the family attaches every member of it to Charles Bon, the avenging angel of concealed blackness.

Who is Bon to be worthy of the love of all the Sutpens but Thomas, and of all their narrators? He is a man who knows what no one else in *Absalom* except Shreve and the lower classes (Wash Jones and the slaves) knows—how to enjoy himself sensually. Doreen Fowler, in a fine Lacanian study of Faulkner, speaks of Bon as representing for the Sutpens "the fullness of being" that they lack, the original plenitude before the repression that constituted the subject (96). She is right, but she does not consider how Bon's insertion into the role of the unrepressed may relate to Faulkner's American Africanism. Bon stands for "the forbidden phallus," "transgression of the Law," and "the unconscious" for Mr. Compson, as Fowler points out (99), because these are things that white Americans have used African Americans to stand for. At the end of the novel, according to Fowler, Bon represents a "completeness of being" that Quentin struggles to attain by telling Bon's story, fusing with Shreve, and ultimately realizing Bon's blackness (115-16). Her idea that Bon "is" (116) an original unity that has been repressed corresponds to a positive potential framed by "race." If one "race" can have the feeling of realizing the true situation of the other, then the greatest separation between people can be overcome. To understand Bon could bring release from Sutpen's curse, bring salvation.

Bon is exactly like his father in appearing from nowhere (*ex nihilo*) to seek respectable connections and a dominant position. Bon also has a vigorous Sutpen temper, unlike that of Henry, the Coldfield (*AA* 95). The cynosure Bon is "phoenix-like, fullsprung from no childhood, born of no woman and impervious to time and, vanished, leaving no bones nor dust" (58). He is "three inanimate objects in one" (59), and his eye is on the sparrow, even if that sparrow is a courtesan (92). His childhood was bitter because his mother was denied the right to have a legitimate child. So he was raised as a love child, and he is killed *"to prove love's immortality"* (120) as he asks why his father has forsaken him. He takes upon himself the human body and is born among outcasts; and the four narratives of Rosa, Mr. Compson, Quentin, and Shreve circle around his sacrifice like Gospels.[21] Even more of a Christ figure in many ways than Joe Christmas, Bon is the *sumum bonum:* he is everything Christian that has been denied by the Puritanism Faulkner depicts. And the central feature of Christ in this perspective is that for the racist system that condemns anyone with any black blood, Christ was certainly black. Such Christians deny this aspect of Christ because it reflects on his Father, as Bon does on Sutpen. The sublime object this order sees as fair-skinned was an African rebel destroyed by European imperialism. Bon as Christ accords with Žižek's idea of a radical Jesus who sacrifices himself to change the rules in political terms so as to speak for denied voices (*Fragile* 155ff.).

If Henry's restrictions make pleasure seem like the most important quality to him, he is right in view of the destructive effects that his ingrained limitations ultimately have. When one side of life is built up at the expense of another, it is on the other side that chances for development will lie. So virtually all of the causes that have stirred the idealism of America's young people since it became settled—the children of Sutpen—have been oriented toward the values of Bon in opposition to the establishment: anti-imperialism, social radicalism, romanticism, natural feeling, ecology, and non-Western spiritual techniques. The major alternative to these rebellious impulses in *Absalom* is the course that Henry is obliged to take in spite of himself—injustice and stagnation.

In *Love and Death in the American Novel,* Leslie Fiedler calls the bond between the white hero and his nonwhite sidekick (Natty Bumppo and Chingachgook, Huck and Jim, Ishmael and Queequeg) the most powerful emotional connection in American literature (198–200, 324–34, 383). *Absalom,* which is filled with ironic images of questers moving toward goals that will shatter them (Rosa, Sutpen, Quentin), climaxes with Henry and Bon riding through the war together. They complement each other as neatly as yin and yang: "Think of the two of them: Bon who didn't know what he was going to do and had to say, pretend, he did; and Henry who knew what he was going to do and had to say he didn't" (*AA* 273).

Bon doesn't know what he'll do for the same reason that attracted Henry to him: he has freedom of movement "like to a cat" (*AA* 252) because he is not bound to any social system. Here is the existentialism that attracts Mailer's hipsters. Bon lives in a void, and the values he subscribes to have no authority and do not allow control: his not knowing what he will do means that he has to improvise. He must pretend that he has an intention so as to claim respect and effectiveness, but he knows that when he tries to act with Judith, it will not be allowed to work. Excluded from the Symbolic system, Bon dwells in a witty series of sensations that are too sophisticated for linear logic, so his brilliance frees him from the hierarchical constraint of authority. His position as the colonized makes him culturally more modern than the plodding Henry. His fluid sensuality links him to ideas that were advanced in the 1860s, such as Walter Pater's aestheticism. Here the outsider is avant-garde, possessing an intellectual and aesthetic advantage that will require a historical transformation to become effective.

Although he portrays African American desperation keenly, Faulkner shows his limits by being unable to imagine that Bon could claim authority of his own that might lead to a goal. Faulkner handles black males best if they have many white features, as do Bon, Christmas, and Lucas Beauchamp of *Intruder in the Dust*.[22] Early in *Absalom,* Rosa and Mr. Compson use monstrous stereotypes to describe "Sutpen's wild negroes" from Haiti (16, 27). Davis (192) notes that Compson is slightly more skeptical of these offensive images than Rosa is (*AA* 36). The images establish the dense miasma of racism in Mississippi in 1833, but Faulkner may see too much truth in them. On another level, their wildness, exaggerated by local racist discourse, shows that these men are more immediately from Africa than any other slaves in the area, highlighting the African nature of the source of Sutpen's power.

While Bon cannot act except to destroy himself, Henry cannot help acting because he is restricted by the Symbolic system. This makes the consequences of every word clear, and makes the doubt in which Bon suspends him unbearable. Though he destroys himself as Bon does, Henry does it by fixation. The sense of stable form on which his will is based is one thing Bon finds attractive about him. Henry's sense of predestination is so strong that he spends his whole life trying not to do what he knows he'll do. Young people who try to rebel usually end up conforming. Sutpen as Jehovah rules Henry's world as a logic that cannot be escaped. Think of the two of them, who captivate the minds of Quentin and Shreve in the twentieth century as a disturbing portent of the relentless American dilemma. Henry and Bon sense that the only possibility of full life for both of them lies in interchange, but they can only go on together by pretending to be what they cannot be. The system that constitutes and divides them, pressing to deform each into half a person, cannot be overcome.

Does Faulkner lack the social imagination to foresee the growth of more flexibility, change, and hope? To some extent he does, but the toughness of his vision should not be underestimated. Perhaps a major social system cannot exist without an authoritative parental figure able to sacrifice his or her children: how else can they be made to fight and work hard? Because Sutpen raises himself from the bottom to the top, he tends to stand for the strongest mobility, the most vital authority. Yet the chain reaction of psychological destruction that Faulkner shows proceeding from Sutpen is appalling. When people are denied humanity by ideological abstraction, they turn around and perpetrate this crime on others. The outrage is passed from Sutpen to Eulalia, Henry, Bon, Clytie, Rosa, Wash Jones, and Etienne Bon so that the negation multiples.

Faulkner's inclination to defend the South—which balances his attack on it—may lead him to overstate the parallels between slavery and capitalism, but my main novelists all emphasize parallels between the two systems for reducing humans to calculable, functional quantities. Such ideological abstraction is described by Faulkner in a nation-sweeping gesture as essentially the same as the orderly systems of thought that run the country, and that are inculcated where Quentin tells Sutpen's story, at Harvard. Harvard is also where Slothrop of *Gravity's Rainbow* is conditioned as an infant with a parody of male drives (*GR* 286). Faulkner sees Harvard as "dedicated to that best of ratiocination which after all was a good deal like Sutpen's morality" (*AA* 225), and finds it suitable that such thinking should be quarantined on campus where "it (the logic and the morality) could do the least amount of harm" (225).

Absalom shows how life is maimed in Sutpen and his followers by a social system of inhuman principles, by personal relations that follow the methodology of power, of mechanical causality, of slavery. The book begins and ends with grotesque images of the deformation left in Sutpen's wake. On the second page, Rosa resembles "a crucified child," and in the last major scene of the book, the 1909 confrontation of Henry Sutpen by Quentin, Henry is a zombie: "the wasted yellow face . . . the wasted hands crossed on the breast as if he were already a corpse" (*AA* 298). Faulkner saves the scene for last because it seals the doom generated by Sutpen's actions. After forty-five years, Henry, unlike Orestes, has not recovered from the loss incurred when he found his principles beyond his capability and gave up the attempt to grant part of himself civil rights. He is finally locked in as irrevocably as Bon was locked out. This realization is traumatic for Quentin because he sees himself as doomed to follow Henry's fate (so he is upset at Shreve's calling Rosa his aunt on 142, 43, 46 and so on), and suspects that all Americans may be children of a power that creates them separate: *"maybe Thomas Sutpen to make all of us"* (210).

Like two children of Sutpen, Quentin and Shreve share such a comprehensive world of perception that they seem to be psychically attached, as is shown by how smoothly they alternate as storytellers. As Spillers points out, it is often difficult to tell which one is talking, and sudden switches from one to the other add to the seamlessness (*Black* 360–61). The debate in the first chapter between "two separate Quentins" (*AA* 4)—one a ghost and the other striving to live—may be continued by the debate between Quentin and Shreve at the end. Shreve, the one who will survive, tends to express the black side.

TWO ENDINGS

Absalom ends with a nightmare vision in which each generation of Sutpen's mixed descendents grows more degenerate. The strongest way to read the ending is as a warning of what will happen unless America gives up artificial, destructive racial distinctions. Such a terrible conclusion accorded with the modernist critique that led to more open, relativistic, and multicultural ways of seeing things. But the ending also reflects Faulkner's worst attitudes in suggesting a biological decline resulting from miscegenation. Fiedler says, "More shocking to the imagination of the South than the fantasy of a white man overwhelmed by a hostile black world is the fear that finally all distinctions will be blurred and black and white no longer exist" (382). Faulkner, however, is a dialogical writer aware of several opposing views at once, and

Shreve stands at the end for an alternative view to Quentin's obsession with southern tradition. Shreve says that "the Jim Bonds are going to conquer the western hemisphere. . . . [A]s they spread toward the poles they will bleach out . . . so in a few thousand years, I who regard you will also have sprung from the loins of African kings" (*AA* 302). Quentin finds this prospect horrifying, but the healthy and jocular Shreve does not. As Parker points out, Faulkner here makes "fun of miscegenation-fear," though he cannot escape it (161).

While Jim Bond figures in Quentin's vision as a symbol of negation, Shreve may simply use him to indicate that the races will mix, which may not be a bad thing. Miscegenation may be a solution to the black-white conflict if it creates a society in which most people are neither. *Absalom* emphasizes the absurdity of the rule that one drop of black blood makes one black, which eliminates all but Aryans. The more advanced side of Faulkner suspects that mixing may not be bad, though his less advanced side is afraid of it.

Since Bond is seen as the channel through which the future will pass, a crucial question is whether his idiocy is a matter of heredity or environment. Whereas Etienne Bon was raised in a supportive environment in New Orleans, his son is born into negation from the start. The very idea that he will pass on his seed and that they will sustain themselves implies that his mental deficiency will not be inherited. In fact, Faulkner could see that the theory deriving degeneracy from mixing was doubtful. Col. William Falkner, the main model for Sutpen, had a mixed daughter, Fannie Forrest Falkner, whom he sent to a Negro college. She married a black college president and had a successful family (Williamson 65–69). While this shadow branch of the Falkners was not recognized, Faulkner's awareness of it would militate against his acceptance of the degeneracy theory.

The Sutpen situation of concealing a black wing of the family may have been the rule rather than the exception in the South, especially for extended families. Jacobs describes a slave who was whipped until there was a puddle of blood under him for complaining that his master had had a child by his wife (759). Among white witnesses, Mary Boykin Chesnut, a member of one of the leading families of South Carolina, says in a diary entry of 14 March 1861, "Any lady is ready to tell you who is the father of all the mulatto children in everybody's household but her own. Those, she seems to think, drop from the clouds" (Dunaway and Evans 241). Chesnut claims that mulatto children exist on every plantation. The county seat of Yoknapatawpha is named for Thomas Jefferson, who had black family.

After his extreme exertion in attacking racism in *Absalom* (1936), Faulkner tended to drift toward more conservative positions, as Weinstein shows, though he kept trying to attack Jim Crow, with diminishing forcefulness (*Subject* 141–52). He made some embarrassingly conservative comments on "race" in his later years, especially in his cups, but he also said positive things. In 1956, while arguing against forced integration, he said that in a century, integration would be accomplished, and that in three, the black race would be completely assimilated into the white one (Williamson 306). While he foolishly assumes that African Americans will become white, the combining of the two races is accepted. Faulkner, then, realizes that Shreve's prediction has its own validity outside of Quentin's disturbance at it, which is therefore seen as limited and pathological. The possibility of escape that Shreve holds out highlights Quentin's entrapment. Shreve is consistently linked to Bon, as Quentin is with Henry (*AA* 237ff., 267), so Shreve may carry on Bon's message in his naturalness and ambivalence. He imagines the Sutpen story accurately from the black side in the language of his period when he concludes that "it takes two niggers to get rid of one Sutpen . . . . Which is all right, it's fine; it clears the whole ledger" (302). Like Bon, Shreve speaks in quotes, using every phrase ironically. His playfulness matches Bon's alienation. Both see the multiple levels of language, and this frees them from being enclosed in the stereotypes of ideology. Despite his irony, Shreve envisions a process of racial conflict in which African Americans are bound to win. The value of black liberation is confirmed by its correspondence to healthy white reactions, for Shreve, like Henry insofar as he has any moral hope, becomes a spokesman for Bon.

BON'S DECISION

Faulkner's insight into the torments of African Americans is shown especially well by the story of Bon, who knows what's good, but also knows the skull *bone* beneath the skin. He is a son without a father because the position of the father cannot be connected to the colonized. So he enjoys great emotional freedom because he is not bound to anything solid, but he wants nothing more than responsibility: "in all the twenty-eight years had never been told by anyone, 'Do as these others do; have this task done at nine a.m. tomorrow' "

(*AA* 246). Faulkner sees that the claim to responsibility has been systematically suppressed with the paternal aspect of the black subculture: if they act
like men, they are troublemakers who must be punished brutally. The power
to run their lives is held by white officials, by the abstract law of the father.
In Bon's case, his life is run by a lawyer who has no feelings except to calculate profit and loss (246, 271). This calculator is the only figure who succeeds
in using the power structure of the novel's world. Though he is continually
tormented by financial frustrations (242), he seems to succeed in murdering
Eulalia and making off with her money (271).

Bon is driven mainly by his mother's rage at her rejection, which is conveyed to him before words as the fundamental reality of life: "he took it for
granted that all kids didn't have fathers too and that getting snatched every day
or so . . . and being held for a minute or five minutes under a kind of busted
water pipe of . . . vindictiveness and jealous rage was a part of childhood" (*AA*
239). According to Lacan's theory of the mirror stage, a baby must be reflected
by parents in order to develop a sense of wholeness (*Écrits* 3–9). For Bon,
however, the mirror that should reflect the child is broken. Since this stage
is the basis of one's self-image, Bon lacks coherence and is self-destructive,
for he has never been reflected as a whole. The passage shows how the psychic afflictions of racism can be passed on silently and unintentionally; so the
problem can seem genetic when in fact it is caused by history, perpetuated by
unconscious actions. So Bon's life is dedicated to revenge from birth without
his awareness. Shreve calls Bon a "fatalist" because Bon senses that no matter
how he thrashes around, he will end up down the same drain. He is free because no action that he takes can have any significance. Until the end, his only
activity is waiting for Sutpen to recognize him.

Even though Bon could not legally claim Sutpen's property as a black de-
scendant in Mississippi (Polk 137), Sutpen can never recognize him, for it
would destroy the principle of Sutpen's design. Sutpen identifies himself with
this principle of superiority, which is not violated if people think that he is
ruthless or inhuman, or that he stole the money for his mansion. But it will
be violated if his legitimate first son is black because it is intertwined with his
male line of descent and its whiteness. Southerners were continually trying to
prove their whiteness. This was the fundamental equation of their existences,
and African Americans were subject to it insofar as they wanted credit in this
fantasy world.

When Bon can no longer stop realizing that Sutpen will never recognize him, he is driven to lash out at the Sutpens even though he will destroy himself. Bon's story is substantially the same as that of *Native Son* (1940), though this is less because of influence than because of a shared knowledge of social realities. Wright's Bigger Thomas is a son so systematically denied significance by the land that gave him birth that he is pushed to self-destructive violence. Bon, Thomas, and Tyrone Slothrop are perpetually manipulated by forces that they cannot identify. When they confront these paternal and institutional forces, it destroys them.

These figures are in tragic situations that are parallel to Hamlet's. Hamlet, caught in a world ruled by an oppressive, false father, must either "suffer / The slings and arrows of outrageous fortune" or rise up against these injustices "and, by opposing, end them. To die" (3.1. 57-60). Hamlet shares such a choice with Antigone, who resists tyranny. In the era of slavery, and often afterward, African Americans had to choose between accepting injustice and taking grave chances of throwing their lives away. From the white side, this rebellion is suicide, but from the black side, it is creative. In dire situations, it may be the only creative possibility, and its creative potential may be enormous. This matches Eagleton's idea that tragedy reaches beyond the individual. The limitation of Faulkner's ability to see this creative dimension in Bon is continuous with the doubt into which Bon's progeny is cast. Yet there is another side of Faulkner's mind that recognizes Bon's spiritual productiveness, just as Rosa sees Bon's sacrifice as giving meaning to the war by proving *"love's immortality"* (*AA* 120). Indeed, the ability of love to reach beyond selfishness is enacted by the breach that Bon initiates in the racial barrier by his fatal protest, so Faulkner ends up giving Bon more potency and generativity than the author can feel comfortable with, making him the progenitor of the only line in the novel's extended family that may survive, an obscured African heritage.

As Bon knowingly goes to his death by insisting on marrying Judith, he takes her picture out of a locket she had given him and replaces it with a picture of his octoroon mistress. The act shows that Bon expects to be killed, for if he were to join Judith, he would want her picture. Shreve says that Bon switches to say, *"I was no good; do not grieve for me"* (*AA* 287; italics in original). This sounds right, and Singal adds that it will tell Judith "that he was the Bon she loved" (211). Yet these may only be Bon's motives toward *Judith.* In the story "Evangeline," realizing that the picture in Charles's locket has "negro blood" makes the anonymous narrator realize why Charles was sent to Mississippi and why Henry could never permit him to marry Judith. This is elliptical, but it indicates something "worse than . . . bigamy" to a Mississippian, so it seems to imply that the picture of the mistress/wife, perhaps combined with other clues, identifies Bon as black (*Uncollected* 609). Likewise in *Absalom*, Bon finally decides that the mother of his son is the woman to whom he belongs, that his real bond is with the black woman. If he will never be admitted by the Sutpens, he decides to assert his black identity by throwing his death in the face of the white family that denies his existence. This will change (really end) their lives so that he will play an active role, though a negative one. Perhaps it is not until this moment that he fully becomes or realizes that he is black, though Sutpen's denial of him is a big step in this direction. Bon insists on inscribing himself on the Sutpen family, so that he ends up memorialized in their cemetery plot (*AA* 157). His black opposition is the source of the Sutpen story, the sand that produces the pearl. Žižek says that the cause of every symbolic system is a resistance or disturbance that disrupts that system (*Metastases* 30). The Sutpen story would not exist without Bon, the core of the story that gives it its shape and its only direct voice.

Bon joins a series of Americans who could protest against slavery effectively only by giving their lives to make history, including Nat Turner and John Brown. This may be the major input that Faulkner's work takes from African Americans. The voices of such figures, of every black impulse of doomed rebellion, established for Faulkner the sense of black resistance, the obscure force that gives *Absalom* its depth and intensity. The African Americans who had the greatest influence on Faulkner, as on Wright, were those who expressed defiance. This voice of terror and pity is the inspiration for Faulkner's strongest statements of protest. Another example is the slave Eunice, who is found to have drowned herself in "The Bear" (*Go* 267), thus moving Ike McCaslin. This black voice is the kernel of many of Faulkner's greatest works, such as "That Evening Sun," *Light in August, Go Down, Moses* (especially "Pantaloon in Black"), and *Requiem for a Nun*.

In this sense, Bon's decision to die is an act of authorship that generates a pioneering story of protest against racism. Writers of both races fed this protest, but Bon makes a powerful contribution to it by inspiring *Absalom*, one of the main works with which Faulkner contributed strongly to the growth of civil rights fiction. This is another way in which Bon is like Christ: his decision to die produces four versions of his story that influence history to promote freedom. Moreover, Bon survives as a spirit, or ancestor who cannot rest, and this prominent aspect of haunting is closer to African religions than to Christianity.

Faulkner recognizes a defiant self-assertion in Bon's claiming of his black identity, which cuts him off from the white side. Perhaps Faulkner does not appreciate the level on which Bon is initiating a new culture on the black side, but we should remember how Bon is alienated. At least Faulkner makes Bon assert a reversal of Western abstraction through the affirmation of the flesh; and he connects Bon to a dream of Africa, though a distorted one. Moreover, Faulkner realizes that the sensitive white people involved in this story, including himself, have no vital choice but to support Bon's Africanist values, though their support may be lame. I will show how the opposing side that Bon represents grows progressively more important and developed in the following novels, starting with Bigger, who is in a position similar to Bon's, but has his own set of conflicts, which lead to a more substantial development of what I call the American African side.

2

Native Son
Bigger Thomas's Complex Vision

SOUTHERN STRATEGY

Native Son is haunted by the ghost of Sutpen distributed as an abstraction. The system in which Sutpen made a place for himself—with its Coldfield aspect reflected by the piety of the Dalton family—is in charge of Wright's Chicago, just as Faulkner saw its irrevocable logic of power extending to Harvard. To the extent that we are all children of Sutpen, which accords with Wright's views, Bigger Thomas is as much controlled by Sutpen's ideology as is Charles Bon. Yet Bigger, who has no father (his father was killed in a Mississippi "race" riot; *NS* 74), is a child of society; so for him the spirit of Sutpen, of white power, can appear only as a demon that negates him by possessing him. The intensity and centrality of this possession reveal that even though Wright rejected African culture, it works powerfully in the novel. And while possession is Bigger's affliction, it is also, as an African pattern, evocative of resistance. If Bon tries to join Sutpen, Bigger struggles to free himself from this demon of condemnation within him.

Bigger's defiance, developed beyond Bon's, entails two fully opposed viewpoints (circles that deny their overlap), products of Bigger's split position as extensions of Du Bois' "unreconciled strivings" (215). One attitude is the need to join the white world, and the other, to reject it. Neither side can get free of the other. Various attempts by critics to reconcile them—that is, to subordinate one to the other—end up reducing the book. Their irreconcilability gives *Native Son* its modernist force and depth. Wright elaborates the philosophical complexity of the postcolonial situation by seeing it as a dialogue between positions rather than aiming at the correct one. This multiplicity of outlooks may be African.

The Sutpen system that Faulkner sees spreading throughout the United States rejects Bigger as a son before he is born. Bigger bears within himself the agency of whiteness that negates him, just as Sutpen carried the owner who turned him away from the door; but Sutpen can assume the voice of the master, while for Bigger, who can succeed only as a servant, this voice can never be possessed. It can only possess him, deny him, and agitate him. Morrison argues in *Playing in the Dark* that the idea of the adventurer who wins fortunes is built on colonialism (34–45). Bigger has no worlds to conquer: he is the conquered. Yet because he aims outside the existing world of Sutpen, his ideas may lead to creation as well as destruction.

The claim that Sutpen haunts *Native Son* is supported by the fact that Faulkner and Wright were both born in Mississippi eleven years apart during a period (1889–1909) that Williamson describes as the most intense concentration of racism since the Civil War: in this period, 293 black men were lynched in Mississippi, more than one a month (157). The foundation that Faulkner and Wright share remains substantial despite the enormous differences between them, differences that often reflect the system in which they are entwined. Faulkner, for example, had "a storybook childhood" as the son of property owners (Williamson 141), while Wright, the son of a sharecropper, describes a series of hardships and disasters in *Black Boy*. It is apparent how these childhoods made each other possible, and how the system that separated them caused both Faulkner's tendency to be conservative, especially in later years, and Wright's staunch radicalism.

During the 1930s and 1940s, however, when the Depression generated a flood of protest writing, Faulkner and Wright were seen by leaders of the Harlem Renaissance as members of the same movement, a wave of social critics of the South. In 1938, Sterling Brown ranked Wright's stories in *Uncle Tom's Children* with Faulkner, Toomer, and Erskine Caldwell (Fabre 161). In 1941, Alain Locke spoke of "The movement by which [T. S.] Stribling, Caldwell and Faulkner have released us from the banal stereotypes," and added, "It is to Richard Wright's everlasting credit to have hung the portrait of Bigger Thomas alongside in this gallery of stark contemporary realism" (Gates and Appiah 19). In September 1945, Faulkner wrote to Wright about *Black Boy*:

"It needed to be said, and you said it well" (*Selected* 201), adding that Wright had said it even better in *Native Son*. He hedges here by fearing that people will not listen to Wright, and his later excuse for resisting civil rights was that one cannot force social change. Yet Faulkner's next novel, *Intruder in the Dust* (1948), may show Wright's influence in exonerating a black man for killing a white one, and Faulkner's letter evinces solidarity with Wright. Both explore the anger of the lower classes with modernist consciousness, mixing naturalism and modernism.[1]

Of course, *Native Son* deals not with Mississippi, but with Chicago, so I will draw on *Black Metropolis: A Study of Negro Life in a Northern City*, by St. Clair Drake and Horace R. Cayton, to explain how Wright saw the two social orders as parallel.[2] Wright's introduction to this lengthy 1945 sociological study of Chicago says that its "scientific statement . . . pictures the environment out of which the Bigger Thomases of our nation come" (xviii). Drake and Cayton state that more than 80 percent of Chicago's African Americans had immigrated from the South (99); and the roots of black alienation and white racism lay down there.

The political leaders of Chicago, though white, were sometimes liberal; and organized, effective black protest there goes back to the nineteenth century (Drake and Cayton 44). Nevertheless, strong racism emerged when prosperity stalled and the influx of poor black people from the South seemed to cause competition. In 1918, there were bombings, and in 1919, a five-day riot had to be stopped by the state militia. It began when a black youth crossed the line of segregation at a beach and was stoned and drowned. At least thirty-eight were killed in the riot, and five hundred injured, the casualties being mostly black (Drake and Cayton 65–69). In 1928, the year after Wright arrived in Chicago, a black political leader was murdered by a bomb.

Margaret Walker, a friend of Wright's during his Chicago years, says that this incident led "toward his discovery that the landlords and bosses of the urban buildings were no different from the lords of the land in the rural South" (56). She refers here to *12 Million Black Voices* (1941), Wright's history of African Americans in the first-person plural. Most of this book compares the rural Lords of the Land to the urban Bosses of the Buildings (*Reader* 152–238). It emphasizes parallels between the two kinds of masters, analyzing how the Bosses of the Buildings manipulate arrangements to "divide and exploit us" by claiming to be friendly, but swindling us and keeping us in menial positions (223). From the radical viewpoint necessary to see the reality of persecution, many liberal gestures, like the claim that Sutpen does not coerce his slaves, are devices to support racism.

Sundquist says, "in the cultural rise of Jim Crow, the North adopted southern plantation ideology" (*To Wake* 230). Wright realizes that his people are susceptible to northern deceptions because their minds are still tuned to southern oppression. Here Wright distances himself from southern folk culture and its African lore not because he is far from it, but because it still clings to him, as suggested by the use of the first person. His opposition to this mindset is active in his condemnation of previous black writers, which Gates discusses (*Signifying* 118–20). Yet his blindness to the positive role of African-influenced thinking does not keep that thinking from operating in his work, any more than it keeps him from following the African American literary tradition. Rather, such thinking sustains its power even while rejected as "naïve": "Our naïve folk minds become lost in the labyrinth of this reasoning. For centuries we have had to rely on the word of others instead of our own judgment and organized strength; so, with the memory of the Lords of the Land still vivid in our minds . . . we are swept by our simple fears and hopes into the toils of the gangster-politicians" (*Reader* 223).

The explanations in book 3, "Fate," locate the source of Bigger's situation in Mississippi. Here we see the system behind the inner voice that controls Bigger and drives him to murder. This arrangement matches a view that remains powerful in America today, that a major cause of social problems is that African Americans have too many privileges. The novel shows the press stirring hysteria to build a backlash against liberals.[3] To emphasize that kindness caused the problem, the *Chicago Tribune* interviews Edward Robertson, the editor of the *Jackson Daily Star,* who argues that northerners do not know how to treat black people. He says that in his youth, Bigger revealed himself to be a "depraved" type of Negro (*NS* 280), and that "only the death penalty, inflicted in a public and dramatic manner, has any influence upon their peculiar mentality" (280). Robertson says that if Negroes get more education "than they are organically capable of," they become "resentful over imagined wrongs," and the best way to bring them "to their senses" is to lynch one of them. As a deterrent, Negroes must be conditioned "to pay deference" to whites: "the injection of an element of constant fear has aided us greatly in handling the problem" (281). This is the fear that moves Bigger to violence in the first book, so Wright's argument is that racism in its urban form is heavily influenced by the South and is the main cause of crime. Colonel Sutpen is injected into the African American subject to become a kernel of self-negation.

Wright expressed recognition that the patriarchal power of racism occupied the position of Bigger's father in a dream sequence that he wrote for Pierre Chenal's Argentine film of *Native Son,* in which Wright starred in 1950.[4] In this dream, Bessie Mears tells Bigger that what he is seeking is there, and points him toward a field. He runs onto this meadow and sees his deceased father holding out his hands to him. Bigger takes the old man's hand and kneels. The camera pulls in to Wright's face bent down because he is overcome with emotion, but then he hears laughter and looks up. He is shocked to see that the hand he is holding belongs to the racist detective Britten, who is sarcastically laughing at him. His horror is caused by a realization that the central source of his life has been turned demonic.

THE ALIEN CENTER

The white Other that forms Bigger's subject confronts him by jumping into his privacy at the start of *Native Son* when Bigger fights the rat. This rat is more aggressive than we expect rats to be, and this is both a matter of Dostoyevskian expressionism and of African American knowledge of rats that leap at people. On one level (as Dorothy Canfield Fisher pointed out in 1940), the rat, with its "long thin song of defiance" (*NS* 6), is Bigger, who strikes out irrationally against hopeless odds. Yet the rat's ferocity also expresses the system that attacks minorities. The animal acts for the colonial power that occupies the position of Bigger's father—Mr. Dalton, the landlord who owns Bigger's home. What Bigger's symbolic father says to him through social machinery that allows him to speak in an indirect, inhuman voice is, "I don't care for you any more than I do for what I would expose to rats, namely garbage." Having such violence invade his space regularly makes Bigger himself violent. In African terms, which may linger from Bigger's southern folk culture, violence is an evil spirit; and so Bigger is possessed by a demon that enters his body and tries to control his identity.

In *Absalom,* Thomas Sutpen is customarily referred to as "the demon" (5, 6, 8 passim), mainly because Rosa, the only narrator who knew him, is certain that he is one. Bigger's demon occupies the place of the father and pretends to be God, as Sutpen did. In encountering non-Westerners, Westerners often used technological advantages to pretend to be gods.[5] Bigger is driven by a desire to find out the truth that cannot be answered because when he looks inward, he sees something that frightens him. So the roots of his perception are pulled out, and the white power that rules him can be seen only as a blur.

The relentlessness with which the white demon attacks him is embodied by a gnawing animal. A powerful vision of this beast appears in Mississippi bluesman Robert Johnson's "Hellhound on My Trail" (1937), in which Johnson likens the days "worrying" him to a "hellhound" on his trail. This use of "worrying" emphasizes its earlier meanings of "strangling" and "tearing with the teeth." The monster that pursues the African American bard is less Cerberus than a bloodhound that tracks slaves. Jacobs says that if such a dog caught someone trying to reach freedom, it "tore the flesh from his bones" (792). Johnson's lyrics, which emphasize that he must keep moving to stay ahead of the hound and suggest that no move the singer can make will hold off this beast for long, indicate that it has been internalized. So has the rat that "leaped at Bigger's trouser-leg and snagged it in his teeth, hanging on" (*NS* 3): it is hard to shake off. Another example of this pattern appears in Ellison's *Invisible Man* (1952) when the narrator speaks to a blues singer who says that he is constantly pursued by an animal: "Caint you see these patches where he's been clawing at my behind?" (171). The Invisible Man, who comes from the South as Bigger did, tends to take confirmation of his identity from folk culture: and the singer's experience is supposed to represent the narrator's own. Early in *Native Son,* Bigger tells his friend Gus that the white folks live "Right down here in my stomach" (21), and then he refers continually to something inside him that drives him to his doom. He sees the whites as exerting this power when they are not there, so they must be within him: "they ruled him, even when they were far away and not thinking of him" (115).

Joyce Ann Joyce points out that the white social structure in *Native Son* plays the role of the gods who doom the hero in Greek tragedy (30). This places Bigger in a polytheistic context that formally accommodates political reality on a naturalistic level. For Wright, capitalism is ruled by groups of men who exercise the power of gods by their concealed manipulation of social codes that shape what is accepted as reality. By determining language precisely, they condition "his relations to his own people" (*NS* 115). Insofar as he wants to be rational, Bigger is told by the educational system to see his language as a series of errors, so his relation to his people in their own words is inflicted with errancy.

The identification of oligarchy with polytheism appears in striking form in Judith's great speech in *Absalom,* when she speaks of the powers that have constructed the social system that is destroying her: "it cant matter, you know that, or the Ones that set up the loom would have arranged things a little better" (101). The capitalized "Ones" denotes multiple deities, and Judith seems to have absorbed knowledge of the classical gods from Henry. The background of Greek tragedy shifts the organization of the world in the direction of an African plurality of spirits. Like deities, the white shapers of society in *Native Son* are both transcendent and immanent, and the psychoanalyst Fanon brings out the interior nature of this force: "what is often called the black man's soul is the white man's artifact" (*Black* 14). The most important, disturbing thing about this construction is that it is at the center of Bigger's being. But his soul may be not so much the white man's artifact as an antagonistic reaction to that artifact.

The core of his problem, and also of his potential, is a voice deep within him that denies him. This voice matches the superego as internalized father. It is a white voice because colonizers assume the position of father for the colonized, and this white authority adheres to the basis of rational judgment. But at the same time, the authority is turned against Bigger in violent denial, so that he feels he must struggle to resist it to survive. The voice tells him to submit, but submission is inseparable from the degradation of the subhuman stereotype. The authority that tells him to be a good boy is an enemy that will never let him in the gate. He has to defy this voice, even if it destroys his body because to obey it is to destroy his soul. And in defying it, he has to go against law and logic, those white machineries of which the voice is a function.

The identity accorded Bigger is either criminal or slave, so the possibility of legitimating himself is not only beyond his kenning, but a self-betrayal, giving in to the voice from Mississippi that tells him he's wrong. His extreme inability to placate this voice causes his sense that the crime is about to happen. Freud found to his surprise that an unconscious "guilt can turn people into criminals." Many young criminals revealed a "powerful sense of guilt which existed before the crime, and is therefore not its result, but its motive. It is as if it was a relief to be able to fasten this guilt onto something real and immediate" (*The Ego and the Id,* SE 19: 52). This corresponds to Bigger's feeling after he kills Mary that he was bound to do something like this, so it is a relief to confront the truth: "he would know how to act from now on" (*NS* 106): "now that he had killed Mary he felt a lessening of tension in his muscles; he had shed an invisible burden he had long carried" (114); "All his life he had been knowing that sooner or later something like this would come to him. And now, here it was. He had always felt outside of this white world, and now it was true. It made things simple" (221). When Bigger refers to "this white world," he means the only existing world, which is white. When he tries to imagine what he wants, it cannot be formulated, for it is outside human language: "Night school was all right; but he had other plans. Well, he didn't know just what they were right now, but he was working them out" (62). Any viable plans for him are outside reality, for reality is defined by the dominant order on his trail.

If Bhabha sees modernism as a consequence of colonial literature, then what makes Wright a modernist is his alienation, his blackness, which displaces him from the reality of any position he could take. Realism depends on the solidity of the middle-class world (Watt 26–27), positing a center of authority that allows details to be evaluated and therefore realistic. But for Bigger, the center is negative; and the furniture and codes, the smiles and concerns of the middle class are extraterrestrial and are constantly seen as attacking him, relentlessly destructive to him. At the Daltons, for example, a chair is so soft that he fears it has collapsed (*NS* 45).

Bigger's black identity is marginal, founded on refusal. He never expresses his blackness more eloquently than when he refuses, a renitence that can generate exalted poetry. When the police tell him that they will make him reenact the rape and murder, he says, "You can't make me do nothing but die!" (*NS* 336). What he refuses is the white center of power, and this center makes him black in that he becomes black by refusing it and turning against white power in a gesture that seems doomed. Yet every refusal is a waking up to a new reality, and Bigger is continually waking, as he does at the start of each of the novel's three books.

When Bigger realizes that he has killed Mary and assumed the position for which he was destined, he has to confront reality: "In the darkness his fear made live in him an element which he reckoned with as 'them.' He had to construct a case for 'them'" (*NS* 88). The whites are at the core of reality because understanding the foe is the crucial requirement for survival. So when he wakes from his first sleep after the murder, things "simply existed, unrelated to each other; the snow and the daylight and the soft sound of [his family] breathing cast a strange spell upon him, a spell that waited for the wand of fear to touch it and endow it with reality and meaning. He lay . . . unable to rise to the land of the living" (97). His construction of the world depends for its reality on the fear that projects "them," and this indicates how his center is occupied by the white Other; for what provides the key to reality is central. Everyone's center is controlled by the Other according to Lacan's idea of the empty center.[6] Bigger is in a position to feel his alienation from his center because the Other is constantly denying him. He can either stay in the spell in which things exist unrelated (as in the realm of spirits) or he can put things together and connect to reality by harnessing himself to the system that denies him.

The limit of the white authority is represented by Blum, who, as a Jew, is between white and black—Jews often lived near blacks—so he is the easiest "white" to get. Bigger spends most of his time in his neighborhood in conflict with himself over whether to attack the white limit by robbing Blum. That he cannot means to him that he is a slave, that he cannot do anything about being controlled by those who hate him. Bigger becomes the leader of his gang by seeming to have the courage to rob Blum, to be a hero of blackness. He pushes the robbery because he is more afraid of going to the Daltons than of the crime. The most terrible fear is realizing that he's afraid of success, afraid of the gentle white people because the power of their system will make him spoil his chances. We are told that "his courage to live depended on how successfully his fear was hidden from his consciousness" (NS 42). This is why he has to attack Gus to show off his courage against his own people. His violence is caused by the construction in his mind that is built and run by white racism, so that from Wright's viewpoint it is law-and-order that causes black violence. This is an analogy to Blake's famous line from The Marriage of Heaven and Hell (1793): "Prisons are built with stones of Law" (Blake 36).

The white power that subjugates Bigger appears most intensely as a white blur. This blur is a loss of definition because for Bigger the position of the whites cannot be looked upon or detected. Like Lacan's Other, it cannot be seen or defined, yet it watches one from all sides, and one gains identity by being reflected by it. Du Bois speaks of "always looking at oneself through the

eyes of others" (*Souls* 215). The fact that the position of the white blur cannot be specified has to do with the way in which colonial subjects are ruled
by technology they cannot comprehend. Since logical explanation is kept beyond them, they cannot see why the whites make their moves, or where they
stand. Historically, the relations of whites to nonwhites have generally been
built on lies. While getting Bigger's confession, State Attorney Buckley tells
him that he sympathizes with him and is concerned: "You look like an intelligent boy" (*NS* 304). At the trial, however, he presents Bigger as a fiendish ape,
a "bestial monstrosity" (408) that should be killed quickly. In the Chicago of
the novel, Buckley stands as the white leader best able to handle Negroes. He
is proud of this ability, which makes him the book's most powerful figure. The
voice that lies most to Bigger has the greatest control over the truth.

The decentered nature of Bigger's blackness, its construction around a
white center of opposition, corresponds to Gates's concept of blackness as an
empty signifier in *The Signifying Monkey*. In his discussion of Ishmael Reed's
Mumbo Jumbo (1972), Gates points out that blackness has been defined negatively in the West, but it has no essence, either negatively or positively (*Signifying* 237). In Reed's novel, Gates argues, blackness is seen as a text that cannot
be defined, a signifier that cannot be linked to a signified (235). The realization that blackness has no essence or center is invaluable for Reed because it
means that blackness can only be embodied by a multiplicity of representations clustered around an empty core—and this corresponds to the true African tradition that Reed calls "pantheistic" (35). For Reed, monotheism is
a pernicious innovation imposed on sub-Saharan Africans by their conquerors. Reed refers to monotheism as "Atonism" because as originally developed
by Akhn*aton,* it was a worship of the Egyptian sun disk called Aton (170, 174).
Reed sees the Atonist efforts to be at one and to atone for sin as limited in
comparison to an African system that "permits 1000s of spirits" (35).

Jacques Derrida, in "Structure, Sign, and Play in the Discourse of the Human Sciences," argues that the model of truth in the Western world has ad-
hered since ancient times to the idea of a single center on which everything
else depends. The main authority for this model is Aristotle's idea of the first
cause in his *Metaphysics.* But Derrida shows that the idea of a single point of
origin is self-contradictory (279), for one thing because a single point cannot exist without referring to other points. Moreover, the supposedly unique
center has been located differently by a myriad of groups, who often fought

to defend their idea of the true center against the false one. In the twentieth century, however, Derrida says that a "decentering" has taken place (280) on many levels with the realization that there are many centers, no one of which is the true one.

It is imperative to recognize how we are blinded by the compulsion to depend on the model of the true center: only by doing so can we perceive the validity of other cultures, their own bases for authority. Lyotard says that each phrase, through the network of linguistic connections that defines it, is the center of its own universe of language (*D* 70–71). So there are as many universes as there are phrases, a view that corresponds to the complexity of pantheism. Monotheism is authoritarian because its insistence on one God demands submission to a narrow view. Pantheism allows for a variety of possibilities, and Gates sees such plurality as matching the freeplay of Derrida's poststructuralism, which he links to improvisation in jazz and to the African-based play of Signifying (*Signifying* 233–38). No position that Bigger can conceive of can solve his dilemma, but his suspension between them contributes an influential decentered paradigm not only to the liberation of African Americans, but to American culture and literature. To see how this suspension works, I will examine the political possibilities implicated by Bigger's two sides; but first I will describe the agency that separates the two.

THE WHITE BLUR

The whiteness that is always a step beyond Bigger's grasp, and conceals its malevolent intention, gives him a feeling that there can be no solution in order to subjugate him. His continual attack on his own center holds him in a perpetual conflict that is both destructive and generative. The split perspective that results from the falseness of his position gives him a potential both for progress and for reaction. While the division that Wright brings out in Bigger is based on Du Bois' double consciousness, another model for this conflict is the split personality of Dostoyevsky's Rodion Raskolnikov, the hero of *Crime and Punishment* (1866), whose last name means "split."[7] The African American and European American sides modify each other, for Dostoyevsky's thinking brings out the conflict in double consciousness, while Du Bois' brings out the progressive charge of Dostoyevsky's conflict. Fyodor Dostoyevsky was Wright's favorite novelist (Walker 75), and *Native Son* is a radicalized *Crime and Punishment*. Both follow the internal experience of a murderer through his crime to his trial, but Wright is far from Dostoyevsky's acceptance of the punishment.

From the start of *Native Son,* Bigger is in opposition to himself, and the forces that oppose each other in his mind lead to opposing ideologies in the novel. In struggling to control his destructive urges, he avoids the truth, withholding awareness of oppression: "He knew that the moment he allowed what his life meant to enter fully into his consciousness, he would either kill himself or someone else" (*NS* 10). He senses that the real meaning of his life is so unbearable that he will have to destroy its manifestation, though by destroying it, he will destroy himself. This real meaning is given to him by the dominant power as a logic of truth based on a center that excludes him, but without which he cannot control his consciousness.

Wright's ability to disturb members of both "races" makes him an equal opportunity annoyer. He shows that the meaning of Bigger's life is unbearable to him so that white audiences can see how badly society has alienated him. But Wright also wants African Americans to confront the worst problems of their less fortunate kin and to realize that they are connected to those problems. He strives to bring intellectual blacks and lower-class ones together, rather than emphasizing the obstacles between them as Dubey does.

Bigger's continuing conflict with his center causes alternation in "the rhythms of his life: indifference and violence; periods of abstract brooding and periods of intense desire; moments of silence and moments of anger— like water ebbing and flowing from the tug of a far-away, invisible force" (*NS* 29). This "invisible force" is the machinery of whiteness, but the alternation it generates is described as internalized here: "It was his own sun and darkness, a private and personal sun and darkness." The opposing motivations interact dialogically within Bigger. The split in Bigger's subject means that there are two motivations involved in his murder of Mary. During the murder, he is seen as beyond control, subject to subconscious forces, moved by disparate areas of his mind that are out of touch with each other: "He felt strange, possessed" (84), "as though he were falling from a great height in a dream" (85). Immediately after the crime, "He felt that he had been in the grip of a weird spell" (87).

The image that represents the forces of which he is not aware or in control as he kills is the white blur of Mrs. Dalton—the immediate cause of his vehemence as he sees her and panics at the indefinable threat. With his pillow over Mary, he resembles Othello, and like Othello, he would not have committed his crime unless driven by white racism. Iago's clever manipulation of selected "facts" impresses Othello as powerfully logical—instilled with a European logic that convinces him that he has failed to realize the truth. Bigger likewise is taken over by whiteness-as-difficulty-of-definition, three lines before he knows what it is: "a hysterical terror seized him. . . . A white blur was standing by the door, silent, ghostlike. It filled his eyes and gripped his body. It was Mrs. Dalton" (*NS* 85). This gleaming demon controls and possesses him in a blur of undefinableness. Earlier, Mrs. Dalton seemed like a ghost who "could see him even though he knew that she was blind" (60). Through the phrase "white blur," which occurs eight times in this scene (85–91), she extends herself as a perceptual level of pure, disembodied incomprehensibility, a unity he cannot grasp.

When Bigger realizes that Mary is dead, he starts to remove her body: "He took her to the trunk and involuntarily jerked his head round and saw a white blur standing at the door and his body was instantly wrapped in a sheet of blazing terror and a hard ache seized his head and then the white blur went away. *I thought that was her*" (*NS* 89; italics in original). Bigger thought it was Mrs. Dalton, but here the white blur is not attached to any concrete form, and it floats without substance for two pages: "He looked again toward the door, expecting to see the white blur; but nothing was there" (89). As Bigger carries the trunk downstairs, "He expected the white blur to step before him at any moment and hold out its hand and touch the trunk and demand to know what was in it" (90). While the blur is uncanny because it is not identified on these pages, it is finally specified in dreamlike terms after several lines of being undefined: "A noise made him whirl; two green burning pools—pools of accusation and guilt—stared at him from a white blur that sat perched upon the edge of the trunk" (91).

Mrs. Dalton's cat, with its accusing eyes, operates as a demonic spirit, active and ghostlike, in the second book of the novel: "the big white cat bounded down the steps and leaped with one movement upon Bigger's shoulder and sat perched there. Bigger was still, feeling that the cat had given him away . . . as the murderer of Mary. He tried to lift the cat down; but its claws clutched his coat. The silver lightning flashed in his eyes and he knew that the men had taken pictures of him with the cat poised upon his shoulder" (*NS* 202). The cat is like the rat in hooking into Bigger, but it goes beyond the rat in being intensely white and infused with intelligence, moral judgment, and intention-ality. In the main picture of Bigger described, the newspaper photo, this ema-nation hovers over him as if it were part of him (224)—the white blur that possesses and controls him.

The irrational thoughts that pass through Bigger's mind may be shaped by African sources. Eugene E. Miller argues that Wright's works refer to Af-rican American folklore that he picked up in his southern youth. Wright's 1946 story "The Man Who Killed a Shadow" presents the belief that "if you were alone with a white woman and she screamed, it was as good as hearing your death sentence" (*Eight Men* 159). Miller cites anthropology to support a claim that this belief shows magical thinking and is linked to folklore about the deadliness of an owl's screech. This explains why Saul Sanders, in "The Man Who Killed a Shadow," is driven to violence to silence a white woman with whom he is alone (Miller 34–39); and it may indicate why Bigger is so frantic to prevent Mary from screaming. Insofar as Bigger believes in this de-monic force, his crime is partly justified. And racism reinforces his belief: so-ciety uses his folk mentality to convince him that he *must* believe that a white woman's scream is death if he wants to survive.

CONFLICT OF VALUES

The killing of Mary is the central action of *Native Son:* the remainder of the book explores its meaning. The external facts present the murder as an ac-cident caused by Mrs. Dalton's appearance when Bigger was with Mary in her room. If the crime is an accident, then Bigger has no idea that he might be killing Mary when he presses the pillow onto her face: his only motive is to silence her. This is true on the conscious level, but on another level of his mind—linked to the blur that controls him during the murder—the crime is not an accident at all. The text makes this clear soon after the murder: "Though he had killed by accident, not once did he feel the need to tell him-self that it had been an accident. . . . He had killed many times before, only on those other times there had been no handy victim. . . . [A]ll of his life had been leading to something like this. . . . The hidden meaning . . . had spilled out. No; it was no accident, and he would never say that it was" (106). This is the meaning that Bigger was avoiding from the start. Here is the core paradox of the book: the murder was an accident, and it was not. The two sides of this paradox are the sides of Bigger's mind. The murder intensifies his conflict so that these two sides are developed as independent arguments. On the rational level, the crime is forced on Bigger by circumstances and society and he is a victim. On the emotional level on which the demon operates, Bigger takes responsibility for the crime as rebellion and becomes a hero.

The heroic response is emphasized in the parts of the book following the murder: "a confidence, a fulness, a freedom; his whole life was caught up in a supreme and meaningful act" (NS 116). Feeling purpose and responsibility for the first time, Bigger senses power and ability. Before this, he was inarticulate and blighted with people, particularly whites. Now he can face them with a sense of being superior because he has (it seems) fooled them: "Like a man reborn, he wanted to taste and test each thing now . . ." (111). "It was the first time he had ever been in their presence without feeling fearful. . . . [H]is nerves were hungry to see where it led" (113). The main focus of the special knowledge that now makes Bigger feel superior is racial codes that both "races" block out of consciousness. When he is with whites, he thinks of how their preconceptions blind them: "Would any of the white faces all about him think that he had killed a rich white girl? No! They might think he would steal. . . . He smiled a little, feeling a tingling sensation enveloping all his body" (113). Questioned by Mrs. Dalton after the murder, he realizes that she is limited because she cannot discuss her daughter's misbehavior with a Negro (128). Here is a hidden system to which he has unusual access and that motivates everyone powerfully. By seizing the knowledge of this system through his crime, Bigger gains a cognitive tool that can compete with the hidden program of the whites. Of course, it *is* their program, but he transforms it.

Bigger's positive transformation after the killing is phenomenal. Earlier he seemed incapable of purposive action; now he is launching ambitious plans: "As long as he could take his life into his own hands . . . he need not be afraid. . . . He was more alive than he could ever remember having been; his mind and attention were pointed, focused toward a goal" (NS 149). Bigger's shifting of the blame onto Erlone, his manipulation of Bessie and others, his writing of the kidnap note, and his elaborate plan for taking a ransom all show a heightening of his capabilities. He seems to go from slave to master, from social liability to dynamic executive: "he would plan and arrange" (129). In portraying this regeneration through violence, Native Son substantially predicts the insights of militant black nationalists. Such views are expressed by Fanon and Amiri Baraka (Leroi Jones), both of whom went beyond nationalism. Clay Williams, the protagonist of Baraka's play *Dutchman* (1964), puts it succinctly: "[A]ll it needs is a simple knife thrust . . . . Murder. Just murder! Would make us all same" (35). This fits both European expressionism and the Black Arts movement. Addison Gayle states strongly the reversal needed to realize the meaning of Bigger's act: "To accept the murder of Mary . . . the reader must willingly suspend rational belief and accept . . . a universe in which all values have been turned upside down, in which murder is not a mark of a man's inhumanity, but of his humanity" (169). To do so, for Gayle, is to enter the New World of black writers. While Wright's vision predicted future developments, such insights were available to radicals in Wright's time. A 1940 review titled "Native Son and Revolution," which the Caribbean C.L.R. James wrote under the name J. R. Johnson, says, "In striking such a blow against his hated enemies, in the struggle to outwit them and evade capture, his stunted personality finds scope to expand" (Kinnamon 49). James hails Bigger as a hero of worldwide black liberation.

It grows apparent, however, as book 2 proceeds, that the effects of the murder on Bigger are not all positive: "There was only one thing that worried him; he had to get that lingering image of Mary's bloody head . . . from before his eyes. . . . [S]he *made* me do it! I couldn't help it! . . . She should've left me alone, Goddammit!" (*NS* 113). Bigger often reverts from the idea of being responsible for his crime to the idea that it has been forced on him. No matter how he justifies Mary's murder, he cannot get her out of his mind, as he cannot get her body out of the furnace. In fact, the furnace, blazing under the white edifice, stands for his mind.

He knows that he must clear the furnace out, but every time he tries, conflict keeps him from acting. This suggests that the furnace is an extension of the white blur, the glowing area at the basis of his mind that he cannot confront. As he stoops to see the ashes that he must clear out, "Mary's face . . . gleamed at him from the smoldering embers and he rose . . . hysterical (*NS* 499, 1940 edition). Later, when he tries to shake the ashes, "He imagined that if he shook it he would see pieces of bone falling into the bin. . . . He jerked upright and, lashed by fiery whips of fear and guilt, backed hurriedly to the door. For the life of him, he could not bring himself to shake those ashes" (501, 1940 edition). The last two passages were added when Wright was revising his version of the novel for the Book-of-the-Month Club,[8] possibly emphasizing Bigger's guilt for white audiences. In all versions of the novel, however, Bigger's downfall occurs because he cannot empty the furnace though he must; and the image of Mary's bloody head returns (100, 116, 118, 132, 207, 218). So the line "for the life of him," added for the published version, underlines a self-destructive impulse outside consciousness, as in the killing.

Yet Bigger was aware that if he killed Mary, he would die for it. Insofar as his killing was intentional on some level, as he insists it was, one of his intentions was suicidal. Earlier he "knew" that if he saw the meaning of his life, "he would either kill himself or someone else" (NS 10). He desires to obliterate himself several times (70, 274), but his self-destructive urge is most developed in his major dream: "he stood on a street corner in a red glare of light like that which came from the furnace and he had a big package in his arms . . . and unwrapped it and . . . it was his *own* head . . . and in front of him white people were coming . . . he did not give a damn what happened to him and . . . he hurled the bloody head squarely into their faces" (165–66). The passage resembles spellbinding dreams in *Crime and Punishment* and illustrates a line of Raskolnikov's, "I killed myself and not the old hag" (Dostoyevsky 433). In a sense, every murder is an act of self destruction (destroying the human image), so Mary's bloody head is Bigger's. By his killing, which impels him to tell people about it, Bigger is figuratively hurling his head at white America. This is confirmed when he thinks that he will be executed "for having flung into their faces his feeling of being black" (NS 311). The crime, like every expressive moment of his life, is breaching the white limit. Here he parallels Charles Bon flinging his death at the Sutpens.

Another indication of the negative effects of Bigger's murder of Mary is that of Bessie. He tells Bessie of the first murder supposedly to force her to join his ransom plot; but on the page in which he confesses to her (NS 178), he thinks of killing her. And once he has told her, he begins reciting a speciously logical formula: "she would not do to take along, and he could not leave her behind" (180). "It would be impossible to take her if she were going to act like this, and yet he could not leave her here. . . . He thought of it calmly, as if the decision were being handed down to him by some logic not his own, over which he had no control, but which he had to obey" (229). He knows his argument well, but not where it comes from—the internalized white blur. On the next pages, approaching the murder, he repeats to himself five more times that "He could not take her and he could not leave her" (235). Obsessive repetition highlights the weakness of the rationalization: Bigger would probably be better off either taking her or leaving her than killing her. His main reason for killing Bessie seems to be that for him murder is the most satisfying form of self-expression. As Bessie says, "If you killed *her* you'll kill *me*" (178).

The murder of Bessie repeats features of that of Mary. As Bigger prepares to strike Bessie, "the reality of it all slipped from him" (*NS* 236). As with Mary, he has trouble retaining self-control and has to keep insisting to himself that his action is necessary: "It *must* be this way. A sense of the white blur hovering near, of Mary burning . . . of the law tracking him down, came back. . . . This was the way it *had* to be" (236–37). Both murders are preceded by sexual excitation and followed by exultation. Bigger feels the same positive feelings after Bessie's death that he felt after Mary's: "a queer sense of power. *He* had done this. . . . In all of his life these two murders were the most meaningful things. . . . He was living, truly and deeply, no matter what others might think, looking at him with their blind eyes" (239). Here it grows difficult indeed to accept Bigger's assertion that his crimes are a positive achievement. Bessie's murder, like Bigger's self-destruction, contributes to Wright's portrayal of his protagonist as a victim, a man whose pathologically violent behavior has been imposed on him by an environment of brutal oppression.

Wright's dreadful vision is an invaluable move forward for rigorous African American self-criticism. Moreover, his depiction of male violence against women reflects a strong impulse toward feminism in his work. While he may have an ambivalent attraction to aggression against women, he chooses to portray it as unjustified and horrible here and elsewhere, especially in the first and last chapters of his first novel, *Lawd Today* (1936, published 1963). In "How 'Bigger' Was Born," written twelve days after *Native Son* was published, Wright says that he has begun work on a novel about "the status of women in modern American society" (*NS* 461). This was never written, but as Michel Fabre reports (321), Wright was interested in *The Second Sex*, by his friend de Beauvoir, when it came out (1949).[9] Bessie Mears is probably named after Bessie Smith, who died in Mississippi in 1937 after being refused entrance to a white hospital, and some of Mears's speeches in *Native Son* have a gut-wrenching intensity (180, 229).

Wright insists on the terrible matrix of violence imposed on Bigger, and stresses the desperation of his thwarted need for manhood. Nothing worse has been done to Bigger than to make him hateful, and Wright has to turn against him rigorously, just as he has to worship and exalt him, in order to convey the fury of his life. As Bigger exults over his murders, his cleverness begins to look pitiful in view of the fact that none of his plans has a chance. His logic and sense of superiority are not rational but emotional, imitations of white leaders. Yet despite this ghastly undercutting, and even somehow strengthened, annealed, and made real by it, Bigger's regeneration through violence and his increased perception continue to have great positive force in the novel. The very clash of his opposition to himself portends important new developments, alternate centers. Bigger's self-division makes him a formidable innovator of new ways of thinking, which is how Wright has sometimes been perceived among intellectuals focused on disassembling traditional authority, starting with Sartre.[10]

We are back to those two tendencies in *Native Son* that contradict each other, two sides of the novel's truth. Bigger's violence is both something imposed on African Americans and their weapon against racism. The split in Bigger's mind recurs after the murder of Bessie: "There was something he *knew* and something he *felt*; something the *world* gave him and something he *himself* had." The world gives what he knows, but he has what he feels. Here blackness is linked to decentering: "and never in all his life, with this black skin of his, had the two worlds, thought and feeling, will and mind, aspiration and satisfaction, been together; never had he felt a sense of wholeness" (*NS* 240). The split between Bigger's reason and his feeling—between the crime as accident, and the crime as desire—is a split in the political values of the book.

SOCIALISM AND NATIONALISM

In the lecture "How 'Bigger' was Born," Wright says, "I drew my first political conclusions . . . : I felt that Bigger, an American product, . . . carried within him the potentialities of either Communism or Fascism" (*NS* 446). He adds that Bigger is not yet either communist or fascist, but his dispossession and frustration impel him toward these extremes. From the start, Wright conceived of the ideology of the novel as dualistic. And he connects communism-fascism with the other dualities I have discussed. The rational side of Bigger is linked to communism, and the emotional side, to fascism. These configurations can be presented as a diagram:

Conflict of Values in Native Son

Murder as accidental, negative	Murder as intentional, positive
Forced on Bigger by circumstances and society	Reflecting Bigger's will and purpose
Bigger as victim	Bigger as hero
Rational	Irrational, emotional
Communism	Nationalism
Whites as humans	White blur

The conflict between rationalist communism and emotional nationalism in Wright's work is pointed out by Russell Carl Brignano. Discussing Wright's nonfiction, Brignano cites a clash between Wright's "rational Marxist" "head" and the angry racial protest of his "heart" (70–82). Brignano finds that the end of *Native Son* takes "the Party line" and that "Wright's heavy handed" Marxism "detracts" from his novel (70–82, 146). This is a common view of *Native Son* that has held many back from seeing the brilliance of the book, as I suggested in 1974. In an opposite view, Eldridge Cleaver's *Soul on Ice* (1968) finds in Wright a "profound" social vision (108), and hails Bigger as "a man" because he rebels against the "totalitarian white world" (106). The nationalist Gayle calls *Native Son* the turning point that allowed black writers to speak their own truth (xviii). But while he sees the killing of Mary as a heroic attack on white society, he calls the murder of Bessie an error on Wright's part influenced by communism. Gayle thus presents "two Biggers," one of whom should be celebrated by black people, while the other should be denied (169–70).

Readings of Bigger as a hero capture an important power in the novel, but block out the book's critique of nationalism. What is needed is a dialogic reading that sees both sides as active. One place that the framework of opposing voices is found is in tragedy, and Joyce Joyce recognizes the active conflict in Bigger, relating it to this statement by Sewall: "In tragedy, truth is not revealed as one harmonious whole; it is many faceted, ambiguous, a sum of irreconcilables—and this is one source of its terror" (Joyce 77). This anticipates Lyotard's idea of postmodernism reviving the critical aspect of Marxism by recognizing irreconcilable outlooks (*PM* 12–14).

Early in book 2, as Bigger gains powers, Wright indicates political dangers in his hero/victim's attitude: "he would know how to act from now on. . . . [A]ct just like others . . . and while they were not looking, do what you wanted. . . . All one had to do was be bold, do something nobody thought of. . . . [I]f he could see while others were blind, then he could get what he wanted and never be caught at it" (*NS* 106–7). Wright makes the connection between Bigger's feelings of superiority and fascism clear when Bigger reflects on his alienation from other blacks. He enjoys news "of men who could rule others," for it indicates to him "a way to escape from this tight morass of fear and shame": "He liked to hear of how Japan was conquering China; of how Hitler was running the Jews to the ground. . . . [S]ome day there would be a black man who would whip the black people into a tight band and together they would act. . . . He never thought of this in precise mental images; he felt it" (115). It fits the division of values in the book that Bigger's fascism is defined in terms of feeling rather than thought. John A. Williams says that Wright understood "that Nationalism . . . was brother to racism" (83). In the introduction to Drake and Cayton's *Black Metropolis,* Wright warns that unless the conditions of African Americans are alleviated, they may produce a black Hitler (xx).

Nationalism and racism are emotional attitudes built on selfishness: the idea that "our" people are the best goes back as far as history. Socialism, on the other hand, is a modern product of rationalism that is based on unselfish principles. For Freud, children are born selfish and have to be taught to be unselfish, so that emotion and selfishness are primary, reason and unselfishness, secondary ("Negation," *SE* 19: 235–42). Wright favored psychoanalysis (Fabre 271–72), and he seems to share this view. He presents Bigger's nationalistic pride as a visceral reaction springing from deep layers of feeling. Bigger's connection with socialism, on the other hand, develops slowly, and the affiliation with Marxist concepts that he may gain is learned with difficulty.[11]

The basis of Bigger's attraction to communism is his desire "to merge himself with others and be a part of this world . . . to live like others, even though he was black" (*NS* 240). The agent who nurtures Bigger's socialism is Boris Max, whose speech in Bigger's defense emphasizes rationalism. Insisting on the need to understand, he uses scientific imagery, comparing Bigger to "a germ . . . under the microscope" (383). Hatred, injustice, and violence are caused by historical, selfish misunderstanding in Max's view, so he argues that all should be forgiven and conflicts resolved by reason bringing all sides together. Here communism follows the ideal of internationalism. As Max later puts it to Bigger, "I look at the world in a way that shows no whites and no blacks. . . . When men are trying to change human life on earth, those little things don't matter" (424). For Max's rationalism, Bigger is not responsible for his crime. It was imposed on him by the racial system of America: "We planned the murder of Mary Dalton" (394). Yet there are motivations involved in the crime that cannot be explained by reason, and Max says, "We must deal here with . . . emotions and impulses and attitudes as yet unconditioned by . . . science and civilization" (387). Although Max says that Bigger had to be a criminal because his life was defined as a crime by America (400), he also realizes that Bigger's killing of Mary was "an act of creation!" (400): "the first full act of his life. . . . He accepted it because it made him free . . . to feel that his actions carried weight" (396). Showing insight into how Bigger feels, Max enacts here the strategy to which JanMohamed refers in his essay "Negating the Negation as a Form of Affirmation"; that is, taking the negative image given to one by racism and turning it around against racism.

The values Max describes here are nationalistic, based on self-assertion through conflict. In this framing, Bigger declares himself independent of white America by the crime and assumes self-determination. Max says that men are not supposed to feel guilty when they kill in war (*NS* 396), and speaks of 12 million Negroes as "a separate nation, stunted, stripped, and held captive *within* this nation" (397). So he is aware of the nationalist position, but he does not see how it can lead to benefits. He goes on to warn that a civil war may ensue unless the "races," especially the whites, learn understanding; and he predicts "riots" in America's cities (404). Thus Max's speech presents both of the novel's main ideologies, but stands up for communist values of reason and boundary crossing.

Wright criticizes nationalism by showing how Bigger's possession by the white blur tends to make all whites look like demons. Bigger finds it difficult to free himself from this incubus for long because the abstraction of whiteness runs his world. Even the left only avoids nationalism with difficulty, and an image of the white blur may occur to Bigger quite late in the book, when he is sentenced to death: "He shook his head, his eyes blurring" (*NS* 417). Yet Bigger does at least temporarily pass beyond the blur toward the end of the novel. When Jan forgives him, "a particle" detaches itself from the "looming mountain of white hate" (289). And in his final meeting with Max, he feels that the "white blur" is no longer "hovering near," and he has to confront a "new" and disarming "adversary" (423). This adversary may be the Real as his own limitation.

When Max asks about Bigger's motive, his response reflects nationalism: "He knew that his actions did not seem logical and he gave up trying to explain them logically. He reverted to his feelings as a guide to answering Max. . . . 'She and her kind say black folks are dogs'" (*NS* 350). This answer is emotional: Mary must have been bad because she was white. Wright, however, has presented Mary as obnoxious, foolish, and hypocritical, but not evil. In fact, it can be argued that she loses her life through her effort to fight Jim Crow. Max says, "But Bigger, *this* woman was trying to help you!" When Bigger says, "She didn't act like it," and Max asks how she should have acted, Bigger replies, "I don't know. . . . To me she looked and acted like all other white folks" (350–51). By demonstrating to Bigger that he killed Mary because of the color of her skin, Max makes Bigger see that in rational terms, the murder was the result of misunderstandings on both sides—and Bigger says so: "White folks and black folks is strangers. We don't know what each other is thinking" (351). The lawyer's searching questions draw out from Bigger both sides of his character: the "bitter and feverish pride" (356) and the ultimate desire "to do what other people do" (352).

BIGGER'S COMPLEX VISION

Personality is generally expanded when its conflicts are seen and diminished by attempts to contain it in unity because, like culture, it is an interplay. So Bigger is most aware of himself when he sees the oppositions of his situation. He expresses himself more completely here than ever before, and the effect is phenomenal: "He could not remember when he had felt as relaxed as this before . . . . [H]e had spoken to Max as he had never spoken . . . not even to himself" (*NS* 359). Max shows Bigger that racist evil comes from human weakness: "Now they're mad because deep down in them they believe that they made you do it" (358). Seeing whites as humans with conflicts allows Bigger to see his own conflicts, whereas while they were a blur, he was dehumanized. His deep exchange with Max leads him to join humanity. He wonders whether "after all everybody in the world felt alike": if Max risks white hatred to help him, then maybe the white "mountain of hate" is "not a mountain" but "people like himself." Then he would hate "if *he* were *they,* just as now *he* was

hating *them*" (360–61). When Bigger stops seeing only from his side and sees
two sides—thinking in terms of interaction rather than conflict—he passes
from the novel's nationalist attitudes to its socialist ones. The Marxist ideal
of interethnic brotherhood appeals to him powerfully because it gives him
a feeling of belonging to humanity that he has always lacked: "If he reached
out . . . through these stone walls and felt other hands . . . . in that touch, response of recognition, there would be union, identity . . . a wholeness which
had been denied him all his life" (362). Bigger's desire for touch is a parallel
to Charles Bon's.

   This passage, removed from Bigger's reality, expresses a level of idealism
that he cannot sustain continuously. He reverts to the idea of conflict, but
now he seeks a conflict based on knowledge and connection to others: "Was
there some battle everybody was fighting . . . ? And if he had missed it, were
not the whites to blame for it? . . . But he was not interested in hating them
now. He had to die. It was more important to him to find out what . . . this
new elation . . . meant" (*NS* 363). Bigger is driven by death to thinking that
is serious and concentrated, as JanMohamed explains, for he is now able to
overcome his social death of fear by accepting his actual death (*Death-Bound*
129–34). As a result, at this end of his pendulum, he can agree with Max that
"race" is insignificant compared to progress.

   In his last interview with Max after the trial, the prisoner leads in asking
questions. The strain of Bigger's "double vision" (*NS* 364) is apparent as he
vacillates between mistrust that Max is not concerned and realization that
Max has communicated humanity to him. Bigger finally manages to make an
impressive statement: "I'm glad I got to know you before I go!" (423). But
Max disappoints him soon after this by not appearing to remember the crucial
import of their first interview. As Joyce points out, Max's relation to Bigger
is primarily professional (103): while he does have an interest in Bigger's personal life, that interest mainly serves his defense of Bigger, which serves communism. Like Bon's lawyer, Max illustrates how the colonial system puts an
attorney in the place of the father.

   Max does try, but as he attempts to comfort Bigger through a comprehensive explanation of his own worldview, the two men run into disturbing
trains of thought. Max says, "they say that black people are inferior. . . . They
do like you did, Bigger, when you refused to feel sorry for Mary. But on both
sides men want to live. . . . Who will win? Well, the side that feels life most,

the side with the most humanity. . . . That's why . . . y-you've got to b-believe in yourself, Bigger. . . ." (*NS* 428; last ellipsis in original). Max may well feel uneasy when he tells Bigger to believe in himself. By his own account, the injustice of their world necessitates conflict. Earlier Bigger had thought that "All his life he had been most alive, most himself when he had felt things hard enough to fight for them" (419). Now he responds to Max's adjuration to believe in himself with searching logic: "when I think of why all the killing was, I begin to feel what I wanted, what I am" (429). His ability to reason, which was blighted early in the book, and stirred to extravagance at the murder, now finds a human focus. Max backs off from this and reacts "despairingly." But Bigger, a page from the end, insists on developing this point intensely for eighteen lines. "I didn't want to kill!" he shouts, "But what I killed for, I *am*!" (429). He himself will be killed by a racist government in a half day, so his need for truth drives him through restless cogitation. Starting with a vague need to believe that his action was "kind of right" (428), Bigger advances to seeing that it defines his ideal or real self. But this self is conflicted because he "didn't want" to do it. Like someone grasping an electric wire, he seizes an identity of anguish in order to issue a flash of insight. The truth of his ethnic dilemma shapes a personality that consists of an attack on himself and that reaches for a future beyond racial negation. This radically decentered identity plunges forward into the transformation of history.

Critics have noticed the great contrast between the philosophical and poetic language used to describe Bigger's thoughts and the limitation of his inarticulate vernacular speech. Laura E. Tanner, in "Uncovering the Magical Disguise of Language: The Narrative Presence in Richard Wright's *Native Son*," is troubled by the description of Bigger's mind in language that he could not understand, and argues that Wright aims to expose narrative conventions (Gates and Appiah 138–46). I think that the contrast between descriptive lines like "reforge in him a new sense of time and space" and spoken lines like "Gee, kid" (both on *NS* 135) serves to indicate the distance between Bigger's consciousness and the psychological, racialized, social, political, and conceptual forces operating in his mind, or operating it. In trying to speak for those who cannot express themselves, Wright may use the artificiality of his representation to reflect the difficulty of capturing what is obscured. Yet in his last speech to Max, Bigger *sees* those concealed forces and articulates them as expressions of himself. As he grows theoretical, he assumes the authorial consciousness that controls him. So he takes over the narration instead of being narrated, a powerful example of metalepsis. As the hidden voice is searched out, black people gain the ability to articulate the feelings that control them, but the heart of what gets spoken may be dreadful.

The problems involved in making such a terrible figure as Bigger represent African Americans are weighty,[12] as are the problems in making the terrible Hamlet or Oedipus representative. So skeptical analysis such as Dubey's is helpful in questioning representative figures. But while we should seek out such questions, the way forward lies in focusing on the possibilities of expressing the lower classes in their terribleness rather than focusing on the difficulties of such expression. Tragic trespassers may speak for the human attainment of freedom. "What I killed for, I am" is a twist on Descartes' "I think, therefore I am" from someone for whom consciousness is fatal. Bigger communicated his inner self to Max so as to connect to humanity, but what he communicated was his motivation for murder. Bigger's manhood as a colonial subject is defined by his ability to resist domination in a way that is chosen for him rather than by him. Indeed manhood has often been measured by ability to kill, but modern society abstracts this so that one earns manhood by excelling in a skill—and one may be called a killer at what one does well. Defeating an opponent is hidden behind the abstraction of scoring points. But for Bigger, who sees such abstractions as attacking him, the existing world must be killed for another one.

Max is disturbed by Bigger's words here, though he recognized their main principle at the trial when he said that Bigger's life was a crime. Now he says, "No; no; no . . . . Bigger, not that . . . ." (ellipses in original). But Bigger goes on asserting the only thing he has to assert: " 'What I killed for must've been good!' Bigger's voice was full of frenzied anguish. . . . 'When a man kills, it's for something. . . . I didn't know I was really alive . . . until I felt things hard enough to kill for 'em' " (*NS* 429). Bigger had no sense of moral responsibility for his actions until the murder that was to lead him from "Fear" to "Fate." It became a murder retroactively because he did not intend it until he discovered the intention. Thus, he killed for something good in that the crime was an act of self-definition that made him capable of action and understanding. This gives him a basis for insisting to Max that he is "all right," and for send-

ing a friendly greeting to Jan at the end of the novel. If Bigger had not murdered, he might never have gained the self-confidence to relate to Jan as an
equal: "Tell Mister. . . . Tell Jan hello" (430).

Yet the reason Bigger sympathizes with Jan is that he has butchered his beloved. Wright is horrified that Bigger's humanity is defined in these terms, but
he realizes that they give Bigger extraordinary philosophical power. Bigger's
existential creation of meaning out of nothingness, which is well delineated
by JanMohamed (119–35), is startlingly advanced for an American novel of
1940. Wright's only peer in this area may be Faulkner. In the late 1940s, Wright
worked with Sartre in France (Fabre 321–22), and his next novel was the existential *The Outsider* (1953). As a writer opposed to the dominant order of
Western civilization, Wright anticipated European thinkers who were moving toward deconstructing that order.[13]

Joyce Joyce points out a reversal in the last scene in which Max becomes
the one who is lost, and Bigger, the one who understands and helps (40-50).
In fact, Bigger, finding a truth to sustain him, does not cry, but Max does. As
he goes out on the last page, Max is unable to look at Bigger: "like a blind
man . . . . He felt for the door, keeping his face averted" (*NS* 429). This parallels the shame of Bigger and his brother on the novel's first page: "The two
boys averted their eyes." In the elaborate imagery of eyesight and blindness
throughout the book, the averted eyes on the last page recall those on the first.
The shame and negation that white America has visited on African Americans
rebound back onto it.

AMERICAN AFRICAN PERSPECTIVES

Visual imagery is one of the most striking means used to convey Bigger's
philosophical complexity and its connection to his political distress.[14] When
Bigger feels seriously threatened—which is often—he characteristically attempts to look in several directions at once. The pattern first surfaces when
the rat is stalked by Bigger, "his eyes dancing and watching every inch of the
wooden floor in front of him" (*NS* 5). A hunter who could not see an animal
in the jungle might use his eyes in this dispersive fashion.

In fact, because European American literature has generally drawn its
imaginative vitality from images of non-Europeans, the first hero of American fiction is identified by the ability of his eyes to wander like the eyes of Native Americans, a trait that earns him his native nickname. This is from the

first paragraph describing Hawkeye in James Fenimore Cooper's *The Last of the Mohicans* (1826): "The eye of the hunter or scout . . . was small, quick, keen, and restless, roving while he spoke, on every side of him, as if in quest of game, or distrusting the sudden approach of some lurking enemy" (22). Natty Bumppo's scattered visuality matches his ability to see vital possibilities that European eyes miss. But his cultural and visual decentering is not as extreme as Bigger's.

The pattern of Bigger's simultaneous multiple perspectives grows clear in the scene of his tense relations with his friends at the pool hall: "With a look that showed that he was looking at Gus on the floor and at Jack and G.H. at the rear table and at Doc—looking at them all at once in a kind of smiling, roving, turning-slowly glance—" (*NS* 37). On his compulsory date with Jan and Mary, "Bigger held his head at an oblique angle, so that he could, by merely shifting his eyes, look at Jan and then out into the street whenever he did not wish to meet Jan's gaze" (66). And at the critical moment when Bigger is silencing Mary, "He held his hand over her mouth and his head was cocked at an angle that enabled him to see Mary and Mrs. Dalton by merely shifting his eyes" (85). The typical pattern of being able to see two threats, one on either side, corresponds to Bigger's political situation of being caught between two clashing ideologies. Africans have often been placed between two competing imperial powers, such as (in *V.*) England and Germany. In America, Du Bois established that black people have been forced by external pressures to cultivate several viewpoints at once.

The pattern is related to offensive stereotypes of black people with rolling or shifty eyes. One of the most famous eye-rollers was Louis Armstrong, for whom rolling was a trademark. Armstrong had more African cultural features than most twentieth-century African Americans because he came from New Orleans, a Catholic city in which Puritanism, as Faulkner suggests, eradicated less of African culture. For example, in the city's Congo Square, early in the twentieth century, African Americans were allowed to play African drums and perform partly African rituals (Atkins 18). African Americans may have used their eyes in such ways partly because they tended to be placed in compromising positions that made it hard to look people "squarely" in the eye. But the American irregularity may well have sprung from African roots: Africans have different ways of using their eyes, if only because of their different environments.

Is there evidence that African eye movements reached America? Spillers, in "All the Things," sees enormous emphasis on the gaze in descriptions of Senegalese in the 1960s. She finds among the Dakarois "a veritable 'grammar' of the look: 'formidable,' 'contemptuous,' 'masked,' 'averted,' 'eyes turned sideways,' 'looks and laughs,' 'looks down (or lowers head)' " (592). She hypothesizes that the Senegalese variety in the gaze "may actually 'translate' into diasporic communities as the analogous stress on looks, prestige, success, and the entire repertoire of tensions that have to do with outer trapping, that is, one's appearance" (592). While she is not thinking of "a transhistorical (black) collective psyche," she does feel that these patterns "could possibly bridge across Old and New World African cultures in a consideration of unconscious material" (593). She suggests here that eye movement could be conveyed across generations and across the Atlantic without verbal instruction, as Eulalia Bon conveys feeling to her son without words. There are indications that some African groups from whom slaves were taken conceived of a person as seeing things from several points of view at once. In some West African cultures, one is supposed to have three or four souls (Nida and Smalley 11); and the image of having more than one mind is a perennial motif of the blues. Wright, in his preface to *Blues Fell This Morning: The Meaning of the Blues* by Paul Oliver (1960), cites a typical line about multiple minds: "I've got a mind to leave my baby an' I've got a mind to stay" (viii). The pattern is given special complexity by Eddie "Son" House in "Louise McGee" (recorded in his old age in 1965): "I gets up in the morning with the blues three different ways. / I have two minds to leave here. / I didn't have but one says stay." Here three different kinds of blues are equated with three minds, and I will later argue that the blues were originally African spirits. Another clue to African thinking about multiple minds may lie in the idiom *first mind,* which Smitherman cites as meaning that one's initial idea is usually the best because it is intuitive (*Talkin* 131).

Concrete evidence for multiple perspectives in African culture may be found in masks. Picasso was influenced by how African masks broke up the face into several different planes as if seeing it from several points of view. This inspired him to invent cubism with *Les Demoiselles D'Avignon* (1907). Here he liberated art from Renaissance perspective that projects a single point of view. Such a view has rarely existed, even in one-eyed people; but Westerners are trained to assume such a unique viewpoint. The term *cubism* has been used for the multiple perspectives of *Absalom,* in which an action is seen first from one viewpoint and then another. This is one way in which Faulkner's absorption in the "race" issue led him toward African perspectives. There are also many African masks that combine several faces turned in different directions (Sweeney, plates 17, 20; Parrinder 73, 77). In representing multiple spirits that can inhabit a "single" person, such masks imply that the wearer speaks and perceives from more than one point of view.

McKee explains African American multivision as a reaction to whiteness. Quoting Ruth Frankenberg, she describes whiteness as " 'a relational category': 'a normative space' that makes it possible to produce and order differences between various racial and cultural identities" (10). Whiteness frames visual representations as abstracted to the point where they become exchangeable (4). It allows all differences to be brought together into a common logical unity, something like capitalism's translating of everything into financial equivalents. It appears to be perfectly inclusive, but it excludes whatever cannot be translated into its logic of unity (14). McKee says that Morrison "refuses the equivalence of discourse and vision that claims clarity and focus as necessary attributes of social meaning. . . . Even if clear, or perhaps because they are clear, these lenses provide only exclusive representations. With less clarity, Morrison represents African American experience as doubled consciousness, doubled discourse, doubled or multiplied vision" (29). Perhaps this multivision is not only a reaction to whiteness, but a heritage from Africa. In her "Characteristics of Negro Expression," Hurston describes the decentered perspective of the multiple body as a typical feature that she calls "asymmetry": black dance has "the rhythm of segments. Each unit has a rhythm of its own, but when the whole is assembled it is lacking in symmetry" (*Sanctified* 55). This matches the scene in *Beloved* in which Baby Suggs bathes Sethe's body "in sections" (109), which could be an African ritual.

Bigger takes pride in his ability to see several things at once as a personal black talent or skill. He draws on this ability when he is being questioned in the Daltons' basement: "he stood in a peculiar attitude that allowed him to respond at once to whatever they said or did and at the same time to be outside and away from them" (*NS* 155). This is a technique for relating to white people, who can be unbearable to Bigger if he concentrates on them. Later, when he is confronted with the Daltons and their maid Peggy, "Bigger's eyes were wide, taking in all three of them in one constantly roving glance" (189).

After his crime, Bigger continually feels that "he could see while others were blind" (*NS* 107) because they do not see the hidden realities of race that he has penetrated. In particular, whites do not realize that he sees the limitations of their perceptions (127). But he also discovers this blindness in his mother: "Whenever she wanted to look at anything, even though it was near her, she turned her entire head and body to see it and did not shift her eyes" (108). Mrs. Thomas's efforts to be respectable may lead her to imitate the stiffness of whites as her need to be proper keeps her eyes directly on the dominant center that controls her. In any case, the blindness of those who follow convention consists in being able to look only in one direction, whereas Bigger, as an outsider, is forced to see in several at once. He connects his plural vision to his highest ambitions. In arranging his kidnap plot, he selects a perfect apartment from those left by urban blight: "By looking from any of the front windows Bessie would be able to see in all four directions" (173). The windows are near a corner and perhaps at an angle, so that by looking from them, one can see streets in all four directions, but the perspective sounds miraculous. And the best thing about Bigger's final refuge on a water tower is that it "had a wide view" (266). In his continual eagerness to see while others are blind, Bigger strives to reverse Foucault's apparatus for controlling people, the Panopticon (*Discipline* 200–202). Instead of being seen by an unseen power, Bigger wants to be the unseen power that does the seeing.

Bigger's final assertion of the nationalist value of his crime is crucial to him because it allows him to see a reality of his own that Max cannot see. Bigger's cultivation of multiple viewpoints leads me to realize that when he accepts the fact that his meaning depends on the murder, he is also aware of the other side. Marginal remarks in his final speech—such as "Maybe it ain't fair to kill" (*NS* 428) and "I know how it sounds" (429)—show a rational side constantly present as a counterpoint in his mind. He knows that his acceptance of the murder he did not intend is not a responsible position that can be held without the pressure of opposition. His nobility finally lies in the acceptance of his terrible fate with a full awareness of both sides, and this is also where his intellectual innovation lies. His two-sided discourse constitutes the *differend,* for Lyotard emphasizes that if the *differend* could be put into coherent language, it would cease to be the *differend* and become mere litigation (*D* 28). But by containing the most radical contradictions, Bigger's increasingly conscious dilemma encompasses the truth about America.

THE PROBLEM OF NATIONALISM

At the end of *Native Son,* the central paradox of the book resounds: Bigger is both the helpless victim of society and the purposeful hero of a racial war. Through his double consciousness, Wright extends the dialogic principle of Dostoyevsky's novels, which Bakhtin (who was not available to Wright) refers to as polyphonic. Bakhtin says that to be alive, an idea has to enter into "genuine dialogic relationship with other ideas" (*Problems* 88); it must interplay with other ideas to avoid becoming fixed dogma. He adds that an idea should never try to be a total explanation, but should be seen as "one orientation among other orientations" (98). *Native Son* builds a dialogue that is intellectually and historically creative in a far-reaching way. It does so by way of Wright's sophisticated ideas about the relation of nationalism to socialism, yet it finally assumes its greatest generative power by going beyond his control.

Wright's "Blueprint for Negro Writing" (1937) says that because "Negroes" have always been separated from whites, their culture is suffused with nationalism (*Reader* 42–43). Only through a sense of group life can African Americans readily grasp the meaning of their suffering, a crucial step toward liberation that Bigger takes. But Wright realizes that this step may be misleading: "Negro writers must accept the nationalist implications of their lives, not in order to encourage them, but in order to change and transcend them. They must accept the concept of nationalism because in order to transcend it, they must *possess* and *understand* it" (42). Because of its reactionary tendencies, nationalism must be subordinated to socialism. Wright enjoins "the highest ... pitch of social consciousness" in a Negro nationalism aware of its "limitations" and "dangers" (42). Such nationalism carries within itself the opposition of the left. Fanon, a later friend of Wright's, also warns that nationalism (which results from and reflects imperialism) will lead to tyrannical native governments unless it is controlled by democracy and socialism.[15] The idea of using the progressive aspect of nationalism leads Shelby into the concept of a nationalism without ethnicity united by a sense of injustice. Bigger may be moving in this direction, but he may only approach it as someone else, without his leading half.

A more actual nationalism appears at the end of *Native Son,* when Bigger asserts the value of his violence and Max is dumbfounded. It seems that the main effect here is pity for a person so dehumanized that murder is all he can believe in, and pity is part of the tragic vision; but Wright emphasizes in "How 'Bigger' Was Born" (*NS* 454) that pity is not what he wants to be foremost. There is also terror, here occasioned by a need for action against the odds. Wright's final assertion of nationalism expresses his feeling for the reality of the lives of the oppressed. This group, in Wright's opinion, has no nation of its own, so it is ironic for anyone with a real share in America to tell it that nationalism is wrong. On the global level, which Max invokes, the world may be divided into a small group of privileged people who are so enlightened by Western education that they can appreciate the merits of democracy or socialism (maybe 20 percent of the world's population) and a larger group who are more concerned about how they suffer because of their ethnic identity. For the people privileged by imperialism to tell the underprivileged that their ethnicity is retrograde unleashes dreadful contradictions.

Bigger's nationalism must be seen as crucial to the truth of black people at the moment when they define themselves as free. Its value lies not in mapping out or fitting into a responsible program, but in showing the falsehood of any such program, in insisting on the *differend*. Bigger's situation has to be expressed in opposed fragments (such as nationalism and socialism) in order to see its actual dynamic as a drive toward future change. The danger would be in making a coherent system by claiming that nationalism includes social welfare (because "we" are so good) or that Marxism can leave nationalism behind (it has not). The justice of socialism and the popularity of nationalism are both parts of the solution. The act that will transform history when it is written about cannot take place without both, but they are from different phrase universes and cannot be reconciled. Because it keeps the relationship between them unresolved and active, it is the perception of their incommensurability that leads to progress. Though socialism should be the goal, it can only be delineated by considering the value of the nationalism that is immediate to the people. The way to make nationalism serve Marxism that Wright moved toward—perhaps without being fully aware—was to express the force and truth of black consciousness as a way of expanding the conceptual limits of rationalist left thinking.

Some of the important truths of nationalism that Wright asserts are based on African thinking, for although Wright was leery of using African culture, his historical position as an African American connected him to it. In *White*

Man, Listen! (1957), Wright says that to be enclosed by African tradition is a "trap" because it keeps one from operating effectively in the modern world (2). Yet later in this book, in the essay titled "The Literature of the Negro in the United States," he takes a positive view of African American folklore based on African sources. Here he says that "the forms of things unknown," which consist of folk utterances, will be "the subject matter of future novels and poems" (83, 87). And in "Blueprint," he says that Negro writers must be aware "of the *whole*, nourishing culture from which they were torn in Africa, and of the long, complex (and for the most part, unconscious) struggle to regain in some form and under alien conditions of life a *whole* culture again" (*Reader* 43–45). Wholeness here probably matches Lyotard's idea of supplementing cognitive knowledge—the only kind legitimated in the West—with the other kinds of knowledge cultivated outside the West.[16] This passage indicates that the survival of African knowledge or lore in America has often been unconscious, and that the effort to recover the coherence of African civilizations is crucial and comprehensive. So it suggests why African elements play active roles in *Native Son*—not merely as affliction, but as vital sources of resistance and of valuable ideas. Wright's African/modernist method of seeing a whole culture is to bring out the division in America because only through dialogic conflict can we see the active form of what has been excluded and denied.

Early in the novel, Bigger and his friends see a movie, *Trader Horn* (1931), that shows "naked black men and women whirling in wild dances" (*NS* 33). He imagines that they are "at home in their world" (34), not considering the stereotyping involved. The scene underscores the gaping space in his life where traditional ethnic culture should be situated; yet Bigger does use African patterns transmitted through his culture. A good example is the scene in which he and Gus "play white," imitating those in power (17–19). The scene is made up of double-voiced signifying techniques that may descend from Esu. We have also seen how Bigger's experience is shaped by demonic possession and by multiple vision. All of these elements use African perspectives to split open the ordinary version of reality, to sharpen alternatives. At the center or centers of *Native Son* is a series of African-based ways of multiplying focuses of consciousness.

Wright, then, contributes to our literature not only a new socialist awareness of a divided America, but a new, decentered way of seeing identity and thought as fields of conflict. It passes through various channels of the underground into a culture of resistance. Whether we trace it through black writers like Ellison and Baraka, through civil rights into the antiwar movement and feminism, or through existentialism into the hipster as "White Negro," the absurdists, and postmodernism, this culture always assumes that the existing order of America is culpable and has to be defied. And it must be defied not by an alternative order that could replace the center, but by a multiplicity of centers that do not seek to coalesce. In this sense, Wright took a step toward Africanizing the point of view of the most vital agencies in American civilization, or perhaps revealing African bases of the American conglomerate. Moreover, the decentering, defiance, and multiplicity described in this paragraph play crucial roles in the thinking of Thomas Pynchon, and Pynchon builds on certain aspects of Wright's worldview. Wright sees African Americans as colonized by the United States in an international Marxist context, and this leads to Pynchon's postcolonialism. Moreover, Max's insistence that "the side that feels life most" will win (NS 428) seems to be related to the force of vitalism in V.

In these conservative times, readers may object to Wright's revolutionary conclusion that America is culpable, which Native Son presents as alienating even Negroes. America has many excellent features, but the purpose of serious literature in the past century has not been to praise America. Such praise consorts oddly with people like Bigger who are born into situations that are both typical and hopeless. The political reality makes it hard to separate praise from the juggernaut that is presently thrusting a bigger and bigger percentage of African Americans into prison and causing the wealth of the top 2 percent of the country to be equal to that of the bottom 90 percent (Lind 190). Today one-third of young African American males are attached to the penal system (Currie 13), and the figure is rising. In cities such as Baltimore and Washington, D.C., the figure is more than half. In a situation in which most of the population is under the law's supervision, Max's argument that Bigger's life is a crime grows concrete as the idea of blaming the individual grows suspicious. As my novelists imply, the issues remain centered on slavery. This is why our best writers have taken such strong positions on the subject of "race."

Yet a certain desperation in the lives of African Americans before the civil rights movement may be reflected in parallels between the endings of Absalom and Native Son. Both insist at the end on rejecting the liberal notion of brotherhood for the harsh truth of conflict. The concluding scene in which Max tries to win Bigger over to enlightenment and Bigger spirals into alienation is parallel to the one at the end of *Absalom* in which Bon responds to Henry's calling him brother by saying, *"No I'm not. I'm the nigger that's going to sleep with your sister. Unless you stop me, Henry"* (*AA* 286). Through their refusal of reasonable compromise, both heroes of the earlier novels give rise to the power to inspire future generations.

Wright conveys a message from Bigger to America, a declaration of independence that has the ultimate purpose of demonstrating interdependence. Wright separates black culture from the white machinery that obfuscated it during earlier centuries; he does so by having Bigger insist that his opposition or resistance is the truth about him. Bigger's refusal of adherence allows a black viewpoint to be seen, and this is a step toward the possibility of reconciliation. In fact, his final gesture is his greeting to Jan, and this may be seen as expressing sympathy and solidarity, mutual engagement in the cause of liberation. Wright, however, confines it to a small point, overshadowed by the fact that Bigger could not connect with Jan until he had connected with his terrible self. Wright senses that to keep both sides active, one must overbalance the gravitational pull to smooth things over. So Bigger's final statement can only be a greeting to the future.

3

Opposing Trajectories in *V.*

THE WORLD BEHIND THE WORLD

Pynchon's *V.* is made up of two books, one a novel set in 1955–56, and the other a book of stories presenting scenes from 1898 to 1943 involving a woman called V. who may be imaginary. There are two main figures in the present action of 1955, a rollicking sailor named Benny Profane and an obsessed intellectual named Herbert Stencil, who projects the stories of V. that make up the second book. The two books shuffle like decks of cards into alternating sections, with a strong sense that the scenes from the possible life of V. are the events that created the decadent 1955 world of eccentrics and bohemians. After studying with Vladimir Nabokov, Pynchon led the shift from modernism to postmodernism by depicting how the alienation of the intelligentsia had caused the United States to be shadowed by theories of history that could not be resolved coherently. Now the narrative of our lives was built over another narrative that could not be understood, or reduced to logical causality.

Joyce had deployed a secondary Homeric narrative behind his primary one in *Ulysses,* but his secondary world is only a series of references, it follows Western mythology, and it does not destabilize his primary one to the extent that Pynchon's does his. Insofar as myth in *Ulysses* does radically destabilize its primary world, it anticipates the postmodern arrangement whereby the undecidability of the past and our relation to it disintegrates the coherence of the present incurably.

Lyotard argues in *The Postmodern Condition* that postmodernism rejects the idea that all knowledge can be unified, insisting that the world is made up of opposing systems that cannot be reconciled. He derives the ongoing opposition from Marx, but says that most Marxists, influenced by Stalin, slip into "unicity," the totalitarian attempt to join everything in one system (11–14). Insofar as oppositions in modernist novels cannot be resolved, works like *Absalom* and *Native Son* anticipate postmodernism, and the insistent conflict in American writers often enacts racial difference. In fact, *Absalom,* like *V.,* moves between a hopeless modern level and a historical sequence on which it depends, and which is composed of uncertainties. We have here parallel critiques of what Pynchon refers to in 1966 as a "white culture . . . of systematized folly" ("Journey").

Yet it is useful to distinguish modern from postmodern. For example, Faulkner, at the University of Virginia in 1958, said that while *Absalom* might present "thirteen different ways of looking at the blackbird, the reader has his own fourteenth image of that blackbird which I would like to think is the truth" (Gwynn and Blotner 274).[1] Here the conservative Faulkner of later years is smoothing over the conflicts of the earlier work. But Faulkner and Wright tend to believe that a single real truth may be discovered behind the various positions they depict, and in this they differ from Pynchon. With *V.,* Pynchon staged the multiplicity of information with so many unconnectable fragments as to sweep away the idea of a coherent center—and to usher in American postmodernism in full swing.

No detail of Pynchon's 1955 world can hold its postmodern existence-in-question without interacting constantly with the sporadic, alienated imagination of history. The life of V. and the world of the 1950s cause each other, as past and present cannot exist without re-creating each other continuously in postmodernist history.[2] As Shawn Smith indicates, Pynchon implies by his dubious narratives that any attempt to see history objectively is fallible (34), and Pynchon criticism has generally emphasized how his fiction subverts linear systems of causality. Yet for this reason, an accidental, pathological assemblage of intuitions such as Stencil's V. construction (*V.* 244) may give more insight than history that proceeds with the blinders of proper authority. If history is as doubtful as Pynchon's text, then the picture of the century that he presents may be as true as any history, perhaps truer insofar as it evades confirmation, or aims at disjunction.

The causality that binds the two narrative time frames together is speculative and elusive because it rests on power effects whose erasure is foundational to conventional history. The shadow world of V.'s story is the history of imperialism, racism, and sexism behind modern European American civilization, or within European history deployed as the basis of American cultural systems. This vision matches ideas presented by Boris Max late in *Native Son*. His account of black America as a nation in bondage (397) leads to a postcolonial outlook of internal colonization; and his claim that "the side that feels life most" will win (428) corresponds to a contrast in *V.* between the inanimate West and the spiritual vitality of the Third World.

The historical action that spans all of *V.* begins with the Fashoda Crisis of 1898 in Egypt and ends with the Suez Crisis of 1956. This sequence emphasizes that conflict over the Middle East—conceived of as a female prize (the fertile crescent that engendered "civilization")—goes on perpetually, with war always imminent. The Suez Crisis, however, advanced decolonization, for Egypt under Gamal Abdel Nasser seized control of the canal. In the twenty years between 1943, when *V.*'s story ends, and 1963, when *V.* came out, the world shifted from colonial to postcolonial as Europe lost direct control over most of Africa and Asia. It is the power shift of history that joins the two books, the two narrative arms of *V.*, at their causal root. The plot of *V.* also has a temporal *v* shape in the order of its telling. The first half of the novel is generally focused on a decline into inanimacy in the West, while the second half portrays a rising action in which humanity is recovered outside the Western order, primarily by Paola Maijstral and her father, Fausto, both of Malta, and by figures associated with them.

Malta is identified in *V.* as a central point between Europe, Africa, and Asia (7, 388).[3] It operates in this scheme so as to imply that the developmental possibilities of the Third World are most visible in the countries that are closest to the West. Yet for the West, the potential for development by any possibility of actual contact is stronger with less Westernized, more culturally distant countries. Cultures framed by the West as extremely different are positioned by fundamental Western exclusions so as to provide moral and philosophical concepts of which the West has need. Likewise, contact with the West, harmful as it may be, shapes the development of the Third World by making its peoples define and activate their cultures as modes of resistance. In this area, as Priya Joshi observes, the colonized reshape the culture of the colonizers by resisting it in translating it (10–11). The focal point of this exchange is the cultural locus where the anxieties of each system pass toward the culture it forms itself by opposing, and then return from that otherness as the signal of the Real, with its beauty and terror.[4] This is any point at the borderline between cultural configurations where interchange is active. As the *differend,* it is also the point where history can change direction, so it is the point on which the *v* of history rests.

At the center of the text of the novel is the low point of its *v,* the point between decline and rise. This is "Mondaugen's Story," Pynchon's nightmare vision of African colonialism. The lowest point of inhumanity is thus the transition point between imperialist destruction and the regeneration of the developing world. This turning point is specifically lodged in a single suffering native woman, the Herero Sarah. She represents the limit of the expansion of empire because she demonstrates that no matter how much degradation is visited on the souls of the colonized, they finally retain their independence and resistance.

From the start of the sequence of historical episodes in *V.,* the hypothetical or virtual woman V. represents the object of desire for the European controllers of power, and she grows increasingly inanimate as the technical means of imperial control grow more artificial and alienated. Paola, her opposite in "mirror-time" (41), is the object of desire for those who seek freedom. Whereas V. first appears as Victoria Wren, who is named for the queen and believes that God is a colonist who fights an "aboriginal Satan" (72), Paola first appears with a link to doubt about colonialism. She has left her U.S. Navy husband, Pappy Hod, and had an affair with a French paratrooper who was tired of committing atrocities against the Algerians. From him she learned a song that indicates her poetic sensitivity. J. Kerry Grant's *Companion to V.* identifies it as "Le Deserteur," by Boris Vian, a 1955 antiwar song that expresses refusal of military service at the time of the Algerian War (8–9).

Several lines of this song, which are first given in the original (*V.* 11, 24) and then translated, speak of going "on the road . . . from the old to the new world" (12). Pynchon says that when he wrote *V.,* he was "attracted" to Kerouac's *On the Road* (*SL* xvi) and saw it as a major aim of his own work to embark "on the road" (xxxiii). This use of the phrase has an African American source that is significant if not originary. Rudyard Kipling uses "on the road" to refer to being headed for a destination in "The Road to Mandalay" (1890), and James Joyce uses it in *Ulysses* (1922) to refer to a traveling salesman (337). But the earliest use of the phrase that I know of to refer to the practice of rambling without a definite goal is in "Kassie Jones, Part 2" (1928), sung by Walter "Furry" Lewis, who was admired in Pynchon's circle of friends.[5] Lewis defines it as the shifting locus of authentic African American identity: "I'm a natural Negro, on the road again." In *Beloved*, Paul D [*sic*] often expects to be on the road permanently. In *V.*, where the destination is always indeterminacy, the transit "from the old to the new world" refers to a removal of focus from the West to the Third World on which the entire novel embarks in moving from America to Malta.

Since V. is attracted to the Third World (Egypt, German Southwest Africa, and Malta), while Paola is drawn to the European-dominated culture of America, they adhere to the two sides of the interface between First and Third Worlds, the margin where culture develops through exchange. Such exchange is enacted by America, a part of the Second World, the colonial world that is neither European nor non-European.[6] From the American point of view, one dominant viewpoint from which they are seen, V. represents European "high" culture as an object of desire. Yet in the course of the century, this European culture is increasingly attracted to non-Western elements that decenter it. What draws each side to the other is the tendency of the other to represent the Real, and America is divided between them.

For Lacan, as Hanjo Berressem notes, the object of desire represents the Real, the lost original object that can never be recovered, but that holds out the possibility of unity and identity (19–20). V. represents the Real of Europe, the desire of Americans to find true identity as Europeans—something that they can never do since they are colonials. This corresponds to the exclusive definition of Americans as Anglo-Saxons, which seems to be V.'s ethnic position. Morrison refers to this Anglo-American tradition in *Playing in the Dark* when she says that to be American has generally meant to be white (47). But there has also been a flourishing *in*clusive definition of America: it involves pride in the ability of the country to allow various ethnic groups to contribute to a diverse national culture that has been identified with such elements as jazz and civil rights. Paola represents the ideal object of this inclusive view of America, so that her advancement represents the progress of the nation. Historically, V. embodies the Anglophone object of desire in the first half of the twentieth century, while Paola embodies it in the second. Between them the dominance of Anglophone culture by the purity of England has been replaced by that of hybrid America.

Deborah Madsen says that V. represents "the link between the fictional world and its metaphysical explanation" and "connects the values shared by a number of disparate historical moments with the perception of the characters that these moments are significant" (38). V. motivates people to interpret history, so she puts a shape on the forces that move events. For Pynchon, the very fact of making the forces of history assume a definite form makes them false and destructive, for history always by-passes in a crucial way whatever it claims to identify. V. plays a destructive role insofar as she expresses the authority of Western civilization; yet she is herself determined and undermined by cultural discourses. Her ability to move men depends on the codes of a civilization that starts with European homogeneity and shifts radically toward non-Western multiplicity, a shift embodied by the transition from Victoria to Paola.

The overall pattern opposing the two women is pointed out by Robert D. Newman: "V.'s descent into the realm of the inanimate is mirrored by Paola's ascent into the realm of human relations" (58). Newman sees that the ivory comb that Paola inherits from V. suggests a transmission of V-ness, and he realizes that colonialism is a central concern of *V.*; but he does not see the cultural shift that moves through the two women. The first vivid image of V. in the book is a vector pointing away from the decadent West toward the non-Western world: "overhead, turning everybody's face green and ugly, shone mercury-vapor lamps, receding in an asymmetric V to the east where it's dark and there are no more bars" (2). This is a signal that any appearance of the letter *v* stands for the force the heroine represents. It also implies that every road, as it recedes into the distance, forms a *v*, a lost highway. Moreover, by pointing from Virginia across the Atlantic, the image suggests that the enigma of American civilization has its roots in colonialism.

The inhumanity of technology here directs the reader to the major part of the world that has not come under its control. Today, when the control of technology has extended further—there are now bars in the East—we have to see Pynchon's views in historical perspective. Active in *V.* is a romantic mythology that idealizes the Third World as a zone free of control. Two problems involved in this outlook must be considered in relation to the novels I feature. The first is what Gates calls "inverted polarities" (*Reading* 8). The idealization of nonwhites may preserve racial stereotypes, while reversing their evaluation. This may be ameliorated by remembering that racial features are codes imposed on people. Yet idealization has served to redress imbalances by highlighting the potential in cultural formations that have been debased. What *V.* and *Beloved* develop more than the other two novels I have treated are countermyths that derive value from opposing the dominant ones, such as the countermyth that people of color are people to be learned from. Moreover, one of Pynchon's main purposes in reversing polarities and having them cross each other in his plot is to call the polarity itself into question. So the idealization of the colonized allows Pynchon to show the truth about the positions not only of the natives, but of the colonists: the dependence of Westerners on culturally formulated fantasies, the limits of their access to the unpredictable.

A sweeping view prevalent during the 1960s was that different oppressed groups shared a common culture, so that minorities, the colonized, the poor, women, and young people could unite in their interests. In *Black Skin, White Masks,* Fanon objects to a statement that colonial exploitation differs from other kinds: "All forms of exploitation are identical because all of them are applied against the same 'object': man" (88). Today, this formula seems to leave out the majority of oppressed people, women. Yet it has a strong logic in its historical position: the more people can be brought into the revolution, the more chance it can be imagined to have. Though these groups may not be able to overcome their differences, focusing on their commonality can encourage change. For Pynchon, black liberation gains power by seeing what it shares with all causes of freedom. This encourages Pynchon to see parallels between the woman-as-object *V.* and nonwhite victims. It weakens his focus by missing great differences between the two groups. Yet all groups that are excluded by the system have similar powers to see alternative links and to create new languages, so the boundary they share is active. What are the progressive implications of this view of everyone as colonized?

The orientation of these minorities who make up the majority reverses that of European males. The natives excluded from civilized roles start in the positions of outsiders from which the faults of the Western system can be discerned. But they are impelled toward an order that they require to develop, so they cannot help needing things the West has. Those ensconced in the Western order are bound, like Henry Sutpen, by a system that determines them. Their need is to take apart their culture, whereas the excluded need is to put theirs together. So Western culture needs to be deconstructed, but non-Western ones need to seek new constructions.

Two articles take opposing views on *V.* as a postcolonial novel, both with some validity, though I prefer the viewpoint of the first. Robert Holton feels that epistemological problems in *V.* break down an objective realism that protects the hegemonic culture of Western society. He says that all of *V.*'s historical sections have imperialism as their subtext, and that the irony of the text supports a central attack on racism (333). Ronald Cooley, however, sees a contrast between *V.*'s attack on colonialism and its narrative complexity, which undercuts any thematic component by reducing it to only one possibility. For Cooley, who sees *V.* as perhaps the best such attempt, this makes it unlikely that a Western writer can attack colonialism effectively (308). Yet Cooley overlooks the likelihood that to attack racism without being aware of multiple viewpoints would be too one-sided to be effective. Pynchon's complexity makes his attacks on racism stronger because they are located (uneasily) in a real world of contingency. Likewise, Pynchon's concern for justice energizes his complexity. The power of his attack on racism has now been confirmed by Patell (89–91).

Cooley makes the dubious assumption that Pynchon's critical and deconstructive techniques should be applied to the radical opposition and to the evidence for the oppression of natives in *V.*—as if those who are already regarded as questionable should be called into question. But deconstruction should be used on what is most securely constructed, and Bhabha sees poststructuralism as a necessary tool of postcolonialism: "To reconstitute the discourse of cultural difference demands not simply a change of cultural contents and symbols; a replacement within the time-frame of representation is never adequate. It requires a radical revision of the social temporality in which emergent histories may be written, the rearticulation of the 'sign' in which cultural identities may be inscribed" (171).

Here is a rationale for Pynchon's unsettling reorientations and his jumps back and forth in history. Bhabha's "rearticulation of the 'sign'" is realized by V. herself, an embodied sign that is framed in uncertainty and changes her name and form, even passing beyond the human. The fragmentary nature of the scenes in which V. appears and the lack of continuity that disconnects them correspond to the "disjunctive temporality" that Bhabha sees in the postcolonial postmodern. Like that of *Absalom,* V.'s story is told out of order in such a way that beginnings and endings are not intelligible: "this arbitrary closure is also the cultural space for opening up new forms of identification that may confuse the continuity of historical temporalities, confound the ordering" (Bhabha 179). Bhabha emphasizes that the " 'indeterminism' " of the postcolonial world is "conflictual yet productive" (172), the key source of new insight in our age. He says that from those who have been oppressed and displaced "we learn our most enduring lessons for living and thinking." Pynchon gives special insight to nonwhites because their exclusion lets them see through the system; they would lose insight if they belonged.

In radical terms, to call the dominant class into question is to undermine its authority, but to question the excluded class only confirms its grievance at being misconstrued. Yet in conservative terms, which have now been sharpened by the terrorist threat, it is dangerous to assume that the underprivileged cannot be criticized. On one level, Pynchon is satirizing as well as enacting the compulsion of liberals to idealize minorities. But he aims to clarify progressive aims, not to defeat them.

THE EXCLUDED REAL

The function of nonwhites as spirits guiding whites toward personal and ethical development is examined in "The Secret Integration," a story Pynchon published in 1964, the year after *V.*'s publication. Pynchon refers to it credibly as his best story (*SL* 22), and its focus on civil rights issues brings out the importance of such issues in *V.* Pynchon's novel *Mason & Dixon* (1997) confirms that these concerns run through his career. In this work, Charles Mason and Jeremiah Dixon see a master whipping his slaves. Dixon seizes his whip, strikes him, and frees the slaves (688–89), yet the scene does not have enough complexity to carry much conviction. "The Secret Integration," which Pynchon says is about "the experiences I grew up with" (20), shows how a group of suburban white adolescents create an imaginary black playmate named Carl. Carl appears as a reaction to the racism they see their parents practicing and to an evening they spend with a black alcoholic jazz musician named Carl McAfee. They are deeply moved by McAfee's desperation, which they see as caused by racism, especially since he gets arrested by sinister white law officers for not having enough money for his hotel room (*SL* 184).

The protagonist of the story, Tim Santora, and his three closest friends all see the imaginary Carl as a real person whom they hang around with and involve in their energetic mischief against adult institutions. Carl is parallel to Charles Bon, for Rosa wonders whether she invented Bon (*AA* 118, 121–22). Though Charles gets much more of a life, he and Carl are both obliged to be fantasms, objectifications of the Africanism that Morrison says Americans have to employ to think about subjects like ethics and metaphysics (*PD* 48, 64). For Tim and his friends, Carl is a spirit they share that gives them access to imagination and freedom, a sort of African spirit. Carl is described as "put together out of phrases, images, possibilities that grownups had somehow turned away from, repudiated, left out at the edges of towns" (*SL* 192). This corresponds to the way the Africanist persona is built up out of what is evacuated by the purification of whiteness. In the story, some white suburbanites, including the parents of the four friends, actually dump their garbage on the lawn of "Carl's" family, the only black one in the area, though the couple is in fact childless. Experiences at the margin of consciousness are rejected by adult rationality, but valued by these young people. Tim used to think of his friend Grover's house as a person, and "still was not at the point where he could give this up completely" (*SL* 148). The imagination reaches beyond established terms, so what is cast off by white men is the source of expansion into new possibilities. Carl's words and gestures are "the kids' own words," but "given by them an amplification or grace they expected to grow into presently" (192). The suffering and exclusion visited on African Americans puts them in the realm of ideal justice, and these young people aspire to this rather saintly black realm to save themselves from what their youth recognizes as a criminal system.

Like Bon in the intellectual and moral supremacy he exerts in *Absalom,* Carl is seen as possessed of a knowledge so real and total that any virtue on their part can only aim at it: "Carl shrugged and sat watching them, as if he knew what, knew everything, secrets none of them had even guessed at . . . which Carl would only someday tell them about, as reward for their having been more ingenious in their scheming, or braver in facing up to their parents, or smarter in school, or maybe better in some way they hadn't yet considered but which Carl would let them know about when he was ready, through hints, funny stories, apparently casual changes of subject" (159). Not only will the reward for any meaningful activity in their lives, any virtue they can imagine, consist of Carl imparting some of his knowledge, but the possibility of goodness beyond what they already know must be attained through him. Not only has he assumed the position of a divinity, as Bon did for Sutpen's children, but for these kids, who may become intellectuals, Carl comprehends the universe of ideas.

The notion of black people as guardian spirits leading whites forward is seen from the dark side in Octavia E. Butler's *Kindred* (1979): here Dana, an African American of 1976, goes back to slavery times to protect and instruct her white ancestor. What she has to convey is the *differend* that has to be made known to carry America into the future and to produce herself. Yet she finds it horribly difficult to reform Rufus Weylin, who finally cannot understand the freedom she offers.

The Lacanian Real that resides beyond language stands for all of the possibilities that any particular language excludes. Berressem says that Pynchon's prose, because it constantly demonstrates the inadequacy of language, "always foregrounds the enigma of the real" (26). He also says of the Real that "Like the unconscious, it can be apprehended only as a cut and a void" (17). Gaps in discourse where language fails are the only way that the Real can ever be manifested to people; and apparitions express something speaking that, in Lyotard's terms, cannot be made cognizable, the cry of the victim (D 30). Any strong manifestation of the Jewish or black holocaust will tend to take the form of a ghost.[7] The Real is a sudden hole in assumed reality, a pattern embodied by Carl, Charles Bon, V., and Beloved—and by Bigger in his blackness, in what Baraka calls "terribleness" (*In Our Terribleness*). In *Kindred*, Butler's 1976 Dana would appear to be a spirit in the 1820s, and may indeed be one.

Carl's method of teaching, "through hints, funny stories, apparently casual changes of subject" (159), matches Pynchon's writing techniques. To change the subject in a surprising way corresponds to inventing a new variation in jazz improvising.[8] By recombining notes in a different way each time, improvising attests that while it is constantly "necessary to link," "the mode of linkage is never necessary" (D 29). The elements of the world can be recombined in unpredictable ways, and the unexpected connections speak for those excluded by the received order. Richard Pearce says that when a gap appears in our representation of reality, the hole speaks for the whole, that is, the rupture of language expresses what has been excluded. By this, Pearce means mainly voices of women, children, and minorities, who do not have languages that can claim effective authority, but who represent the great majority of humanity (10–12). To speak for the Real as a whole is to speak for alternatives to established reality, and this is an approach to the correspondence between non-Western people and postmodernism. To move toward the new world is to open oneself to alternative connections suggested by those who are outside the established order.

OUTSIGHT

The characters who best understand the encompassing poststructural values of *V.* are the two men to whom Paola is closest: her father, Fausto, and her African American lover, McClintic Sphere. They hold understanding because much of the identity of each is situated outside Western civilization. Fausto is convincingly portrayed as a genius who analyzes the phases of his life so as to indicate a shift in the order of world culture. After being colonially educated to cultivate British traits, Fausto was brought close to inanimacy when Malta was pounded for years by fascist bombing. Just as Bigger Thomas felt himself attacked from two sides, colonial people are often objects of wars between imperial powers. During the war, Fausto came to see Malta as a point surrounded by "radial arrows—vectors of evil—pointing inward . . . . Malta in siege" (*V.* 376). Fausto says that his generation came "further from the University-at-peace and closer to the beleaguered city than any were ready to admit, were more Maltese, i.e., than English" (365). He recovered after the war with a negative view of the role of British culture in his world: "Shakespeare and T. S. Eliot ruined us all" (337). "Anglo-Maltese intercourse was a farce. . . . Keep the natives in their place" (368). He also developed a sense of moving back toward life that may involve a new crisis-born respect for the Maltese culture formerly seen as subhuman: "his slow return to consciousness or humanity" (336).

Fausto develops advanced ideas about literature and history, such as his theory that the purpose of the poet in the twentieth century is to lie, to show that the truth is a series of metaphors (*V.* 360). What he has been through on the receiving end of imperialism (which killed his wife, Elena) enables him to see the illusory nature of metaphoric constructs so that he rejects "the fiction of cause and effect, the fiction of a humanized history endowed with 'reason'" (335). Fausto rejects the prime mover so radically that he anticipates poststructuralism. His dense chapter is the philosophical heart of the novel and unfolds its comprehensive theories.

Fausto's status as the person most able to comprehend both the West and the Third World is related to his being one of the two people who see V. and survive to speak to the 1956 characters. The other, Kurt Mondaugen, does not appear directly, but he delivers a blistering message through Herbert Stencil. To see V. is to confront the spirit of history in an electrifying form. Fausto regards Paola with thoughtful consideration and insight, and this may be a big factor in her qualifying to replace V. Fausto's confessions are addressed to "Paola: my child, Elena's child but most of all Malta's" (*V.* 367). He selects the material of his meditation for her: "I would never be telling you this had you been brought up under any illusion you were 'wanted'" (379). Whatever ideas Fausto develops, then, he must intend to transmit to or through Paola; but this applies to virtually the entire intellectual structure of *V.*

A key statement of Fausto's about the organization of the book is ostensibly about himself, but also about the division between Benny Profane and Herbert Stencil: "Perhaps British colonialism has produced a new sort of being, a dual man, aimed two ways at once: toward peace and simplicity on the one hand, towards an exhausted intellectual searching on the other. Perhaps Maratt, Dnubietna and Maijstral are the first of a new race" (*V.* 339). Fausto and his friends combine a division that is created by colonial hierarchies, and that is separated in the two "protagonists" of *V.*: Profane aims at peace and simplicity, while Stencil virtually consists of exhausted intellectual searching. Perhaps the most obvious *v*-formation in *V.,* they are the two sides of a narrative that alternates between them. Fragments of the alienated potential protagonist of the book, they extend outward from T. S. Eliot's "dissociation of sensibility," a failure of contact between thinking and feeling in the modern world (Eliot 95). They add up to a *differend* because each speaks for a different phrase regimen. Profane acts without thinking, while Stencil thinks without acting significantly, since all he can do is follow clues in relation to his father's references to something called "V." (*V* 51). The division of Bigger Thomas has generated a protagonist made up of two irreconcilable figures. These two are both extensions of Pynchon, who served in the navy (1955–57)—linking him to Profane—and who imagined V., as Stencil does.

V. alternates freewheeling Profane chapters set in the book's present (1955–56) with antiqued chapters recounted to or re-created by Stencil and depicting the life of his putative mother and unreachable goal, V., who may have lived from 1880 to 1943, though she may be represented by any word beginning with *v.* The six Stencil chapters (3, 7, 9, 11, 14, and the epilogue, with a few pages excepted) add up to exactly the length of the eleven lighter Profane ones. If one arm of the *v* were longer than the other, it would become a check. The two balanced narratives differ in style. Profane's never stops mocking itself in phrases alienated from meaning, "made up of nothing but wrong words" (*V.* 144); Stencil's seems to take itself more seriously, but it is a series of impersonations that change identity and style to fit shifting narrators and historical settings. Stencil himself is a series of personifications having no identity outside the arbitrary roles he assumes: "he was quite purely He Who Looks for V. (and whatever impersonations that might involve)" (244).

The possibility of intelligent action is foreclosed by the sundering of Profane and Stencil in the contemporary world. They are like Bon and Henry without a common Sutpen to focus on. Yet Fausto is able to hold both sides in his mind, and Sphere, as Newman observes (59), realizes the need to combine the outlooks of Profane and Stencil in his famous line "Keep cool but care" (406).[9] The last European who was able to combine thought with action in *V.* was Sidney Stencil, Herbert's father the British agent. The story of how he comes to be the terminus of intelligent Western action is at the center of the novel, and is intertwined with the story of V. The events of her imagined life trace a series of steps by which she and the men she encounters are caught up in a historical process of deanimation.

THE CURVE OF V-POWER

V. traces a progressive "deterioration of purpose; a decay" (*V.* 104) in leadership through scenes from the life of a woman who embodies the goal of desire for Western civilization as she pursues her powerful drives into the twentieth century. The life of V. illustrates from a partially non-Western perspective how body and spirit come to be sundered in modern Europe. Moreover, changes in the nature of woman as goal are changes in man, so the course of V.'s life defines the course of Western manhood in this century, which declines from activity to consumption, from expansion to tourism, and from adventure to concern for security. Her spell shifts men from extroversion to introversion.

Though V. is first seen as a good girl who believes in forces of light and purity struggling against those of dark and evil around the world (*V.* 72), by next year, in Florence, she has renounced England, become a free agent, and shown attraction to forces she should be fighting. She shows this by choosing an ivory comb made by one of the Mahdists (Moslem rebels who massacred the supporters of England in Khartoum in 1885) that shows British soldiers crucified: "Her motives in buying it may have been as instinctive and uncomplex as those by which any young girl chooses a dress or gewgaw . . ." (177). Victoria is not aware of her attraction to forces opposing the civilization she occupies; her action is as instinctive as the sexuality that seems to cause her to be cast off by her father. "[A]ny Victoria" (72) can be taught to revere the Empire, but "any young girl" can have feelings that break out of its machinery.

The third chapter is hard to read, plunging us into the chaos of the world as it takes on the points of view of inhabitants of Egypt who do not see what the Europeans are up to, which is espionage. V.'s appearance, the birth of V-ness, entails non-Western viewpoints because she embodies a force that reaches beyond Western civilization. The undercurrent of feelings in V. that run counter to her culture is introduced as she is in this chapter. Hearing her name, Aïeul, the Alexandrian waiter, and Stencil's first impersonation, imagines a swarm of possibilities surrounding her:

> This fat one [Goodfellow] was out to seduce the girl, Victoria Wren, another tourist traveling with her tourist father. But was prevented by the lover, Bongo-Shaftsbury. The old one in tweed—Porpentine—was the macquereau. The two he watched [Porpentine and Goodfellow] were anarchists, planning to assassinate Sir Alistair Wren. . . . The peer's wife—Victoria—was meanwhile being blackmailed by Bongo-Shaftsbury, who knew of her own secret anarchist sympathies. The two were music-hall entertainers, seeking jobs in a grand vaudeville being produced by Bongo-Shaftsbury, who was in town seeking funds from . . . Wren. (63)

Excluded from knowledge, Aïeul proliferates contradictory hypotheses. His playful, multiple way of thinking, not tied to Aristotelian causality, is close to V.'s principles of contingent connection, and he may notice what Europeans miss. There is no way to be sure that any of his theories is false, for all of the characters may be playing complex roles, but his first sentence seems to be true, and there may be something to his impression of V.'s "secret anarchist sympathies." Because he can entertain many contradictory interpretations at once, Aïeul exemplifies philosophical advantages possible to the colonized. Bhabha says that the postcolonial subject inscribes a "cultural incommensurability where differences cannot be sublated or totalized because 'they somehow occupy the same space'" (177). The words in single quotes are from Charles Taylor, who is trying to define a "'minimum rationality' as the basis for non-ethnocentric, transcultural judgments." Bhabha hails the use of "incommensurability" to go beyond "'merely formal criteria of rationality . . . toward the human *activity of articulation* which gives the value of rationality its sense'" (177). The philosopher Taylor is striving to gain access to Aïeul's mode of thinking as a path to the future, to an advanced mode of communication. A further extension of Taylor's thinking is the entire chapter, with its eight alienated voices, each with its peculiar focal point. In this, as in all of the V. chapters, revolution is in the air. The exception, "V. in Love," centers on an artistic revolution in dance and includes a Bolshevik, Kholsky (*V.* 450). In chapter 3, the revolutionary feeling is a simmering desire—distributed in various modes among the Africans—to get rid of the Europeans. This picture of the Middle East is the opposite of Orientalism: each voice is different, and the emphasis is on resistance.

The next section is taken by Yusef the anarchist, who keeps "abreast of current events" and dreams of "the elegant woodwork [of the consulate] crusted with blood" (*V.* 65). Yusef sees V. as "A balloon-girl" (65), a title Fausto later applies to her successor Paola (366). It suggests vacuum or void, and the anxious British phrase "up goes the balloon" (something is launched), but it also suggests the buoyancy of beauty, for V. steps like a Botticelli, "Hardly seeming to touch the waxed mirror beneath" (65).

The third impersonation through which Stencil views V. raises the question of her hidden corruption. The pedophile Maxwell Rowley-Bugge briefly wonders if eighteen-year-old Victoria could be Alice, a ten-year-old whom he seduced eight years ago in Lardwick (*V.* 69). He soon decides that Catholic Victoria couldn't possibly be Anglican Alice, but it later appears that V. was from Lardwick (176), so Victoria might have done things that would appall her namesake. Yet this may only show that V. cannot be free from suspicion in the male mind, in this case Stencil's. He later speculates that as a small child she might have known Rimbaud in Africa, and served as "mascot to the Mahdists" (430). V. is constricted and shaped by the male fantasies with which she is surrounded. Rowley-Bugge feels that satisfaction can only be found with girls not yet conditioned to self-conscious repression: "Which was why he drew the line at sixteen or so—any older and romance, religion, remorse entered like blundering stagehands to ruin a pure pas de deux" (69).

His section ends with his being demolished by V., perhaps in revenge, when she says to Porpentine, "Do finish with your cripple. Give him his shilling and come" (76). This so upsets Rowley-Bugge that he rejects the money he's been angling for all evening, and sees his future as grim.

The first three impersonations begin to depict V. as a magnet for male desire. Her attractiveness rests on a quality of will in her, a vitality shaped by the tensions of Western culture, but pointing beyond it, to a world outside it: "receding in an asymmetric V to the east where it's dark" (*V.* 2). As the strength of Western civilization has been measured by its power to expand outside the West, so much of V.'s force field can only be seen by the outsiders who narrate the chapter. For example, Aïeul's impression that V. and Bongo-Shaftsbury threaten Goodfellow has a basis that the principals do not perceive, for in effect she ends up cooperating with the enemy agent to defeat the chubby seducer. V.'s overpowering of Goodfellow portends how power will be sexually organized in the coming century.

Stencil's fourth impersonation is unusual for V. Waldetar the train conductor is a gentle, happily married man whose banter with his wife, Nita, shows healthy, liberating love: " 'Great king,' she yelled: 'Who?' they both started to laugh like children" (*V.* 79). Unfortunately, this playful affection serves to contrast with the operation of power in the political arena as Waldetar is appalled by the European violence and unable to comprehend it. The Sephardic Waldetar shows feelings that are negated by the Empire's power system. Though he is seen as "merely train's hardware," his mind swarms with imagination, and he has a radical vision of vital spirits excluded by the European system mapped out by Karl Baedeker's tourist guides: "A grand joke on all visitors to Baedeker's world: the permanent residents are actually humans in disguise. This secret is as well kept as the others: that statues talk . . . that some government buildings go mad and mosques make love" (78). To give life to something is a definition of love, and Waldetar introduces a non-Western perception that what seems to be inanimate is really animate; but his animist notions are seen as pathological by those who control the world.

Max Horkheimer and Theodore W. Adorno, in *Dialectic of Enlightenment* (1944), define Enlightenment in these terms: "The disenchantment of the world is the extirpation of animism" (5). This suggests that the Enlightenment sees animism as the Church sees sin, as a weakness to which everyone is so prone that one must struggle against it constantly, do all one can at all times to see things objectively, as objects. Animism is so childish, perverse, and anti-intelligent that the main goal of the Enlightenment is to wipe it out of people's minds. To do so, their thinking must be controlled in unprecedented ways that match statistics, that can be translated into mathematical terms. People who cannot be calculated are what Du Bois called the Negro, "a problem" (213). Patell unfolds at length the attack on the Enlightenment in Pynchon and Morrison (82–140).

Such control is attained only by reducing living people to abstract, inanimate concepts. Power is engrafted to machines in the modern world because conflicts are increasingly decided on the basis of technological advancement. Bongo-Shaftsbury, by announcing that he is an "electromechanical doll" and showing an "electric switch" "sewn into the flesh" of his arm, wins a signal victory by frightening Sidney Stencil's friend Porpentine. Bongo-Shaftsbury is a superior agent because he is inhuman. He warns that Porpentine will be in danger as soon as he forgets himself "enough to admit another's humanity," for "Humanity is something to destroy" (*V.* 81) because it is less efficient than machinery. To see how far this principle extends, consider the following chapter, in which Esther gives up a piece of her individual humanity, her nose, to take on a standardized part for efficiency. Plastic surgery has increased vastly since 1963, and it often follows racist, sexist, or classist norms, as it does for Esther, who switches her hooked nose for an upturned one. In a parallel set of terms used by Bongo-Shaftsbury's German partner Lepsius, Esther gives up her "soiled" (75) southern identity for a pure northern mask. The racist distinction between clean Nordic types and unclean Mediterraneans was strong around the turn of the century,[10] and the link between the rational, mechanical mind and the whiteness of the North reaches a climax for Pynchon in the parts of *Gravity's Rainbow* set in Peenemunde, the Nazi rocket-making center on the Baltic Sea.

V.'s defeat of Goodfellow in this chapter appears in a context of the increasing technological sophistication of power. The Fashoda crisis, which is in the background in 1898, was one of the first of a series of crises, often over colonies, that led to World War I. This war is central to *V.* because it consolidated the mechanization of Europe by reducing war from a matter of individual virtue to one of dehumanized masses and machinery. It also led to America's taking the lead from England as the center of Empire. With the disposition of power so impersonalized, the individual can exert ability (*virtú*) only through a specialized technical skill such as flying or spying. Since most crucial action in the modern power struggle takes place *sub rosa,* in secret machinations—such as the plot of Lepsius and Bongo-Shaftsbury to assassinate [Evelyn Baring] Lord Cromer (*V.* 93)—the spy plays a powerful role.

Goodfellow's skill as a spy is reinforced by his ability to seduce women, but what Porpentine sees through the window of Shepheard's hotel is that Goodfellow is impotent with V. This is clear in the first version of chapter 3, the story "Under the Rose" (*SL* 127), but is indicated here only by an understated "A bit thick, you know" (*V.* 88). Goodfellow's failure disturbs Porpentine as badly as his enemies do. Just as he fell after Lepsius touched him (68), he falls outside the hotel, and seems shaken up. Because sexual prowess is an indication of manhood, Porpentine realizes that his team is in trouble as he imagines Bongo-Shaftsbury already present: " 'But perhaps the sun, and what is happening down the Nile [at Fashoda], and the knife-switch on your arm, . . . and the frightened child, and now—' he gestured up at the window he'd left—'have thrown me off. . . . Put your revolver away, Bongo-Shaftsbury' " (*V.* 89). This leads inevitably to the shooting of Porpentine by his inhuman enemy (*V.* 96).

V.'s ability to disarm professionals indicates rare power, and mythic tradition holds that the woman who can destroy the most men, the princess for whom suitors take risks, is the most desirable. That Sidney succeeds with V. in Florence in 1899—an act not confirmed until the end (*V.* 542) and possibly leading to the conception of Herbert—shows that Stencil is more of a man than his doomed colleague. Since the younger Stencil is born in 1901, the relationship of V. and Sidney must be seen as lasting many months for her to be Herbert's mother. So the greater the love or lust in this affair, the better the chance of her motherhood.[11]

THE DEATH OF VENUS

Sidney Stencil proves himself capable of using the power system, but he also sees beyond the system. His ability to be inside and outside makes him the most important male in *V.,* the last complete Western man. The destruction of Stencil by V., which is also the destruction of V. by Stencil, begins in 1899 in the second Stencil chapter and reaches its culmination after the Great War, in the epilogue, in 1919. The relation of V. and Stencil really goes on throughout the Stencil narratives; moreover, it is behind the Profane narrative, for it produces the children of this century. The breakdown of Stencil and V., who both start as practitioners of Machiavelli's "virtú, individual agency" (*V.* 213), polarizes thought and feeling to render real action impossible, leading to the division between Herbert Stencil and Profane.

The Stencil–V. bond at the center of the stories of the past is reflected and paralleled by everything around it. The Egyptian chapter has been shown to prefigure it, and it repeats through the Godolphins, who are foregrounded in the Florentine chapter (7). Hugh Godolphin, born in 1845, is the last explorer in that he discovers Vheissu, linked to the South Pole as the last or deepest place of mystery on earth. Vheissu stands for the possibility of secret or new realities. Sidney, born 1859, contrasts with Hugh as an agent who maintains power by technique in a world in which there are no new areas to explore. The decline shown by contrast between these fathers also appears in their sons. For Evan Godolphin may be a playboy (*V.* 166), but at least he is capable of action as a pilot. He loses his face when shot down because virtue is weakened by technological advances that make war faceless. Herbert Stencil, "the century's child" (48), is born in 1901, two decades later than Evan. Herbert is absorbed in the abstract scheme he inherits—V.—and fears contact with reality. The term "world adventurer" (48) can only be applied to him with a good deal of irony. The earlier father at least sees his son occasionally, and has a body of belief to communicate to him. The Godolphins share the knowledge of V., the source of dreams, which the explorer perceives as an unknown country, Vheissu. The younger father Stencil, however, has no dream to believe in; and his technologized life does not allow him to see his son, just as it does not provide any mother for Herbert (48).

The Florentine chapter is the most lyrical of the book, an oasis of youthful dreams of love and revolution—but these dreams fail. The point late in the chapter at which the decadent Rafael Mantissa fails to steal Botticelli's *Venus,* to effectively consummate his relation to politics, is also the point at which Evan fails to stay with V. because of his obligation to his father. This juncture parallels the void of Sidney's union with V., which is advancing offstage— together with still another failure to secure V., the foreign office's inability to explain Vheissu.

Hugh's stories about Vheissu make Evan see it as preeminent among the "outlandish regions where the Establishment held no sway" (*V.* 166)—an area not controlled by rationalization. American slaves direct from Africa—

as opposed to "seasoned" slaves who mixed cultures—were called "outlandish" because they were furthest from European civilization (Mishkin 26), and Roony Winsome records Sphere for Outlandish Records. When Evan is arrested, the police say, "You may be from any country in the world. Even one we have never heard of" (*V.* 187). The Godolphins represent Vheissu, the incalculability that the ministries aim to curb. Sidney Stencil laments that because the international Situation of political crisis exists in several heterogeneous minds, it has more dimensions than one can comprehend (203). What Fredric Jameson (after Louis Althusser) calls the "absent cause" of history— a multiplicity too complex to delineate its causation (*Political* 82)—is here equated with the incomprehensible part of the world as the crisis focuses on Vheissu. The Third World rebellion from Venezuela that the Gaucho heads serves to manifest the greatest possible distance between cultural frameworks, the multicultural reality that makes monologic planning go wrong. Vheissu is also V., the unknown part of woman that can never be understood.

The contrast between the dreams inherited from his father's more expansive world and "the Establishment" (*V.* 165) of settled order in which he grew up led Evan to rebel and become a cynical hedonist; but his dreams revive in a Florentine spring charged with the drive toward V-ness. His first pass by Victoria is a conjunction of youthful spirits, for she has also rebelled against the establishment to follow personal feelings (168, 176–77). He is stirred by her and by the context of Vheissu to regain a youthful capacity for wonder: "from now on he would perform like penance a ready acceptance of miracles" (215). To confront the unknown is to be alive, relating to the world rather than to known, inanimate patterns.

Hugh Godolphin, however, has followed his dreams to their end or lowest point in a drive to explain or penetrate them; and found that when all mystery is subdued, when one possesses the world for one's system, there is no possibility of life except to find a deeper level of mystery. This is shown when he reaches the South Pole and looks under the ice, only to find another gaudy integument of illusion (*V.* 221). So he has lost faith in the dream his son is reviving—a disastrous gap in timing, as parenthood often is. Evan's very rebellion against his father makes him fear hurting him. So Evan movingly gives in to his father's demands and goes off with Hugh rather than confronting V. in the unknown (224). He will receive Vheissu as an outworn story rather than as living reality. Likewise, it can be inferred that Sidney, in his tryst with V., follows his disillusion or cynicism rather than his idealism, for he does not form a lasting union with her, or doesn't realize that he forms one.

V., cast off by Evan, turns for satisfaction from love to power, from accepting to controlling, in a scene that links violence to desire: "She saw a rioter . . . bayoneted again and again. . . . [S]he saw herself embodying a feminine principle, acting as complement to all this bursting, explosive male energy. Inviolate and calm, she watched the spasms of wounded bodies, the fair of violent death, framed and staged, it seemed, for her" (*V.* 224). Sidney Stencil later reveals that Victoria joined the riot after Evan's departure, flaying an unarmed policeman's face with her fingernails (542). Her equivalent of Sidney's disillusion is a sense that it is safer to use power than to take a chance on another person.

Profane's notion in chapter 8 that "all political events . . . have the desire to get laid as their roots . . . . anybody who worked for . . . inanimate objects was out of his head" (*V.* 230) is fundamental in its insistence that one must either have an animate goal or an inanimate one—either allow an other person to live, to surprise one, or maintain such control that the other is kept at the level of an object, making one a tourist of human relations, a consumer. The joke and the pity here is that Benny himself cannot escape the pattern he denounces as crazy, cannot help treating women as inanimate objects of mechanical processes constructed on standardized outlines. When Rachel Owlglass appears to Profane "perched like any pinup beauty" with her "girl's ass one hand moved to automatic," he feels regret that she is "inanimate as the rest" (398). Just as the natives are human beings hidden behind automata (78), so Rachel is a spirited woman, but poor Ben can only relate to her as a fetish. The typical Pynchonian replacement of an adverb with an adjective ("automatic") is not only vernacular—a hip pretense of stupidity, but replaces an action with an object. Here lovemaking is not a creative activity, but a series of prefabricated units. Pynchon's language relentlessly undermines the conventional connection that Fausto demolishes between motive and action (335). Lyotard says that this connection cannot be formulated because motive and action involve two different genres of language (*D* 48–55).

THE LOW POINT

The link between motive and action has grown subject to manipulation. Technology has given modern people so much control, so many extensions, that they seem able to avoid external opposition. All they apparently need to do is to control the external world to answer their fantasies. This is the situation in "Mondaugen's Story," which, as Patell puts it, "brings the sadomasochism of slavery out into the open" (88). This stark chapter portrays the earth as seen by the eyes of the moon (Mond-augen). The relation of European civilization to the rest of the world—the part "below" European consciousness—and the fashionable one of individuals to each other and to their ids in Europe—has ceased to be the Victorian one of striving for virtue and become one of control for pleasure. How much is conceded to non-Westerners by Westerners depends on aesthetic factors—such as the vividness of a photo of a starving baby—on what will make the Westerners feel good. Foppl's fortress represents Europe, with guests from ten of its countries (*V.* 253–54); and its attitude toward the natives and toward its own soul is one of excess control, overkill, as symbolized by the scene of airplanes bombing natives. Mondaugen has a series of fever dreams that apparently share Foppl's memories. That Foppl, "the siege party's demon" (or their Sutpen), is "coming more and more . . . to prescribe their common dream" (277) indicates that the violence that supports the luxury of their lives is unconsciously shared. Mondaugen has Foppl's visions because the whites in the fortress share what Morrison would call the rememory (*B* 43) of the extermination of the natives, just as the ex-slaves in *Beloved* share the rememory of the Middle Passage, a terrible procedure that keeps going on in the present: "All of it is now it is always now" (*B* 248). In this part of *V.,* the gang rape becomes a model for mutual male involvement in erotic cruelty. Such brutality could not be practiced without a male commonalty that sanctioned it. Wright points out in 12 *Million Black Voices* (1941) that the crews of the slave ships satisfied their sexual desires on the slaves with no restraint while the other slaves had to watch (*Reader* 149).

In Mondaugen's dream, Foppl relives his experiences of 1904–7, when an order was given by General von Trotha to exterminate the natives, an actual historical event. The narrator points out that "von Trotha is reckoned to have done away with about 60,000 people. This is only 1 per cent of six million, but still pretty good" (*V.* 265). The phrase "pretty good" is a striking example of Pynchon's technique of using "wrong words" (144). His postmodern style gets its strongest effects not by using words that suit the subject matter exactly (as in modernism), but with words that do not fit—by how far those words *diverge* from the actuality of subject. As with the African American use of *bad,* the words act in opposition to the normative frames of standard usages. In this case, the shocking confusion of registers involved in referring to genocide as "pretty good" forces the reader to displace her framing of the concept. She may recall that civilizations usually gain status through their ability to kill people in wars; or that by slaughter, nations have been empowered to define the sacred, so that there is no definition of virtue that is not built on murder.

This section puts us in the mind of someone committing genocide. Foppl realizes as he murders and rapes that he feels free of his chief obstacle because he doesn't have to struggle with morality any more: he can enjoy what he feels as his instincts. Justified by beliefs in the dominant ideologies of technology and racism, he need not fight his desires. He can project them on others and be in control, achieving an ecstasy through violence that he calls "functional agreement" (*V.* 284). The rationale for this cold, sadistic sexual stimulation leans on the pleasure of a job well done. Killing natives is satisfying because it exerts manhood as technical ability. Male sexuality tends to feature control, attack, technique, and quantifying (scoring points). A man may be more excited if he has to give less money or commitment, for that makes him seem more potent. So the more criminal his treatment of a woman, the more enjoyable it is, and five women are better than one. In *Gravity's Rainbow,* when Slothrop makes love to Katje Borgesius, he is referred to as "Mister Technique" (222).

"[F]unctional agreement" assumes that the job of killing natives has to be done for the sake of a more efficient world, ultimately for their own good because they are getting in the way of the technical development of their country. Native culture is an obstacle to progress. Lyotard sees functionalism involving a giant machine with a single center that allows one to measure efficiency precisely (*PM* 11–12). *Functional agreement* also assumes that natives enjoy being killed, just as some men assume that women enjoy pain, and some Nazis assumed that Jews liked to suffer. Profane, when he works clearing alligators out of the sewers, comes to believe that the gators want to die (*V.* 154). A refinement of skill in such work is to put the victims into positions in which they seem to enjoy their destruction, a parody of excruciating sexual stimulation. For example, there is a teenage girl who is raped by the platoon, with Foppl last: "After he'd had her, he must have hesitated a moment between sidearm and bayonet. She actually smiled then, pointed to both, and began to shift her hips lazily in the dust. He used both" (287). To satisfy his fantasy, he must avoid realizing that what she wants most is to be done with him. To harness the force necessary for efficient killing, the men must share a manly pride in being able to do terrible things, a pride fed by lust. Atrocities are conceived of as spiritual exercises toward greater control: "Before you disemboweled . . . her to be able to take a Herero girl before the eyes of your superior officer, and stay potent" (279). Because the soldiers could not do their jobs without shaping their desires in this way, Pynchon shows that colonialism and the European culture based on it (and shared with America) must be based not only on the rational motives it keeps insisting on, but on the satisfaction under the rose of unspeakable sexual desires.

The idea of a superstructure of culture based on violence is allegorized when Mondaugen visits Foppl's planetarium. This orrery is powered by an African on a treadmill, so that as Holton (334) observes, the Western construction of the world runs on the labor of those it holds under. Beneath this level, in the basement, Mondaugen finds Foppl sjamboking Andreas Orokumbe. At the root of the European world-machine at this point is the urge to whip a bound man. Foppl is not concerned with winning or being right—what he wants is pleasure: "You like the sjambok, don't you, Andreas" (V. 259). Andreas's wounds smile and his vertebra winks: he gives gratification. The choice of power over love—or satisfying oneself by hurting others rather than helping them—leads to a "progress of appetite or evolution of indulgence" (296), an advance of erotic technique toward greater satisfaction in destruction.

The atrocities of "Mondaugen's Story" are exaggerated in the manner of Louis-Ferdinand Céline to insist that the moral horror of colonialism is beyond realistic conception. If a black writer were to produce this chapter, he would be accused of overstating reality, so this is an example of Morrison's idea that writers on each side strengthen their positions by concessions to the other (PD xi). And it shows how in certain ways white writers can be especially effective in attacking racism.

In German Southwest Africa, V. apppears as Vera Meroving, a cruel temptress with an artificial eye that contains a clock. She is seen flagellating her Nazi lover, Lieutenant Weissmann (white man; V. 255), and annihilating the soul of Hugh Godolphin, perhaps in revenge for his taking his son from her. Indications of how she reached this inhuman state appear in later sections. In 1913, after a series of venal relationships with men, she fell in love with

Mélanie L'Heuremaudit, a ballerina, in Paris. She loved Mélanie for her perfection, making love to her with her eyes (455). In jazz argot, to love someone is to have eyes for that person. Dahoud sings, "I Only Have Eyes for You" (489), and when McClintic is struck by a girl at a party, he says, "Give me back my eye" (326). After Mélanie's death, an apparent suicide, V. may have torn out or removed her eye in remorse, and replaced it with a more perfect prosthesis. In 1919, as Veronica Manganese in Malta, V. already has the clockwork eye, and a sapphire sewn in her navel (542), and she has become a sinister fascist force. Yet she is capable of holding the devotion of the ruined Evan Godolphin, and of generating warmth from Sidney Stencil. It seems to be her loss of Sidney, whom she may be said to destroy by her political role, that makes her turn against life permanently. She reappears in Malta during the 1940s as "the Bad Priest," who is so completely opposed to life that "he" urges Fausto's wife, Elena, to destroy her gestating child (379).

Complementing and balancing the low point of V. as Vera is another story. Mondaugen's dreams of Foppl's experiences end with memories of Sarah, a "Herero child" (*V.* 293) whom Foppl apparently tried to make his mistress around 1908. The protagonist of the dream orders her to sleep with him, and she persists in refusing even after he whips her and holds her head under water with his boot till she almost drowns (295), even though she knows he can kill her. Now he becomes obsessed with her, suggesting that her resistance adds to his attraction. So he has two women hold her while he whips and then rapes her. At a certain point, while he is raping her, she stops resisting; and that night, she comes to his house and slips into his bed. The only word of Sarah's speech given is her name, and it is left a mystery what she thinks; but she may give in to him not only to save her life, but out of a feeling that now that he has taken her, "She was his" (295), so she may as well try to find love here.

Sarah might have become "the closest thing to a wife" that Foppl "ever had" (*V.* 296), but the men of the platoon share their native women, and while Foppl is out, they rape her in a series of deviant ways. Natives serve as receptacles for the forbidden aspects of the group's male sexual mentality. When Foppl returns, he finds Sarah "drooling," and when he unlocks her chains, she springs by him with "an incredible strength" (296) and runs into the sea. Later he finds her body and decides to leave the outpost he was helping to build and to return to a more settled area where he will consolidate his fortress.

Sarah's suicide confronts Foppl with the realization that women and natives do not really want to suffer, that they have a spirit that finally can't be broken, a beauty unattainable for him. He continues to brutalize natives, and to enjoy it, but his active role in expanding the empire is ended. It occurs to him that he could not practice genocide again with the same sense of adventure that he would later celebrate about 1904, and that the remainder of his life, with no indication of any other love, is "meaningless" (297). Moreover, Sarah's death ends Mondaugen's dream-sharing of Foppl's mind. He awakes revived., and soon (after getting Weissmann's solution to the riddle of the sferics and witnessing the bombing of the natives) decides to leave Foppl's fortress. He takes off and ends up riding with a native—and *Gravity's Rainbow* reveals that Mondaugen then spent some time with the Hereros and derived a kind of wisdom from them (*GR* 403–4).

Faulkner presents a parallel to Sarah's suicide in "The Bear": Isaac McCaslin discovers in his family's ledgers that his grandfather Lucius had a daughter by his slave Eunice, and then conceived a child by the daughter. When Eunice realized that her master had impregnated the daughter he had by her, she drowned herself. This suicide clashed with stereotypical images of blacks, and two days after recording her death in 1833, the ledger reads, "Who in hell ever heard of a niger drownding him self" (*Go* 267). So Eunice's death, like Sarah's, is an assertion of humanity in the face of extreme denial, a gesture that has a revelatory moral power to which whites rarely have access. Isaac's discovery of Eunice's suicide leads to his decision to give up the land he inherits.

In *V.* as a whole, Sarah's insistence that her dignity and the possibility of love are more important than her life concludes the low point of the *v* and turns the direction of the book—from heading toward the inanimate to heading toward the animate. From here on, the action of the novel is relentlessly headed for Malta, a scene of regeneration at the edge of the Western world. In the chapter following "Mondaugen's Story," McClintic Sphere passes up another woman to realize that he loves the one he calls Ruby: "When had it become a matter of having her or losing her?" (*V.* 327). Paola has had the courage to pose as a Harlem prostitute in order to find love with the only person capable of it in the Whole Sick Crew. This arrangement diminishes the problem of Sphere's being attracted to her because of the status of her whiteness. Apparently, once they have found real love, Paola and Sphere are able to let it go when she has to return to her father, Fausto. In this regard, they contrast with

Evan and Victoria in the first half of the novel, who cannot afford to part because they have not really found love. So the second half develops the idea of responding freely to changing situations, which Evan Godolphin conceived of in Florence (215), but was unable to enact effectively.

The idea of taking on a series of identities or languages for different situations unfolds in the stages of Fausto's "Confessions," but it is enacted in a more immediate form by the improvisatory lifestyle of Sphere. His falling in love with a prostitute goes against his expectations—the assumption that "A whore isn't human" (*V.* 317)—and an explicit statement of his adaptability to new contexts is "*Set/Reset.*" After talking to an recording engineer about digital computers and flip-flop switches, he writes a piece with this title, and it becomes his theme song for each "set" (319). This found title follows a procedure similar to one used by Thelonious Sphere Monk, after whom Sphere is named. When the composer would play a new tune and someone would ask its name, often whatever Monk answered became the title. Pieces by Monk from the 1950s include "Think of One," "Let's Call This," and the romantic "Ask Me Now." This postmodern use of titles focuses on the arbitrary, spontaneous nature of naming.[12] Monk often ended his sets with a theme song that had an abstract title, "Epistrophe."

Sphere is the only male in the Crew capable of love, and he may be the only real creator in this collection of pseudocreators (*V.* 400). The main model for Sphere, as Stanley Edgar Hyman pointed out in 1964, is the innovative Ornette Coleman (509). Coleman had not yet appeared in 1955–56, but Pynchon may have decided to base Sphere on Coleman despite the anachronism in order to refer to the radical upheaval of Coleman's "free jazz." Sphere's "ivory alto" Africanizes the white plastic alto sax that Coleman played when he arrived in New York in 1959. And the pianoless quartet Pynchon describes at the V-Note (based on the Five-Spot Cafe), seems to be Coleman's. Intellectuals of all races liberated their minds through free jazz's surprises and "rising rhythms of African nationalism" (*V.* 56).

DISAPPEARING DESTINATIONS

Having spoken of Sarah, Fausto, and Sphere, I will focus on two more examples of the rise toward humanity late in the book, Paola's reunion with Pappy Hod and Sidney's role in the epilogue. The reunion is hard to accept because Pappy seems to be a limited figure, and he was abusive to Paola in the past (*V.* 11). Paola's earnest protestation that she will act as Penelope to Pappy, whom she now calls "Robert," seems out of keeping with the tone of the rest of the book and hard to believe: "I will sit home in Norfolk, faithful, and spin. Spin a yarn for your homecoming present" (492). Yet there has been earnestness all along in Paola's restless turning from one man to another for love. Her disguising herself as a prostitute has a touch of earlier drama, such as Oliver Goldsmith's *She Stoops to Conquer* (1773). It acts out the insecurity of her borderline identity as a hyphenated American.

Cooley argues that this scene undercuts *V.*'s serious content, including its attack on imperialism; he finds irony in the phrase "spin a yarn" (492). The scene has an ironic level, but irony does not keep Pynchon from being emotionally effective at his best. It is important to realize that Pynchon does have emotional power (though it declines in the 1990s), for his works are sometimes dismissed as lacking feeling. "Mondaugen's Story" is a stupendous modern version of the Dance of Death. Even *The Crying of Lot 49* touches us when Oedipa Maas meets a forlorn old bum in San Francisco (125–26). In *Gravity's Rainbow,* the story of Franz Pökler, whose family is sent to a concentration camp, can make a reader cry, and the sublime ending of that novel, the sacrifice of the child, is quite moving though the irony remains.

The reunion of Paola and Pappy is affecting and dignified because of the social disorder and doubt that it counters. Chapter 16 shows the crew of the Scaffold trying to protect Hod because they know how he has been suffering over the loss of Paola. She has worked through her critique of marriage and pursued freedom into experience. Having been a barmaid and a prostitute, she may be expressing the views of the exploited in concluding that the solidest relationship is the best. Moreover, Pappy may have learned through separation from Paola to respect her. In any case, it seems clear that he loves her: "He'd been saying it every night to a steel bulkhead and the earthwide sea on the other side" (*V.* 492). Having lost Paola, Profane realizes that the one he didn't get is the "one unconnable (therefore hi-valu) girl" (504). This tends to confirm her V-ness, but she reverses V.'s trajectory, for V. starts respectably and becomes an outsider, while Paola starts the novel as an outsider and ends by assuming a respectable position. Yet it is respectability with a difference, for the text indicates that Paola does not need makeup to pass for an African American (388), so social progress may be made if Paola and Pappy succeed in 1956 as an interracial couple. Their reunion enacts the best potential of America, so the following words near the end of the scene may not be entirely ironic: "The American flag, skewered by spotlights, fluttered limp, high over them all" (493).

The other major action to contribute to the affirmative movement of the second half is saved for the epilogue: Sidney Stencil's last mission. The year 1919 finds Stencil horrified at the war and convinced that a universal blindness makes war inevitable and meaningless. It has been recessed only because its organizers have run short of money and young bodies: "this abattoir, but lately bankrupt" (*V.* 510). He sees that the separation between "Right and Left; the hothouse and the street" (520), which will eventually be manifested by his son Herbert and Profane, makes it impossible for his world to contact reality. This is parallel to the dilemma of nationalism and socialism that Wright saw in modern society. Now Sidney confronts V. again, yet he realizes that he has "passed and repassed you, or your work, in every city" (542), for she is the force behind the machinations of power. Even before he actually makes love to her (in a hiatus on 541, during which he learns of her sapphire navel), he realizes that "he'd be little use henceforth" to Whitehall because his affair with her was not over: "What he had thought was an end had proved to be only a twenty-year stay" (541). He is bonded to her by nostalgia, and she is inanimate, entangled in fetishes, a symbol of a civilization too encased in possessions to take on fresh experience. His fatalism is clinched by sex with her semi-animate body.

The opposite of V.—Carla Maijstral, pregnant with Fausto, but in danger of being destroyed by V.'s temptation of her husband—confronts Sidney with some consequences of his political role. The swelling life in her body reverses V's spreading cancer of inanimacy, and her dependence and defenselessness also oppose her to V. She feels that if Maijstral continues to spy for the British at V.'s house, he will be caught and killed by his fellow workers. And if he continues to stay away from her in the orbit of V., she will not wait to be destroyed by infidelity, as her mother was, but will kill herself (*V.* 537). Fausto writes that she would have walked into the sea with him inside her (351). So Sidney saves her from drowning, reversing Sarah's fate. Sidney's recognition of Carla is his last contact with reality, as signaled by the Real. He stops Maijstral from seeing V. only by threatening to expose him to the workers (546). But in saving Carla and her baby, he gives up Maijstral, his last spy in V.'s camp, betraying his duty drastically and alienating V. by removing her toy Maijstral. So Sidney negates his whole life of service to the Empire by one vital gesture, and from here on, the distance between his reality and his values will remain such that, like Herbert, he will be unable to live in the present. As he dismisses Maijstral, "He forced himself into the real present, perhaps aware it would be his last time there" (545).

Sidney's mysterious death may be illuminated by comparison to the mysterious death of Fausto's wife, Elena. Both lose their attachment to life, and then get blown away by the contingency of the world, as if they submitted to the disorder of existence: she is hit by a bomb, and he, by a waterspout. Just as he loses his life when he loses his agency as a spy, she loses hers when her connection with Fausto breaks down. This occurs in the nightmarish scene in the park in which Fausto realizes that he does not know her, for she has slipped back, under the influence of wartime stress and of V. as the Bad Priest, into atavistic superstition: "Was she even seeing the same pavilion . . . was she here in fact" (V. 373). She gives up life because she is unable to escape her cultural background into the real world of the West; Sidney gives it up because he is unstrung by confrontation with the Real outside the West. Together they enact a realization in V. that the Third World needs to move toward the West and the West needs to move toward it.

The reality that destroys both characters is precisely the interface between the two sides, which they are unable to handle because each is invested in one side or the other. This interface, or v, the site of the Real in which language breaks down, can be a terrifying scene of chaos and conflict. Fausto sees it as such in the park scene: "As if winds were blowing today from all thirty-two points of the rose at once to meet at the centre in a great windspout to bear up the fire-balloon like an offering . . ." (V. 371). The windspout–fire-balloon seems to combine the waterspout and the bomb. The way to deal with such disorder is to make it comprehensible by building connections on different sides, as the progressive figures of the rising action do.

Bomb and waterspout are linked again in a passage that suggests that what controls them is a factor of randomness so tightly linked to women as to be virtually a function of theirs, though they cannot control it. Fausto's journals reflect that "Mothers are closer than anyone to accident" (V. 355) because pregnancy is so unpredictable. The function is that of making the inanimate animate: "they do not understand what is going on inside them; that it is a mechanical and alien growth which at some point acquires a soul. They are possessed. Or: the same forces which dictate the bomb's trajectory, the deaths of stars, the wind and the waterspout have focussed somewhere inside the pelvic frontiers without their consent, to generate one more mighty accident" (355). The forces that generate colossal disasters are located in woman's powers of birth-giving, which are manifested whenever the rules are broken, when something supernatural appears.

The deaths of Elena and Sidney are presided over by a female spirit, for the Valletta area is said to be ruled by the destructive Mara, whose name means "woman" (*V.* 513). The second half of the book is generally either in Malta or headed for it, so a female deity may be in charge once Sarah dies. In this realm in which the inanimate becomes animate, the feminine spirit punishes those who deny life, randomly killing the Bad Priest (379). This female deity may suggest possibilities for a post-masculine, post-Western outlook that will carry further the transformation of violence to compassion, an outlook like Morrison's. In the second half of *V.,* women take on new powers of resistance, like the Sultan's harem inspired by Mara (514). Esther Harvitz denounces Shale Schoenmaker (323–24), and Rachel sees the pitiful emptiness of men in Profane: "you all live inside us" (411).

Stencil's sacrifice, because it contacts reality, is productive. The colonial father who exerts authority over his colonized "children" can have horrible effects, which are indelibly depicted in "Mondaugen's Story"; but a creative function of the father is to sacrifice himself for his children, and one positive role the West can play is to sacrifice itself for the developing parts of the world. By his listening to Carla and restraining Maijstral so as to save her, Sidney makes it possible thirty-seven years later for Fausto and Herbert Stencil to have a great potential for communion—though Herbert's obsession limits it. When Fausto says, "I only made it into this world through the good offices of one Stencil," Herbert says, 'It may have been his father," and Fausto says, "Making us brothers" (*V.* 494). Though Herbert has to reject Fausto's claim that the original Anglo-V. is dead (494–502), the scene shows how the colonizer Sidney, in sacrificing his authority as father, enacted the vital paternal function of giving life.

The connection and continuity between Sidney and the Maijstrals is indicated as he watches Maijstral walk away from his release with a step "less sure." Sidney pronounces a postmodern benediction: "let him be less and less sure as he gathers years. . . ." (*V.* 546; ellipsis in original). Sidney may finally realize that he has been regenerated by his opposition to the ruling order, the source of sureness. This adjuration is fulfilled in the life of Fausto, who advances toward greater ability to sustain uncertainty, so we may say that Sidney's relation to Fausto is a working fatherhood, just as Paola's returns to her father and Pappy bind up connections between generations and "races." The generosity of the West gives non-Westerners like Fausto the ability to be free, whereas the stringency of the West impels them to resentment and intolerance.

Both Paola and Sidney obliterate themselves by joining the other side. But because Paola moves from the dark side of the social construct toward the white side, she loses creativity to gain security—while Sidney, in moving from the white side toward the dark one, loses security to gain creativity. The Stencil-Maijstral story develops the notion that the best thing a Westerner can do is to turn against his role in the Empire: it saves lives and provides for perception of both sides. When *V.* was written, this attitude was growing in America. Bob Dylan's 1964 song "Chimes of Freedom" praises "warriors whose strength is not to fight." The war that young people were repudiating in 1963 was against communism. Perhaps this argument does not apply today to a war against fundamentalist terrorism, but we should still oppose the atavistic imperialism unleashed by this threat.

Though *V.* insists on the inhumanity of the century it depicts, it is not an inhuman book: it aims to complete humanity. Like Joyce's *Ulysses,* it searches into the failure of human connections as bleak actuality, but suggests other possibilities. The fragmented world of scattered links and forlorn hopes deployed in *V.* evokes the dream of a new ordering. This new world sought by Pynchon's hipster questers is introduced at the start when Paola sings of straying "over land and sea" "*au nouveau monde*" (*V.* 11), and its potential swells as the book proceeds toward Valletta. Sundquist uses the term *New World* with the reservation that it is "problematic" because of social ills imported from Europe to America (*To Wake* 136), but *V.* aims at a world that is truly new. To some extent, it corresponds to the world that Addison Gayle talks about in *The Way of the New World: The Black Novel in America* (1975). Yet Gayle is too exclusive in making anger and blackness the criteria of this world. He is right in maintaining that through black anger the truth can become visible, but the new world will have to accommodate more, including the sympathetic aspects of white people, the excluded world of women, and minorities, such as the Native Americans whose spirits are submerged in our land and culture.

A more recent, eclectic view of the hope for a new articulation of America that conjoins radicalism with visions of African culture appears in Robin D. G. Kelley's *Freedom Dreams: The Black Radical Imagination* (2002). Kelley reviews the relation between the left and the black freedom struggle, arguing that for a century black radicals like Du Bois and Wright tried to persuade socialists to see the centrality of the "race" issue to social advancement. But Marxists generally responded that nationalism was a distraction, and that the problem of "race" could only be solved by socialism. Kelley argues that this resistance to confronting "race" is racist and is one big reason that the left has done so poorly in America (36–59)—a debatable view, but perhaps significant. Kelley thus sees cultural nationalism as having potential to reform the left. He admits that hopes for social and cultural liberation have faltered in recent decades; but he celebrates these dreams of a new land in which the established system of privilege and prejudice would be replaced by one of freedom and tolerance. Hoping to inspire a new generation, Kelley reaches out to more people than Gayle addresses, including feminists and progressive whites. Yet appealing in 2002 to people's senses of beauty and liberation, Kelley presents freedom as a dream more inspirational than practicable. This dream is powerful in Pynchon's world, yet Pynchon may fear that it will remain a dream. The new dispensation imagined by both is to replace the white empire with a new human planet, and it will be approached by focusing on what can be reached of the nonwhite feeling and intelligence that has been denied. In this sense, there is a deep movement in *V.* from the inanimate to the animate and from the masculine to the feminine. The same movement continues in *Beloved,* where it is embodied by flesh filled with spirit.

Yet this movement is suspended in doubt, and having given it my best try, I must now admit that there is much truth in Cooley's point that any belief within *V.* can only be one possibility among others. None of the main characters in *V.*—Benny, Herbert, or *V.*—can engage this movement actively. Those situated substantially outside the West—Sarah, the Maijstrals, and Sphere—should be able to move forward, but all seem stalled. Sarah is gone, Paola's reunion with Pappy seems uncertain, it is not clear where Fausto is going, and Sphere seems to lose Paola. Perhaps the countermyth finally shows the reality of the Third World when it fails, showing that the residue of oppression still limits the potential for new life. As I have suggested, on one level, Pynchon satirizes the dream of reconciliation and progress, which is a compulsion driven by the injustice of colonialism and racism. On this level, by following *V.* with "The Secret Integration," he was expanding on a critique of the unreal fantasy of the idealized non-Westerner as a projection of white need. The vast and terrible irony of his great works of 1963–73 can swallow any dream, but it can also contain the life of their yearning. Today, faced with terrorism, we are likely to see the idealization of the Third World as a dangerous delusion; but the danger of demonizing that world, as the terrorists want us to, may be greater. While *V.* sees the world moving forward and backward at the same time, it does not fail to recognize the value of forward movement; and it sees that this movement must center on nonwhite people.

Insofar as forward movement is a significant element in this fifty-eight-year narrative, it moves toward a new vision that seeks to pass beyond a millennium of white supremacy. It does so by multiplying realities to undermine the sense that civilization is coherent. Therefore the dissemination of the plots—in which each new historical chapter adds a crucial causal level that is incomprehensible—is a geometrical progression of possibilities to grow "less and less sure" (*V.* 546). For this reason, the postmodern expansion of the book operates to unfold a divided consciousness meant to speak for the excluded. If the postcolonial vision of freedom is only one possibility, it is the one that encompasses the drift of the book and speaks in its divisions.

The postmodern antinarrative and the narrative of liberation alternate with each other in the novel, as do the Profane chapters in the present and the V. ones in the past. Yet it is not possible to identify the present action as postmodern and the past as liberatory (or vice versa), for each has elements of continuity and discontinuity, entrapment and freedom. There is a fundamental *différend* here in that the drive toward freedom is necessary, but so too is the disassembly of the hierarchically framed linear logic of such a forward movement—a disassembly that works against idealizing, as does Bigger's anger.

The general reversal of oppression that cannot be accomplished in any near future by some Third World utopia is already operative in moral choices on the side of freedom. The pointless flurry of the Profane plot only highlights the need for the countermovement whereby Herbert, without realizing it, joins the Maijstrals and Sphere in supporting a forward thrust by revealing behind history the generative activity of his father. In turning against "Whitehall" (*V.* 541), Sidney generated the life of his son's intellectual enterprise, and thereby sustained V.'s maternity as a mental construction that engages one in undermining the Establishment. However widespread intolerance and blindness may obstruct progressive awareness, there is still a path of shared vision that leads beyond history's nightmare. In the midst of its labyrinth, *V.* traces this path. Herbert does not see it any more than Profane, or V., but human connection is there for people who reach out, and it is felt by Fausto, McClintic, and Paola.

The construction of the novel suspends the truth between its two semi-protagonists. Herbert Stencil uncovers the way forward, but is unable to see it because he is looking for the way back. Profane is looking for a way ahead, but is so skeptical that all he can perceive is the backward drag of an impasse. His last line is, "I haven't learned a goddamn thing" (*V.* 506); but Stefan Mattesich, in *Lines of Flight: Discursive Time and Countercultural Desire in the Works of Thomas Pynchon* (2002), gives Profane credit for refusing to attach himself to the social machinery of power (38). That progress lies in a conception that cannot be undivided suggests that a viable program cannot be mono-logically assembled. But it is envisioned between the various characters insofar as they apprehend parts of it. So the scope of the book's vision takes its vast historical power from its ability to encompass the full complexity of its fearful oppositions; by doing so it denies the dominant fantasy of unity.

The *v*-structure of the book aligns two sides to point toward a future, and it resonates with longing for that future when those of its figures who are capable of it cross borders show concern, and experience change. A *maijstral,* or mistral (*V.* 342, 516), is a wind, something that moves across borders, and it is the characters linked to the Maijstrals who undergo these changes. This is less because of anything inherent in them than because of the dynamic positions that they are placed in by a history of racism. A stirring passes through them toward something they seek in their several ways to express through Fausto's theories, Paola's love, and McClintic's art. This something is a world of consciousness that expands the established order, and it is manifested in *Beloved.*

4

American African
Postmodernism in *Beloved*

THE CULTURAL POSITIONS OF BELOVED

The title character of *Beloved* is both a human being and a ghost. Human characters abound, but there are hardly any central figures in major novels of the twentieth century who are ghosts.[1] Beloved upsets the usual expectations by succeeding brilliantly as a character despite her supernatural unnature. This polarized figure—being both inside and outside of the Western concept of humanity—is a departure for Western literature, giving a commanding role to an American version of African spirits. In what ways could this development be an intellectual advance?

In her essay "Rootedness: The Ancestor as Foundation" (1984), written while working on *Beloved,* Morrison says that "Black" people combine practicality with "another way of knowing" linked to "superstition and magic." This other knowledge is "enhancing, not limiting," but it is discredited "only because Black people were discredited. . . . That kind of knowledge has a very strong place in my work" (342). The knowledge that Morrison affirms is clearly derived from Africa. Her use of "only" shows that she is ready to make an extreme statement in order to oppose the denigration of this knowledge. *Beloved* finally recognizes, as Dubey does, that such knowledge must be suppressed for practical reasons, yet the novel enshrines this African-based insight as the foundation of progress for African Americans.

To fight the assumption that African thinking has little intellectual value, we need to build on the progressive force of non-Western modes of thought that speak for those who have been silenced. We must distinguish the beneficial aspects of communal thinking from its conformity, and sift out the philosophical aspect of religion from its superstition. Didier S. Kaphagawani takes such a perspective in "What Is African Philosophy?" He cites Kwasi Wiredu in speaking of "the re-examination and re-appraisal of traditional culture in the hope of identifying and preserving what is useful and worth developing from what is obsolete." For example, Kaphagawani speaks of proponents of "traditional African socialism," which has to do with communal sharing (C&R 96).

In relation or opposition to Western authority, African cultures may operate as forward-looking, though on the other hand, colonialism may aggravate native intolerance. In this cultural ecology, sub-Saharan religions may have great advantages because they are polytheistic; so they involve multicultural structures that combine contradictory beliefs without insisting on one center. Thus they exemplify constellations in which differing groups can share. In "Mami Water in African Religion and Spirituality," Kathleen O'Brien Wicker, who did research in Ghana, says, "Adaptability, flexibility, tolerance, and openness . . . . differentiate African spiritual traditions from Western religions, where faith usually involves . . . beliefs posited as absolute truths" (Olupona 198). Another merit that animist religions may have for America is that they are unlikely to attain the level of belief claimed by orthodox, institutional faiths. In fact, one role they play is like that of classical mythology in modern times: they present without mandate a range of images of opposing values—the gods of love, war, reason, frenzy, and so forth—that inherently deconstructs in advance any particular set of totalizing values and the dogmas they frame.

Andrew Sullivan, a conservative Catholic, sees a parallel between the crusades and inquisitions of Christianity and the intolerance of some fundamentalist Muslims: "almost as if there is something inherent in religious monotheism tht lends itself to this kind of terrorist temptation" (46). Judeo-Christian and Islamic belief that their version of God is the only true one has led to a war between them for over a thousand years that seems lately to be intensifying. Their aggression may spring from the form of a system controlled by a single center that claims total or catholic comprehension of the universe. Such systems spur moral obligations to attack unbelievers.

African Americans have been strongly attached to Christianity, and though

it was imposed on them, it has supported them effectively. Eugene D. Genovese concludes his appreciation of the role of Christianity among slaves as follows: "It enabled the slaves to do battle against the slaveholders' ideology, but
defensively within the system it opposed; offensively, it proved a poor instrument. The accomplishment soared heroically to great heights, but so did the
price, which even now has not been paid" (284). He seems to mean a price of
reduced resistance, and yet Christianity has inspired a series of fiery preach-
ers to struggle for black liberation, from Nat Turner to Cornell West.

Žižek defends Christianity in *The Fragile Absolute,* analyzing Christian
love as a focused effort toward knowing the otherness of the other (129). His
ultimate example of such an effort to consider the other is Sethe's sacrifice of
Beloved to keep the child from slavery. He sees her act as revolutionary because it redefines morality: by suspending existing ethical boundaries, "it has
the structure of a *political* decision" (155). Yet her infanticide could not escape damnation in Christian terms, for she never concedes that there was any
wrong in what she did. The epigraph of *Beloved,* which includes "I will call
them my people, which were not my people" (Romans 9:25), may suggest that
a person need not belong to a particular religion to have moral virtue. Sethe
has little interest in Christianity: her values seem to be defined by the likely
religion of her mother, who did not speak English (*B* 74)—African spiritism. In fact, Morrison's fiction from 1978 (*Song of Solomon*) to 1997 (*Paradise*)
often seems to propose among its possibilities that if African Americans realize their connections to their original religions, they will have access to systems that insulate them from the European order and combine political protest with cultural multiplicity.

Yet the insulation may be more from thinking that is monotheistic (an idea
invented in Africa), from thinking that is "centric" rather than from thinking
that is European. The ancient Greeks may have derived their productive polytheism—which often allowed a variety of city-states to coexist with different main gods—from Africa. In her essay "Unspeakable Things Unspoken,"
Morrison approves the thesis of Martin Bernal's *Black Athena,* that much of
classical Greek religion was derived from African sources: "It is difficult not
to be persuaded by the weight of documentation Martin Bernal brings to his
task and his rather dazzling analytic insights" (7). Modernism often nurtures
aspects of ancient culture that go against monologic Eurocentrism, as suggested by Yeats's occultism, H.D.'s Hermeticism, and much modernist use of

myth. In portraying Ulysses as a Jew, Joyce gives credence to Victor Bérard's theory that the original of Odysseus was Phoenician (Ellmann 488). Early moderns, Romantics, and modernists all used multiple deities to deconstruct the monocentric viewpoint of the Establishment—more as intellectual tools than as religions. For example, Nietzsche's *The Birth of Tragedy* (1872) unfolds a tragic vision divided between two opposed gods, Apollo and Dionysius. From a perspective that is not founded on obliterating African influences, Greek mythology and Nietzsche might both be seen as carrying on African oppositional principles, as intermediaries between African thinking and poststructuralism.

The recovery of African culture by Americans, which built momentum with modernists in Harlem and elsewhere, may be compared to the European Renaissance's recovery of classical culture. Like early modern Europeans, African Americans from the South had lived in a feudal system of bondage dominated by an authoritarian monotheism. For both groups, the recovered paganism provided alternative framings of reality informed with cosmopolitan conflicting beliefs. Through their double consciousness, African Americans apprehend multiple centers of authority that reconfigure the multiple gods of their ancestors. This polycentrism may serve America's need for models of thought that are plural and inclusive rather than unitary and exclusive. African religions can also correct Christian hatred of the body and European scientific abstraction because they maintain a living connection with the objects of the world by investing them with feeling or spirit, making them alive. Jacqueline Rose says, "Access to the object is only ever possible through an act of self-identification" (138). Like *V.*, Morrison's *Beloved* moves from an inanimate world of European values to an animate world of non-Western ones. In *Beloved*, the living world is defined in terms derived from Africa, yet the movement toward it ends up looping back into connection with Euro-America. The book moves through a world of African spirits who haunt the inanimate world of Europeans that they cannot escape. Yet matter is inanimate without spirit, and from an Africanized point of view, Morrison's characters have to pass through intimacy with the realm of spirits to regenerate themselves from the cultural isolation of slavery—what Patterson calls "social death" (32–44)—in order to return with effective vitality to the factual world.

Helene Moglen argues that Morrison re-creates the fantastic in a realistic frame (23). The supernatural aspect of her work can be explained in realistic or political terms. In this framework, Beloved as a person who seems like a spirit expresses the *differend*, what cannot be spoken because of social conflict, what has been excluded and suppressed (*D* xi–xii). This view has a solid role in the novel, but any explanation of Beloved that overlooks the sense (not the fact) that she is literally a spirit is drastically inadequate: it cripples the book by cutting off its most original and intense half, imposing a European model on what I call American African material. While African American refers to American culture modified by African influences, American African refers to African culture modified by American ones.

Morrison speaks in *Playing in the Dark* of the Africanist persona, an ensemble of fantasy images of Africans that European Americans have to use to frame their thoughts about value, morality, desire, and feeling (*PD* 6, 44–52). African Americans also orient themselves continually toward Africa to define themselves. Their images of Africa are truer in many ways because of deep experiences of identification; yet black Americans cannot really be African: they have to use Africa for their own needs. As Morrison indicates, European Americans often use the Africanist persona as a negative example against which to form their own positive virtues, such as independence. But I have shown that visionary white writers like Faulkner and Pynchon have to use Africanist images to create spiritual values and to embody freedom. (Morrison suggests this positive use of Africanism in *Playing in the Dark* [47–48].) Likewise, it is logical that African Americans tend to idealize images of the homeland; yet the horrors of history intervene so that visions of Africa must be associated with terrible things. Only by facing these terrors can one earn the affirmation that gives value to identity. By realizing the extent of the injustice, African Americans can comprehend that rather than being ashamed of past griefs, they should be proud of surviving them. The beauty and terror of American African identity are everywhere in Morrison's works, but they may find their most concentrated form in Beloved herself.

Barbara Christian frames the African aspect of *Beloved* well. She argues that in an African perspective (she rejects the term *Afrocentric* as imitative of Eurocentricity), what appears to Europeans to be a fine novel is rather a profound ritual of remembrance. She says that in a context of African cosmology, the book is designed to bring back the spirits of ancestors torn away from African people by the dreadful passage into America. Christian says that she has found *Beloved* effective in healing disturbed African Americans by putting them back in touch with their ancestors. In "Rootedness," Morrison says, "When you kill the ancestor you kill yourself" (344).

Yet at the same time, *Beloved* is an experimental and advanced work in a Western modernist tradition. As in Picasso's masks and Stravinsky's rhythms, the African elements in *Beloved* charge and inform its modern vision. Conversely, Weinstein says that European modernism provided Faulkner with "artistic tools for diagnosing" the insanity of racism (*What* 172), and it gave similar tools to Morrison. Her dual African and American perspectives here correspond to what Baker calls "the classical in Afro-American expressive culture," a mode in which African possession by a spirit is modified into performance (*Workings* 74). Here the loss of control through possession is balanced by elements of role-playing, fabricating, and manipulating that combine African trickster patterns with European skepticism and drama. This conception matches the view of Denise Heinze, who describes Morrison's use of double consciousness as "orchestrating this sense of connectedness between cultures rather than attempting to dissolve the differences" (10). Jeanna Fuston-White, in " 'From the Seen to the Told': The Construction of Subjectivity in Toni Morrison's *Beloved*," sees the novel as a postmodern text that "deconstructs the Enlightenment notion of subjectivity" to make room for what bell hooks calls a "radical black subjectivity" (461). For Fuston-White, it is urgent to tell the story of slavery intensely through black narrative modes that combine critical theory with African fields of perception.

I will examine how the African and Western sides of *Beloved* work against each other to shape from two perspectives the language of the text, including two typical figures of speech—starting with a statement that must be seen from two sides. It issues from Baby Suggs's final stage of collapse, the subject of the novel's second paragraph. Like most thematic elements in *Beloved,* this event returns periodically in the text to get filled in and further explained. Such sporadic development, using motifs that may include entire scenes, is also found in *Absalom.* This is not only because Morrison is influenced by Faulkner, but because both go back to oral storytelling traditions that tend to follow associations that return to incidents again and again. The tale-telling Morrison builds on has African affinities, and Fuston-White sees Morrison's use of narrative fragments as influenced by tribal *griots* (470).

Baby Suggs's final position is, "There is no bad luck in the world but whitefolks" (*B* 105). It is repeated as the main point of her final announcement (122), so it has weight. Suggs is a woman of tremendous spirit, yet this conclusion is forced on her by a lifetime of oppression: "After sixty years of losing children to the people who chewed up her life and spit it out like a fish bone" (209). Not only was her life lived in the mouths of people who ground her in their teeth, but they treated her worse than food, spitting her out because they wanted only her agony. The feeling of being chewed comes from having her eight children taken from her, in one case after she slept with the boss for months to keep her son (28). But the final blow to Baby is Sethe's murder of Beloved and the fact that Baby cannot make up her mind whether it is right: "she could not approve or condemn Sethe's rough choice. One or the other might have saved her, but beaten up by the claims of both, she went to bed. The whitefolks had tired her out at last" (212). What wears her out most is being put in a position, even after her supposed freedom, in which no matter which choice she makes, she is dreadfully wrong: either the children are to be killed or sent into slavery. This grinding loss infixes Baby's lack of a center (165) and rankles every moment of her consciousness so that, as with Bigger, whiteness becomes a force that fills her entire field of perception and keeps attacking her even when no white person is present. The last sentence quoted, "The whitefolks had tired her out at last," is thought by Stamp Paid, who narrates this version of Baby's decline. He speaks for reasonableness, urging Baby to return to serving the community, but even Stamp sees Baby as perpetually being attacked by white people.

To explain the absolute nature of Suggs's conclusion, I will cite examples of black reactions to slavery as demonic possession. One of the earliest accounts we have of the Middle Passage is the Life of Olaudah Equiano (1791). Equiano says that he had been a slave in Nigeria, but he was so horrified by the cruelty of the white men on the ship that he was sure that they were evil demons (55). I have cited Robert Johnson's image of the hellhound on his trail. This image is such a strong reflection of the experience of African Americans that it appears in a writer who may not intend to invoke it.

Near the end of Hurston's *Their Eyes Were Watching God* (1937), as Janie Crawford and Tea Cake Woods are caught in a flood, they encounter an unnatural dog, "shivering and growling" with "teeth uncovered" in "fury," who opposes her attempt to save herself by clinging to a swimming cow (157). On the previous page, they were not allowed on a bridge because it was crowded with white people, so the dog plays a role parallel to racism in keeping them from safety. The dog gives Tea Cake hydrophobia, destroying one of the most beautiful marriages in American literature. The symptoms of this disease resemble the effects of racism, which *Beloved* portrays over and over as poisoning the ability of black people to enjoy objects of desire. Tea Cake wants water very much: "It was so good and cool! . . . . he rushed the glass to his lips. But the demon was there before him, strangling, killing him quickly" (167). Hurston does not indicate that she means this to refer to racism, and she may not, in which case the passage confirms how pervasive such demonic possession has been for African Americans. Yet as an authority on the blues, she may have known what the hound stood for, and she might expect her African American readers to pick up a submerged message about being bitten by the mad dog of racism.

Nothing less extreme than Suggs's ultimate statement could express her experience or show how badly she was crushed, yet Morrison is aware that Suggs's generalization is illogical. It means, for example, that if she is crossing an empty field and she stubs her toe, a little white demon must be responsible. Through Sethe's account of Suggs's end, Morrison repeats that Suggs's final position gave the lie to her earlier preaching (*B* 105). Baby's calls to the people to love their flesh because the whites hate it—accompanied by therapeutic acting out—were clearly a great inspiration to the community, and provide one of the glories of the text (103–4). But in the final phase in which she sees no escape from the white devil, she "proved herself a liar" (104) in her earlier affirmation of the life force. So there is irony in Morrison's concluding of the narrative of Baby's last words by saying that she "pulled up the quilt and left them to hold that thought forever" (123), for her final "lesson" (122) is a warped shadow of her former greatness. Baby's last testament, then, is suspended between an African awareness of the demonic effect of oppression and a Western irony about how Baby's vision was finally distorted. Neither side should invalidate the other. They both work together to give a three-dimensional picture of how badly slavery could injure an African American soul—an injury whose enormity is measured by the distance between the repeatedly emphasized greatness of Baby's heart (102) and the narrow bitterness of her final conclusion. Yet Baby may be using hyperbole consciously at the end to mix her emotion with African exaggeration.

This twist of Suggs's thought runs counter to the main movement of

Beloved and defines that movement by its opposition. Both as an American novel and as an American African memorial, *Beloved* portrays the shift from death to life in the resurrection from slavery to freedom. Yet this shift drags against a counterforce because, as Amy Denver says, "Anything dead coming back to life hurts" (*B* 42), a key line. To move into freedom causes pain because the mind is fixed in ways opposed to life, ways that emanate from the white power structure. The central enactment of this fixation takes place when Sethe sees slavery as inevitable in her situation, and so tries to kill her family. If she had spared her baby in 1856, they would have had reason to hope in five years, for Kentucky was a Union state in the war.[2] The narrator says, "Freeing yourself was one thing; claiming ownership of that freed self was another" (112). This refers to a long process of freeing one's mind. When Frederick Douglass first came north, he realized that he "had somehow imbibed the opinion that, in the absence of slaves, there could be no wealth, and very little refinement" (359). He did not think that people would work hard without force because his mind was set in destructive ways by the violence of the criminals that had conditioned him. In a poem she read at a Morrison reading at Temple University on April 8, 1998, Sonia Sanchez declared, "In the beginning, there was no end." This indicates that some of slavery's worst effects rested on the pretense that it was a permanent, natural system.

Morrison's formidable analysis of the mind-poisoning effects of slavery is balanced by an awareness that the African ideal is problematic. In a 1994 interview, she said that "it may be a little too romantic to think of Africa as a kind of Eden, before corruption" (Furman 83 n. 21). Nevertheless, because the ideology of slavery reaches its tentacles so deadeningly into the mind, it is only a myth of African understanding, which involves spirits, that can free her characters from mental slavery and allow them to confront themselves. *Beloved* takes place in a world made up of spirits that animate language.

BLUE SPIRITS

Lacan says that to make something into a symbol is always to kill the thing itself (*Écrits* 101), and Europeans live in the Symbolic, whereas Africans distinguish themselves from Europeans by living more in a realm of images with which one identifies. By projecting life on objects, many Africans allow them to exceed prefabricated definitions. An African may see an object in a more complex way than the European one by seeing it as a subject not of one system, but of competing systems. So the perceptions of many Africans may be in touch with the Real, what is outside language; for the Real appears through disjunction. Europeans tends to see things quantitatively and systematically, which always is fatal: two equal units are always dead, for two things that are alive are never equal. What is dead is fixed, but what is living is caught in change. In the animistic world of *Beloved*, as in visionaries like Blake, everything is alive but oppression. In the first sentence of the book, a mathematical fixity surprises the reader by undergoing emotion: "124 was spiteful." This corresponds to the revolutionary poetic language of modernism, so that houses are alive in *Absalom* and in Woolf's great story "A Haunted House."

Modernist opposition to convention parallels black opposition to white values, as Paul Gilroy argues (*Black* 30–36), and Morrison's style expresses black liberation in language that combines modernism and spiritism in ways that are often harmonious. One source from which she absorbed Afro-modern signifying techniques was the blues tradition, which resonates through *Beloved* and her other novels, especially *Sula* and *Song of Solomon*. Baker, in *Blues, Ideology, and Afro-American Literature*, emphasizes key modernist features of the blues, that they are virtually always "in transit," with "multidirectionality" (7), and "already 'gone'" (5). Paul D, who sings the blues (*B* 48, 310), uses a high concentration of blues phrases. He remembers, for example, that when he was on a chain gang, living in a box "drove him crazy so he would not lose his mind" (49). Morrison seems to be referring here to "Louise McGee" (1965) by Robert Johnson's teacher Son House, in which he says, "if I don't go crazy . . . I'm gon' lose my mind." In this multilayered construction, one can lose one's mind on one level while holding it on another, and this matches the aforementioned pattern in the blues of having more than one mind.

The idea of extra minds leads to that of spirits, and the likelihood that the term *blues* originally meant evil spirits is indicated by Bessie Smith in "The Gin House Blues," by H. Troy and Fletcher Henderson (1926):[3] "I've got to see the conjure man soon [repeat] / Because these Gin House blues is campin round my door. / I want him to drive em off so they won't come back no more." This equates blues with spirits by saying that a conjurer can drive them away. Blues also appear as spirits in one of the key definitions of the genre: the spoken introduction to "Good Morning Blues," by Huddie "Leadbelly" Ledbetter (1947), speaks of the blues as living creatures, saying that if you can't eat or sleep, the blues have "got you. They want to talk to you. You got to tell 'em something." This segues to the song, in which Leadbelly demonstrates that the blues are speaking beings by conversing with them: "Good morning blues. Blues how do you do?" The animated blues respond, "Well, I'm doin fairly well. Good morning. How are you?" In the second stanza, the blues take bodily form by walking round the singer's bed, and when he tries to eat his breakfast, "the blues was all in my bread." Thus, they follow the pattern of interfering with sustenance that Tea Cake was subject to in *Their Eyes.* The demon on Robert Johnson's trail *is* the blues, and Leadbelly's phrase "got you" refers to possession. Gerhard Kubik, in *Africa and the Blues* (1999), indicates that this second stanza appears in similar form in "Long Lonesome Blues" (1926), by Blind Lemon Jefferson, Leadbelly's mentor (36). Kubik, who researched for decades in Africa (34, 42), says that this morning situation resembles scenes in African songs: "The moment one wakes up, blues is around and seems to permeate everything. In such cases, the blues almost become personified, as "Mr. Blues," or—on another level of perception—like little blue devils emerging from the most unexpected, innocent objects" (35).[4]

Paradoxically, the blues that stalk Johnson are both soulful African spirits and the white demons that haunt African Americans. Blues are dominated by the negative aspect that speaks of trouble. Whether it be trouble in love, trouble with the law, poverty, substance abuse, or the unhappiness of existence, the troubles of African Americans have generally been shaped by limits imposed on them by racism. If one turns to the happier side of the blues (linked to the term *boogie*), one shifts toward spirits less infected by social toxins. Likewise, if one turns from culture toward nature, one grows more able to imagine positive African spirits. (Is this a shift from the city's monotheist conquerors to the vulnerable animists of the countryside?)

NATURE SPIRITS

A striking line illustrates animistic blues figures that the narrator of *Beloved* uses: "RAINWATER held on to pine needles for dear life and Beloved could not take her eyes off Sethe" (*sic; B* 68). Personification here mixes registers, using natural objects to describe unnatural passions. Such skewed animation often appears in blues, as in Ida Cox's "Nobody Knows You When You're Down and Out," which Bessie Smith recorded in 1929: "Ever get my hand on a dollar agin, / I'm going to hold on to it till the eagle grin." She affirms that she will wait until the eagle on the coin starts smiling. The use of exaggeration to upset conventional scale is also bluesy. Furry Lewis's 1961 version of "I Will Turn Your Money Green" claims adhesion: "If you be my baby, you can be my boss. / I'll stick closer to you, honey, than Jesus to the cross." Morrison's optional (signifying?) deletion of the comma after "life" brings the water-spirit Beloved (who emerges from a stream and seems to return to it at the end) together with water itself—both involved in the same activity of clinging to life. Central to spiritism as a projection of self into nature is the way in which the intricate bond between the water and the clustered pine needles is seen to embody human passion. If Beloved is water itself, then she would be attached to life, for life only exists where water does, and our bodies are 90 percent water. Plants shrivel and fade in drought, when Beloved is not running through them.

As the margin between animal life and what the West calls inanimate, vegetation is a logical focus of animism, and *Beloved* teems with active plants. For example, Paul D is fond of a tree he calls "Brother," to whom he talks (*B* 25, 26, 32); and Sethe has to bring herbs or flowers to her workplace at Sweet Home to make slavery bearable. These plants operate as spirits not only through their scent or beauty, but by preventing misfortune: "The day she forgot . . . butter wouldn't come or the brine in the barrel blistered her arms" (27). The most animated image of vegetation in the book is the scene of Sethe and Halle's honeymoon in the corn. Corn, also known as Indian corn, was often sacred to Amerindians, so this scene has undertones of Native American spiritism as well as African kinds. The intercourse of the lovers spreads in living waves through the vegetation, so that their love is transmitted like an aura to be shared communally (though not without discomfort and jealousy) by the other black men on the farm. Jouissance becomes continuous with and interfused in vegetable life, and the corn is presented as conscious, filled with human feeling, as is shown by the image of its disrobing: "The pulling down of the tight sheath, the ripping sound always convinced her it *hurt*." The sentient words that I have italicized charge the imagery with eroticism: "As soon as one strip of husk was down, the rest *obeyed* and the ear *yielded* up to him its *shy* rows, *exposed* at last. How loose the silk. How *quick* the *jailed-up* flavor *ran free*" (32–33). The corn released from bondage and transformed into delight—"the jailed up flavor ran free"—is the spirit of the lovers revealed to all when they see the stalks stirring, and taken in by all through a ritual feast. Slavery cuts down love, while the spirit of love inspires freedom, as Halle and Six-o are inspired to escape by their women.

Morrison was subject to a tendency to extol Third World solidarity that makes her overlook differences between African Americans and Native Americans. In her African American/Native American vision of spirit culture, the most sublime passage on vegetation begins with Paul D asking a remarkably sympathetic band of Cherokee in Georgia how he can go north, and their telling him to "Follow the tree flowers" (B 132). Because trees that bloom later are at higher latitudes, Paul D looks out for the latest blossoms, and goes from dogwood to peach, cherry, magnolia, chinaberry, pecan, walnut, prickly pear, apple, and plum (133). Here he is described as a "dark ragged figure guided by the blossoming plums." He enters into a world of Native American vision in which the spirits of the trees, the life forces that move them through their transformations, actively guide him to freedom. The array of plants in *Beloved* speaks for the land of America before Europeans chopped it up to make much of it inanimate. Michelle Bonnet, in " 'To take the sin out of slicing trees': The Law of the Tree in *Beloved*," shows how trees play active roles because they are seen in African terms as filled with spiritual energy. She explains the power of sacred groves such as Denver's boxwood bower (34) and the Clearing where Baby Suggs preaches to people "among the trees" (102–4). Here the life force of the trees inspires people beyond merely human action (Bonnet 42–44).

Paul D relates to the ambience of tree spirits because it is like the one his ancestors came from, and there are several passages showing kinship between African Americans and Native Americans. Sixo finds an empty Indian structure and asks permission of "the Redmen's Presence" to use it (B 29). Later Paul D continually hears the Miami Indians from their graveyard "old as the sky" outraged at how their "holy" land has been cut up. He senses their spirits throughout the city: "they growled on the banks of Licking River, sighed in the trees on Catherine Street and rode the wind above the pig yards" (182). The spirit lore of the natives evokes the similar beliefs of Africans, stirring in the main characters a sense of alter-native views of reality that were suppressed in them, a reality that feels like it is deeply their own.

In grappling with the difficulties involved for a Westerner in describing African religions and their transmission to America, my most practical objective is to delineate a ghost or idealized vestige of African spiritualism that the characters of *Beloved* imagine and cling to, as found in the text. This is a strong version of the American African vision, one of its greatest literary embodiments. Another, from a Caribbean source, is Derek Walcott's Pan-African Homeric epic *Omeros* (1990), in which the hero, Achille, has a dream of returning to his African homeland (book 3). The first chapter of *Omeros* presents the consciousnesses of trees, smoke, and a waterfall (3–5), evoking the animist belief that there are spirits in things.

John S. Mbiti, in *African Religions and Philosophy* (1969, 1990), objects to the term *animism* because it has usually been seen as primitive—the first stage of an evolution that leads to polytheism and then to monotheism (7–8). Mbiti insists that animism "is not an adequate description" (8) of African religion, for most of Africa's thousand or so religious systems have long included pantheons of gods as well as spirits, and many feature a central divinity who dominates. A correction of the sweeping concept of animism is given by Wiredu. Avoiding talk about all Africans, he says that among the Akan of Ghana, "God is not apart from the universe: together with the world, God constitutes the spatio-temporal 'totality' of existence" (C&R 187). This suggests that "he/she" is present in everything, but Wiredu denies the presence of spirits everywhere: "Some objects, such as particular rocks or rivers, may be thought to house an extra-human force, but it is not supposed that every rock or stone has life" (C&R 189). Malidoma Patrice Somé, in *Of Water and the Spirit: Ritual, Magic, and Initiation in the Life of an African Shaman* (1994), his account of village life in Burkina Faso (near Ghana), says, "The life energy of ancestors who have not yet been reborn is expressed in the life of nature, in trees, mountains, rivers and still water" (20).

My aim is to show ways in which animism is a highly advanced form of religion. If it is common in West African religions to have a group of gods who are subordinated to a single one, the god principle usually extends into great latitude. As Robert Farris Thompson puts it, "The Yoruba religion, the worship of various spirits under God, presents a limitless horizon of vivid moral beings" (5). Divinities proliferate as active presences on earth that are associated with natural objects, so that if the world is not filled with spirits, they are scattered throughout it. Despite the problems involved in trying to sum up "African thinking," it is safe to say that the novelists I discuss all had images of African culture aligned with animism. Morrison in particular was writing in the 1980s in a culture in which writers like Reed, Thompson, and Janheinz

Jahn were adduced to promote positive images of African spiritism. In "Rootedness," Morrison sees spirits everywhere in her last novel as they would be
in the one she was writing, in the service of "Black art" (342); "all of nature
thinking and feeling and watching and responding to the action going on in
Tar Baby, so that they are in the story: the trees hurt, fish are afraid, clouds report, and the bees are alarmed" (341).

Therese E. Higgins perceptively explores African concepts in Morrison's
work in *Religiosity, Cosmology, and Folklore* (2001). Higgins handles the difficulty of the multiplicity of African faiths by using a survey of nine different
African cultures and showing how many of them share features that match
Morrison's vision; for example, the dead may eat and make love (x). Many
of these features involve spirits who may represent ancestors or be attached
to bodies of water, which are widely thought to have sentient forces in their
depths. Though most of these religions give the highest position to a central
divinity, this divinity may be distant from the world, whereas the spirits are
present in charged objects or in ancestors who return to disturb or advise their
families (x, 3).

Historically, as Sundquist relates, African Americans were under great
pressure to deny or forget their African roots from the nineteenth century
until the Harlem Renaissance (304–5), so a general increase in awareness of
Africana proceeds through the century. But this is undercut as older people
closer to the original African-based folklore keep passing away. The main basis
of Morrison's use of spiritism must be her wide knowledge of her people,
much of it personal.

Sundquist sees forms of animism in the antebellum slave world of North
Carolina, as remembered late in the century by Uncle Julius, the storyteller
of Chesnutt's conjure tales (1899). Sundquist calls this world "the spiritu-
ally saturated world characteristic of much African belief" (314). In some of
Julius's tales, the slaves use their powerful conjuring spells as their main means
to deceive and oppose their masters. In "Mars Jeems's Nightmare," Julius tells
how the slave Solomon gets a goopher (potion) from a conjure woman that
turns the cruel master Jeems McLean into a black man, so McLean gets beaten
by the overseer for resisting. Then he is returned to his "race," remembering
his passage as a dream, whereupon he fires the overseer and is considerate to
his slaves from then on (Chesnutt 29–38). Spiritist beliefs as focuses of resistance were suppressed both by slavery and by Jim Crow.

Because it is so different from Christian doctrine, animism has served to evoke for African Americans the spirits of their homelands. Moreover, as presented in countless modernist texts, from *Cane* to *Beloved,* animism is modern, presenting new ways of supplementing the inadequate philosophies of the West. In the enormous "Circe" chapter of Joyce's *Ulysses,* for example (350–497), things like doorknobs and fans talk. My in-spiration here comes from Reed's *Mumbo Jumbo,* which says that "to interpret the world by using a single" god is like "filling a milk bottle with an ocean" (24). Pluralism derives force from giving life to the various outlooks it recognizes, seeing their personalities. Reed's energetic support for pantheism leads him to postmodernism here, and Gates sees that Reed is following an African tradition into poststructuralism by glorifying "indeterminacy" (*Signifying* 227). Pantheism is more advanced than polytheism because it frees the subject further by deconstructing the permanent pantheon of gods, allowing one to find spiritual vitality in the immediacy of any situation. Derrida sees the value of such a nonarrangement when he praises *bricolage,* the worship among Brazilian Indians of objects found at random ("Structure" 285–86). Such a free, rich, sensitive receptivity to experience may have to combine with other, more stable arrangements, as it does in Africa. But the freeplay of animism is the leading edge of new discoveries: something new is discovered when what was formerly frozen in a category comes *alive* and breaks out of its category. So animism should not be considered outmoded just because it has been suppressed by monotheists.

Janheinz Jahn, in *Muntu,* cites an early, anonymous French report from Haiti: "The slaves are strictly forbidden to practice the dance which in Surinam is called 'Water-Mama' and in our colonies 'Mae d'Agua' (Water mother)" (30). Africans in America were forbidden to practice their cultures, which were demonized and obliterated, so that most African Americans do not even know where they came from or what their languages were. The traces of African civilization that survived tended to be shaped by gaps in the master's control. These retentions made islands of refuge for the slaves, places where they could feel at home rather than controlled by a system that negated them. The images of animism that American African figures in *Beloved* imagine have the potential to give them feelings of freedom and strength.

Beloved seems to be a water spirit, an incarnation of the fact that in Africa, bodies of water are generally "believed to be inhabited by powerful beings"

(Parrinder 83). In *The Dictionary of Global Culture*, Appiah and Gates give the term *Mammy Wata* for such a figure, a female spirit in West Africa who lives at the bottom of rivers and lakes and often tempts young people to follow her underwater (429). Paul D recalls that when Beloved drew him into making love to her, he felt as if he were "drowned" (*B* 311). Her first appearance seems supernatural: "A FULLY DRESSED woman walked out of the water" (60); and the last concrete image of her, seen by a child, appears "by the stream": "a naked woman with fish for hair" (315). The American and African levels work together in this striking image. The naturalistic interpretation of "fish for hair" is that this child has never seen a bathing woman with shiny, wriggling tubes of water running out of her hair. But the accuracy of this interpretation confirms and specifies the fact that the child did indeed see hair made of fish. So the American level enriches the African one that tends to be linked to the intensely animistic imagery. In fact, paintings of the Mammy Wata—five of which are reproduced in Jacob K. Olupona's *African Spirituality* (219–22)—portray her with long, streaming hair and a fishtail for legs.

As a child, Denver saw Beloved under the surface of the stream and played with her (*B* 255). Moreover, Beloved typically sees herself as submerged: "I come out of blue water" (252). In the cold house—when she says to Denver, "I'm like this" and curls up (146)—the visual scene, with "minnows of light" (144) rippling above darkness, seems underwater. Her curling suggests that she is *in utero* when she is at home, and Sethe's flood of urine when she appears is compared to the breaking of water in birth (61). So when Beloved drinks "cup after cup" (61), she is symbolically imbibing her mother's birth fluid. In Uganda, a certain river "was said to have been caused by the birth flood" of the daughter of King Tembo (Parrinder 87).

Sabine Jell-Bahlsen, in "The Lake Goddess, Uhammiri/Ogbuide: The Female Side of the Universe in Igbo Cosmology," holds that Mami Water is a Europeanized name for a powerful female deity whose original Nigerian name is Nne Mmiri. She stands for the fluid, creative, feminine side of life and protects nonconformists who do not fit the norms of the earth goddess, such as active women (Olupona 39–41). So the water spirit represents a female power that has been suppressed by Western patriarchy, a goddess demonized under colonialism (Olupona 38, 207–8); and Beloved, as such a spirit, represents women as well as Africa. Nne Mmiri is linked to change, and one must pass through her by crossing a river to enter new life (Olupona 44), as Sethe does with the Ohio, which is animated in the line "near enough to hear it" (*B* 98). Wicker's "Mami Water" adds that in the New World, Africans saw water divinities as protectors and liberators from slavery (Olupona 202).

Relief from oppression would tend to work through African spirits, yet racism tends to make such spirits appear in negative terms. Morrison's latest American water spirits are the Police-heads in *Love* (2003): "*dirty things with big hats who shoot up out of the ocean to harm loose women and eat disobedient children. My mother knew them when she was a girl and people dreamed wide awake*" (5–6, 106, 201; italics in original). The speaker, who seems to bear ancestral knowledge, is a cook named L (love?) who recurs as presiding narrator of the book and turns out to be the voice of a dead person (*Love* 189) or spirit.

When Sethe finds that her daughter's African spirit has returned to her, Sethe can indulge in a nature worship that corresponds to the advanced European technique of impressionism: "Now I can look at things again because she's here to see them too. After the shed, I stopped. Now, in the morning . . . I mean to look out the window to see what the sun is doing to the day. Does it hit the pump handle first or the spigot? See if the grass is gray-green or brown or what" (*B* 237). The sun is a playful artist here, and the grass is chameleonic, both animated by extension from Beloved's spirit.

In African religions, ancestors often remain present after death. Charles Larson, who taught in Nigeria, says that the spirits of the dead are dispersed through the environment. As Parrinder puts it, "Even supposedly inorganic nature is not dead" (15). Larson and Jahn cite Birago Diop, a poet from Senegambia, a source of American slaves:

> The dead are not under the earth:
> They are in the tree that rustles,
> They are in the wood that groans,
> They are in the water that runs,
> They are in the water that sleeps,
> They are in the hut, they are in the crowd,
> The dead are not dead. (*Muntu* 108)

These lines depict a world of highly differentiated spirits: one from the rustle of the tree, another from the groan of the wood, a third in water that runs, and a fourth in water that stands still. Though the context of these lines is problematic,[5] they have often been cited as a strong vision of the prevalence of spirits, and might be called fashionable at one time.

Morrison depends on spirit lore that she derives primarily from her own experience of African American folklore. In an interview with Wendy Steiner on 7 November 1996, she said that she did not believe in researching African culture to plant it in her work, but in letting African undercurrents reveal themselves in the actions of her black characters. Christian says that in the culture she grew up in on this side of the Atlantic, African religious practices were prevalent: "In the Caribbean, spirits are everywhere. . . . [T]he ancestors, to quote a song by the black women's singing group Sweet Honey in the Rock, 'are in the wind, in the trees, in the waters, in the rocks.' In an interview, Morrison herself reiterated that point: for African Americans, at least until the recent past, the experience of spirits communicating with the living was a natural one" (9).

In the period portrayed in *Beloved*, African spirits were widely recognized, and most members of the black community of Cincinnati in *Beloved* are ready to grant that Beloved is a spirit, but the character whose African concepts pervade the novel is Sethe. Her idea of the presence of the past varies an African pattern: she believes that intense events remain as permanent scenes attached to places in the landscape (*B* 43). Mbiti says that ancestral spirits are linked to the land in Africa, and that this makes it difficult for Africans to be uprooted (26). Morrison addresses such concerns in "Rootedness."

Sethe's attachment to the spirits of her people is shown being passed on in Denver's recollection of her mother's struggle both to reach the new world of freedom and to give birth to Denver. The two goals are one because Denver represents the free future. She completes the story magnificently while telling it to the African spirit: "Denver was seeing it now and feeling it— through Beloved" (*B* 91). In the story, Sethe is ready to give up when the image of an antelope within her spurs her to go on. Probably the antelope was a sacred animal for her mother's tribe. Morrison specifies that it has no American source by saying that Sethe "had never seen one" (37). Sethe associates this graceful beast with her visceral memory of the freedom of the bodies of people in her childhood who did a dance called the Antelope: "They shifted shapes and became something other. Some unchained, demanding other whose feet knew her pulse better than she did. Just like this one in her stomach" (37). They stopped moving to the white compulsion and moved to their own complex rhythm. This spirit knows her pulse better than she does because it expresses an old truth that has been submerged by white conditioning. Deborah Horvitz points out that Sethe identifies the antelope with the image of her mother dancing (162–63); and Higgins says, "The two images—her dancing mother and the ramming antelope—embody Africa and forever link her mother of Africa and her daughter of America" (41).

The antelope keeps Sethe going by repeatedly kicking her womb when she stops, so she identifies her baby's movements with the ancestral spirit. Finally, she feels that she can't move her agonized body any further, "but the thought of herself stretched out dead while the little antelope lived on . . . in her lifeless body grieved her so she made the groan that made the person walking on a path not ten yards away halt" (B 37–38). The extension of herself into the past and future represented by the concept of ancestors to be carried on by her baby gives her strength to go on, defying and changing material reality. So *the spirit of the antelope saves her.* And she has to feel that this extension belongs to her people—as opposed to the ones that have ravaged her. Without this American African spirit, she would not survive. Yet she also would not make it if not for the person who hears her, Amy Denver.

IN DEBT FOR LIFE

Morrison is generous to white people in *Beloved,* yet her generosity strengthens her case against their system. Of the four main groups of whites in the book—Amy, the Bodwins, the Garners, and schoolteacher and his boys—only the last group is fully racist. This is probably a more benevolent breakdown than could be found by sampling whites in the Kentucky-Ohio area at the time. Even the slaveholding Garners resist the worst effects of slavery. Yet their virtues turn out to cause trouble for the black figures in Morrison's analysis of the twisted dependence of black people on white ones in racist societies.

If Sethe had been stronger, she might have killed Amy before realizing that she was sympathetic, for she was about to bite the face of the white person who discovered her (B 38). By helping Sethe to keep moving, ease her wounds, find shelter, and give birth, Amy—at risk to herself—saves Sethe repeatedly, just as the antelope does. As an African American, Sethe owes her life to both African and American sources, so every element of that life has an African side and an American one. On the American side, Amy may lead

Sethe toward a world beyond racism by being a Caucasian who helps her to move forward.

The birth scene is one of the most moving in the book because so rarely did black people and white ones get to break through the system that enclosed and opposed them. Sethe and Amy achieve a climax of reciprocity: "'Push!' screamed Amy. / 'Pull,' whispered Sethe" (B 99). The feeling that they are working together in a complementary way, which is most evident in the balance of "Push!" and "Pull," is effectively reinforced by a counterpoint in which Sethe, who is in pain, whispers, while Amy, who is only vicariously involved, screams. This scene, in which both women unite into a single creature, a pushme-pullyou,[6] may suggest that African Americans have to be assertive and whites, receptive in order to give birth to the hope of the future (Denver).

Morrison follows the birth with a stunning visual image as the air fills with bluefern spores: "they are seeds in which the whole generation sleeps confident of a future. And for a moment it is easy to believe each one has one" (B 99). That only a few seeds will survive underlines the unlikelihood of the survival of Denver made possible by the meeting of the women. The spirit of life in nature swarms with possibilities that exceed logical comprehension, just as life itself begins at the point where causal explanation breaks down. Morrison ends the paragraph by saying that neither the moment of hope nor the typical spore lasts long. The liberating emotional intensity of the scene must be balanced by skepticism, for dreams of going beyond racial limits carry the danger of sentimental escape from the reality of the conflict.

Amy does insult Sethe several times, considering her stupid because she has been forced into an almost hopeless position and assuming because Sethe will not give the name of the man who made her pregnant that she does not know it (B 92). But these offenses seem negligible in view of the extent to which Sethe's oppression is shared by Amy, a runaway indentured servant who has been deceived and abused. Wright argues in *Black Power* (1954) that America first tried to supply its labor with indentured servants in the seventeenth century; but it found that it could not get enough of them, so it turned to African slaves. Wright says that the white servants, who were generally charged with some crime, were not treated much better than the slaves (9–10).

In fact, Amy also shares Sethe's animism because the common people of

Europe cling to vestiges of the paganism eradicated by Christianity. One of the most familiar of these European retentions is fairy lore, and Amy invokes it in a feminine form to comfort Sethe by singing a song Amy's mother taught her about "Lady Button Eyes," who seems to be an animated doll: *"Where 'pon the haunted green / Fairies dance around their queen"* (*B* 95). In this matriarchal poem, nature is filled with spirits. Amy's offenses seem minor not only because she saves Sethe, but because Sethe is enchanted with her. In fact, Morrison said in the 1996 Steiner interview that Amy was a favorite character who sometimes visited her. *Beloved* does not seem to question the validity of naming Denver after the woman who saved her. Yet Morrison recognizes Sethe's debt to Amy as one of a series of debts to white people that are caught up in the disturbing ambiguity of "race" relations. I will examine this ambiguity through the two white pairs who give Sethe help.

The Bodwins and the Garners are both involved in ameliorating the effects of slavery. Though the Bodwin siblings work on a higher level because they are northern abolitionists, while the married Garners are slave owners, the parallels between the two pairs are extensive. They both give many benefits to Sethe and her family, while both white pairs retain racist attitudes. In the case of the Bodwins, this is indicated by the statue of the servile black boy that they own (*B* 300), while the Garners clearly aim to support slavery by improving it. Yet if the Bodwins have a more enlightened attitude, they pay a lower price. Bodwin is insulted and roughed up for being an abolitionist, his face being "shoe blackened" (306), but Garner is "bruised" in a number of fights for insisting that his slaves should be men (12). In fact, Garner seems to be murdered, for he has a hole in his ear, and Sixo's explanation of "gunpowder" seems more credible than Mrs. Garner's of "an exploded eardrum brought on by stroke" (225)—though we later hear that there was no blood (259). Since Garner's neighbors hate him for his racial views, it is not hard to explain his murder. If he was killed for being a "nigger lover," there might well be an automatic agreement among the whites to explain his death as natural.

The benefits that Sethe and her people derive from these two families are enormous, but therein lies the problem. The Bodwins provide a house, a job for Sethe, and fine touches such as the cologne that Miss Bodwin gives Denver (*B* 34), but the gifts garnered from the Garners reach deeper and involve stronger conflicts. If Garner had brutalized his slaves in the usual manner—

instead of proudly risking his life to make them men—the "thrashing" of their "year of yearning" for Sethe would have driven them to violence: "when rape seemed the solitary gift of life. The restraint they had exercised possible *only* because they were Sweet Home men—the ones Mr. Garner bragged about while other farmers shook their heads in warning at the phrase" (*B* 12; my italics). Although Mrs. Garner is amused when Sethe requests that a black couple be married formally (31), the Garners make it possible for Sethe and Halle to have a real marriage. In fact, while slave owners often sold slave families apart to prevent conspiracy and make profit, Don H. Doyle, in his study of the historical background of Faulkner, says that owners in Mississippi often felt that slaves worked better when they were married: it could Christianize them and reduce their rebellion (145–46). The Garners play a role in the great humanity of Paul D, who prides himself on being a Sweet Home man (*B* 7, 8, 13, 21).

Here is a grave dilemma for Morrison's characters: many of their finest qualities are owed to their enemies. And since the good moments of white people are exceptions, if black people take comfort from them, their hopes will be dashed before long. This conflict of good depending on evil runs continuously through Sethe's mind from the fifth page, where she blames herself for seeing Sweet Home as beautiful when she should see it as terrible (*B* 7). Weinstein, following Terry Otten, claims that in Morrison's fiction it is morally necessary to see oneself as implicated in evil (*What Else* 115). Can one fully respect oneself when many of one's best qualities are granted by the whims of those who run a system that depends on humiliating one endlessly?

Before turning from the world, Sethe reflects on the earrings Mrs. Garner gave her, the shining things that identified her as special for Beloved. She took them with her "not so much to wear but to hold. Earrings that made her believe she could discriminate among them. That for every schoolteacher there would be an Amy. . . . But she had come to believe . . . Baby Suggs' last words and buried all recollection of them and luck" (*B* 222). These objects of beauty gave her a sense that she possessed a self that was refined, that could secure itself by using judgment among white alternatives. But her skills could not save her from disaster, so she gave up and withdrew like Baby.

Yet Sethe's withdrawal may accomplish what Baby's could not. In her final focus on colors, Baby was trying to recover a sense of beauty untainted by racism; and Sethe, in her retreat with her daughters, is trying to develop an

American African sense of refinement that is hers rather than being imposed by whites. This would amount to recovering African ideas of elegance that were obliterated with their languages by slavery. Thompson (an art critic) says, "The Yoruba assess everything esthetically" (5). By decking themselves in flowers and bright colors (*B* 282–83), the women in 124 were "going native" to reconstitute a personal beauty linked to African decorative arts. Until they have their own grace, the imposed white one will remain too hurtful.

In practical political terms, the legacy of the Garners and Bodwins could not save Sethe because they did not represent the majority: schoolteacher, who first took over the Garner farm and then assaulted the Bodwin haven, could not be escaped. James Berger sees Bodwin as an allegorical figure for the liberalism of the 1960s, and *Beloved* was written during the 1980s, when the American government was turning toward schoolteacher's views: that black people suffer from too many privileges and must be controlled and forced to work, and that learning should focus on listing their genetic "characteristics" (*B* 228–30) so as to translate changeable sociology into inherent biology. In this perspective, liberalism was a temporary aberration, and the enduring goal of American government is to keep African Americans in their place.

The killing of Beloved is seen from schoolteacher's point of view because this is the best way to justify it. His name is not capitalized because it is generic: he speaks for a system, not an individual, and his feelings are firmly subordinated to economic calculation. It is true that he is quite disturbed by something that he cannot explain about Sethe's destruction of her family: the nephew who had sucked Sethe's milk is shaking uncontrollably, and schoolteacher repeats to himself four times, "What she go and do that for?" (*B* 176–77). But as Boris Max points out in *Native Son*, the sense of how wrong they are has usually made white Americans insist more strongly on their justification (449); and schoolteacher's gut feeling that he has done something terrible makes his racism rigidify. So nothing that he sees has any chance of changing his certainty that African Americans are animals whose significance is to be measured in terms of profit and loss: "Unlike a snake or a bear, a dead nigger could not be skinned for profit" (*B* 174-75). Schoolteacher has a technical term for the mistake that made Sethe go wild, *overbeating*. He says that if you "beat the hounds past" a certain point, you will not be able to "trust them" afterwards (176). As with Sutpen's morality, the important question has to be one of quantitative measurement: the real issue is the correct amount of beating. The volition involved when slaves go wrong is that of the owner's mistake, for slaves have no control over their minds. If they go berserk and destroy themselves when pursued, this only shows how irrational they are. The real problem is that Garner treated them like human beings, and that made it hard to calculate the amount of beating necessary to subdue them. The term *freedom* applies to black people only as a dis-ease that whites could give them: "All testimony to the results of a little so-called freedom *imposed* on people who needed every care and guidance in the world to keep them from the cannibal life they preferred" (177; my italics). Schoolteacher is sure that what he is doing is the best thing that can be done for the benefit of "niggers," and that the profit motive will naturally coincide with what is best for everyone.

The United States does not stop schoolteacher, but Sethe understands him well and does exactly what is needed to stop him. When he sees that she has killed her child, he realizes that there is "nothing there to claim" (*B* 175), for she looks too wild to care for the other children. One could argue that America would stop schoolteacher through the Civil War, but Jim Crow turned out to be almost as bad as slavery.[7] A positive view can say that America does progress, but it tends to involve three steps forward and two backward, and that we are only going two steps backward at present. What torments Sethe is just such an alternation. She sees her life following a rhythm in which a short period of happiness is followed by a long one of misery (*B* 204). This can hurt more than mere despondency.

In the passage in which she reviews her life while turning away from the world, Sethe realizes that the implacability of schoolteacher, or of the system he teaches, drove her to take up Baby's final negation for many years. After this, she recalls that Paul D revived her, "gave her back her body," and brought news. When he heard her awful secret, however, he fled, so she will have to withdraw again (*B* 222); but this time it will be with a difference, with Beloved, a manifestation of her love and of vestiges of African religion. Sethe has alternated between despair and hope that there is something to be gotten from whites: she finds it hard to conceive of any major advancement or positive personal quality that does not emanate from white hegemony. What she needs to develop is the ability to hope for something from her own side, so that she will not remain subject to the cruel zigzag of backlash imposed on her. (The word *backlash* is meaningful to her.) She heads for her retreat with

Beloved not in despair, but eager for a revelation. It is true that her hopes do not include any effective way of relating to the factual world that whites control, but she will have to pass through an inner world of the spirit before she can return to the outer one.

IN THE REALM OF BELOVED

Spirit operates as an extension of human feelings in the imagination, though it confronts people with the need to go beyond feelings they already know into the Real. Beloved is a helping spirit at first, but she turns out to be a demon. One thing spirits can do that Western psychological abstractions cannot do is change. Beloved guides Sethe and others through themselves to terrible realities that they must confront in order to be liberated. Morrison's decision to make Beloved as spirit preponderant in *Beloved* allows her to enter the mind-set of her characters. It would be unrealistic to depict uneducated nineteenth-century African Americans living in a world in which ghosts did not exist. This is especially true for people who retain touches of African spiritism, but it is also true for Emily Brontë's *Wuthering Heights* (1847), set in rural England early in the century. Morrison seems to have decided to take spirits seriously with *Song of Solomon* (1978). The great ending of this novel suggests that African Americans must either claim the spiritual powers of their ancestors or they will not survive. Spirits of African descent, with a Latin American admixture, are also present in *Tar Baby* (1981) and *Paradise* (1997); and *Jazz* (1992) is about a couple, Joe and Violet Trace, who spend their time communicating with a dead girl, Dorcas Manfred. The usual explanation of Morrison's supernaturalism is that it derives from Garcia Marquez; yet in interviews, Morrison minimizes his influence (Taylor-Guthrie 46–47, 242). Insofar as this was one of her sources, it should be noted that Garcia Marquez was hugely influenced by Faulkner, and that *Absalom* is all about haunting.

On the third page of *Beloved*, Denver says, "For a baby she throws a powerful spell." Sethe replies, "No more powerful than the way I loved her" (*B* 5), implying that the more she loves the ghost, the more strength it has. Coupled with her statement four lines earlier—"But if she'd only come, I could make it clear to her"—this suggests why the physical age of the spirit Beloved is what it would be if she had lived. Sethe must have given the ghost her attention and thoughtfulness every day, and this articulated its development through the years. Denver may see Sethe infusing life into the spirit when

she sees her mother kneeling beside a kneeling dress (35). A similar vivifi-
cation is seen in Jorge Luis Borges's "The Circular Ruins" (1940), in which
a shaman in a jungle meticulously imagines a being into life, body part by
body part and thought by thought: this creation ends up seeming to be a real
person (45–50). Morrison may have known this famous story. In any case,
her own practice in animating characters parallels Borges's postmodern portrayal of a shaman or animist priest. In her "conversation" with Gloria Nay-
lor, Morrison says of Beloved, "bit by bit I had been rescuing her from the
grave of time and inattention. Her fingernails maybe in the first book; face
and legs, perhaps, the second time. Little by little bringing her back into living life. So that now she comes running when called—walks freely around
the house . . ." (Taylor-Guthrie 217). Since most of Morrison's characters are
historical, her usual pattern of giving them life must, like this passage, be parallel to the way Sethe gives life to Beloved, so that Sethe is a kind of artist of
imaginary mother love, as well as a conjure woman. And Morrison creates
Beloved not as a crawling baby, but as a grown person who "walks freely."

Characters continually infuse spirit into each other in *Beloved,* and Beloved
herself enacts this pattern in ways that make its operation manifest. When
Sethe attends to her, Beloved grows (*B* 285, 295), but when Sethe turns away,
Beloved begins to disintegrate. This is a concrete enactment of the fragmentation that threatens Lacan's mirror stage, which is where Beloved's mind is
situated. She represents an extension of black selfhood that is nipped in the
bud by schoolteacher. Even after the mirror stage, people can fall apart if they
are not reflected. The pattern appears vividly after Sethe's first reconciliation
with Paul D. Beloved seduces Paul partly to take Sethe's attention from him;
so when he and Sethe make up, one of Beloved's teeth falls out and she thinks,
"This is it. Next would be her arm, her hand, a toe. Pieces of her would drop
maybe one at a time, maybe all at once. . . . [S]he would fly apart. It is difficult keeping her head on her neck, her legs attached to her hips when she is
by herself" (157). Everyone begins by being unified as a reflection of parents,
but someone who has not made it past the mirror stage needs constant reflection to avoid disintegrating. The traumatized mind operates like a spirit that
can be dis(re)membered.

Morrison's use of Lacan's ideas is probably conscious, for her praise appears on the back cover of the paperback edition of *The Location of Culture,*
a book saturated with Lacanian concepts. Likewise, *Playing in the Dark* is a

deconstruction of white American literature, following Derrida's methods of focusing on internal contradictions and showing how the excluded side of a polarity is necessary to the privileged one (Eagleton, *Literary* 115–16). Most likely Morrison is not presenting African American elements that happen to coincide with poststructural ones. She is, like Gates and Bhabha, intentionally combining the ethnic material and the poststructural, so that the distinction is not always discernible. Beloved, for example, is an African spirit who embodies the critical principle of "the word . . . a presence made of absence" (Lacan, *Écrits* 64). This matches Morrison's remark that the experience of African American women in the nineteenth century was postmodern (Gilroy, *Black,* 221).

At the risk of contradictory language, I will say that the essence of Beloved is her division, that her identity consists of being opposed to herself. The need she extends to others, which makes her irresistible, is a gap at her center, the opposite of self-possession. The reason we are told at the end that no one could "remember or repeat a thing she said" (*B* 324) is that what she says tends to be opposed to sense. Her ostensive line "I'm like this" (146) identifies her with something obscure and submerged. She also asks Denver "if there are flowers in the dark" (142). Her doubt about whether things exist if they are not perceived is parallel to the African belief that spirits only exist as long as they are remembered (Mbiti 25), and the Lacanian idea that signs constitute reality (*Écrits* 65). Fuston-White says that while essentialist definitions of black identity should be avoided, the concept of black subjectivity that *Beloved* develops avoids specificity by being based on conflict and division (470–71).

To understand what Beloved says is to be lifted outside of the ordinary world. The Latin root of *ordinary* means giving orders, and ordinary reality has tended to be defined by whites. In *The Bluest Eye,* blacks in the 1920s feel driven to stay within the ordinary because they sense that they are marginal, "on the hem of life" (*BE* 17). Beloved is the American African outsideness in African Americans that they need to avoid. The oppositions that she poses are beyond comprehension both because they involve an African world of otherness and because they are dispersed in postmodern indeterminacy. But to realize the intellectual conflicts that Beloved embodies, they must be seen as rooted in terrible social conflicts, in injustice.

Sethe's line about how powerfully she loved her baby is followed by "and there it was again" (*B* 5)—the scene in which she allowed the engraver to copulate with her in exchange for carving "Beloved" on the tombstone. This proves her love because it was so horrible to give her body, with a boy watching (5). The scene in which Beloved gets her name prefigures retroactively the one in which she gets her being, her "perfect death" (116), the ultimate proof of Sethe's love. Sethe is forced by white men in both scenes who have the power to invade the core of her creativity. She determines that they must not "dirty" her best thing (295), yet they still pollute her ideal creation with destruction. This is the incandescent, broken center of the contradictions in the dream child Beloved. It is a rape consisting of the forcing of murder that leads to a negative impregnation of the spirit. The division that haunts her is imposed by domination.

That Beloved combines the body of a young woman with mental features of a baby corresponds to Sethe's divided needs. Her insistence that the baby understands perfectly (*B* 236) entails an endless need to explain to her that can never succeed. That Beloved seems able to read minds (79), yet entirely misunderstands Sethe's conscious motive for the murder—seeing it as an act of desertion (254, 309)—shows how deep Sethe's conflict is. On some level, she suspects that her desire to protect Beloved from the hands of others ("if I hadn't killed her she would have died"; 236) was a turning away from Beloved to her idea of Beloved. This does not mean that she was wrong to do it, but that doing it involved this extra level of self-division, as I read the formula that Morrison quotes: "It was the right thing to do, but she had no right to do it" (Taylor-Guthrie 272). The painful awareness that her act was wrong from other points of view adds to its rightness, making it a stronger assertion of love and courage. Within her knowledge, it was right, but that knowledge was limited. The withholding of knowledge from her by racism makes her lack of right political. The denial of her rights distorts her choice, enforcing her possession.

If Beloved can be seen as a living person, this should not at all be taken as resolving the conflicts in which she is involved as a spirit, but rather as adding to their complexity. Elizabeth B. House develops an elaborate and credible argument that Beloved is an actual woman who came on an illegal slave ship late in the 1850s. The importing of slaves was banned in America in 1808, yet until the 1850s large numbers of slaves were smuggled into the country (Sundquist, *To Wake* 191). House maintains that Beloved was taken as a child, probably by an officer of the ship, and kept as a sex slave until 1873. Before Paul D leaves, Sethe thinks that Beloved must have been locked up by some white man (*B* 140); and Stamp Paid later reports that a white man died and that the black girl he was imprisoning escaped around the time that Beloved appeared (277). Such traumatic events might make her mind regress, and confinement might explain her smooth hands. Sethe wants a daughter, and the woman who was called Beloved in the dark (88) wants a mother, since her own jumped overboard, so the two get involved in a mutual delusion.

House shows that there is a level on which Beloved is flesh and blood, and this level has political force in showing that Sethe's haunting is caused by human mistreatment. But it must be seen as only one level of the book, a Western one that leaves much unexplained, from the red light at the beginning (*B* 10) to the coda at the end (323–24). The realistic reading reduces the characters to ignorant victims, and it depends on coincidences. In fact, Morrison said in an interview with Marsha Darling (1988) that two Beloveds coexist: "She is a spirit on one hand, literally she is what Sethe thinks she is, her child returned to her from the dead. . . . She is also another kind of dead which is not spiritual but flesh, which is, a survivor from the true, factual slave ship" (Taylor-Guthrie 247). The two sides may be combined comprehensively by saying that Beloved is a living person inhabited by the dead baby's spirit.

Morrison's insistence that Beloved is a spirit is confirmed quite extensively in the text. I have mentioned that she seems to reside underwater (*B* 60, 255, 324) and to cause Sethe to urinate unnaturally (61). Other evidence includes her name, her cut throat, her weird strength (67), her apparent ability to strangle Sethe from a distance (113–16) and to disappear (145, 315), her moving Paul D out of his room and the house, her singing the song Sethe sang her as a baby, her hands without lines (299), her remembering Sethe's earrings (75), and so forth. One point that has not been noticed begins on the second page of the novel, long before Beloved's arrival, when Sethe and Denver try to call out the poltergeist: "Come on. You may as well just come on" (4). Later Beloved calls on Denver to dance with her: " 'Come on,' said Beloved. 'You may as well just come on' " (87). It is as if Beloved remembered the words earlier addressed to the ghost.

Beloved is a figure of dizzying complexity, a living woman who is also dead, an American African spirit who was generated by white racism. America created the spirit of Africa because, as Genovese argues, the Africans who reached America did not share a Pan-African identity until slavery forced them to live together and speak one language as a multicultural black nation (281). Beloved's aspects as child, woman, sister, ghost, and African may be parallel at the root by being excluded. The level that defines her most would seem to be her blackness because this is what causes her destruction, but Sethe may also kill her first because she is a daughter as well as because she is the most beloved. In *Incidents in the Life of a Slave Girl*, when Jacobs hears that her newborn is a girl, her "heart was heavier than it had ever been before. Slavery is terrible for men, but it is far more terrible for women. . . . [T]hey have wrongs, and sufferings, and mortifications peculiarly their own" (823).

Sethe kills Beloved first because she loves her most, and the most disturbing implication of the murder is that racism makes African Americans destroy what they love most, their best things.[8] This idea is supported by a chain of indications that slavery makes one afraid to love strongly because one's love will be taken from one. So Sethe and Paul have both learned to love small, and to lock up their feelings in metal boxes within themselves (*B* 133, 207). Weinstein emphasizes that America has traditionally defined identity in terms of self-possession (*What Else* 89–93), but Morrison portrays such self-possession as repression, locking up one's love in a constricting container. We will see that Beloved emerges from this container and returns to it. Some of the most pernicious effects of white racism involve reversing human values. African Americans with virtues such as courage, beauty, and intelligence would suffer more, getting punished and raped for them; whereas weaknesses—docility, falseness and obtuseness would tend to be rewarded. A slave owner like schoolteacher who believes that he is justified because slaves are not human will reward animal features and punish human ones. Moreover, as Douglass states, the creative activity of slaves benefited their masters, not themselves (353). If a slave had a child, it made the master richer, and the child could be taken away. For this reason, as Elizabeth Fox-Genovese shows, slaves sometimes killed babies in protest, especially if pregnancy was forced (329).

Sethe's mother, known only as Ma'am, killed several of her babies who were born as a result of white rape. This is told to Sethe by Nan, a woman who works as a nurse because she has lost an arm, a weakness rewarded. Nan wants Sethe, whose mother has been hung, to know that Ma'm resisted white rapists; and that Sethe was named after her black father, presumably named Seth (*B* 74). Nan conveys to the child the courage of her mother's resistance, which must have led to Ma'am's execution. In passing this on, Nan is parallel to Morrison, who retrieves a lost legacy of black ancestors. On the other hand, as Jill Matus points out (110), Sethe fears that Ma'am may have run away, choosing to leave her.

Many West African traditions hold that each person contains the spirits of his or her ancestors. Thus Larson says of a childless African woman in a story who commits suicide that she has "trapped her ancestors, broken the cycle of life" (468; see Mbiti 131). One is obliged to pass on the spirits one bears within. Moreover, a person who dies tends to join the ancestors, even if that person is young. The idea that Beloved as a spirit contains her ancestors suggests one reason why her monologue recalls the Middle Passage, even on the level on which she was born in Kentucky. The blast-furnace ordeal through which Africans were wrenched into America erased their culture by generations of terror and constraint. Sethe, for example, remembers two main people who continued to speak African languages, Ma'am and Sixo, and both died horribly for their resistance. Virtually all African Americans have this black hole in their cultural background, and in this sense the Middle Passage is submerged in their minds, so that their mental worlds could not be represented without their being haunted by it.

Sundquist says that as recently as the early twentieth century, "the most pressing racial question" for black intellectuals was, "Could the race advance culturally" or gain equal social rights without "discarding the traces of its enslavement and African origins?" (*To Wake* 291). Blacks who wanted to move upward were under pressure to erase their roots. The cast-off lower level appears in Chesnutt's tale "The Wife of His Youth" (1898). Mr. Ryder has risen in status and is about to marry an elegant light-skinned lady when his wife turns up. She is an uneducated dark-skinned woman whom he had lost track of decades ago during the chaos of emancipation. He assumed she was dead, and now he has to decide whether to recognize her and give up features of his social standing. The story indicates that she must be reclaimed.

Only by embodying the magnitude of what has been lost can Beloved hold out the hope that draws everyone to her, the hope of recovery expressed by Sethe's desire to reclaim her daughter. Yet Beloved, having been denied, returns filled with excessive need and an evident desire for revenge. The need and the resentment feed each other, and they are polarized intensely because she is outside the margin of life. Trudier Harris, examining Beloved in a context of African American folklore, says that she has the features of a demon or succubus (151–63). She separates Paul from Sethe, and seems to be destroying Sethe near the end. Pamela Barnett expands on Harris's view to focus on horrific images of Beloved draining the life out of Paul D and Sethe.

Beloved's fearsome demonic aspect, however, must be seen as only one side, a bitterness that results from suffering that exalts her. Morrison's foreword to the 2004 edition of *Beloved* presents the beginning of the novel in Morrison's positive vision of Beloved: "She walked out of the water, climbed the rocks, and leaned against the gazebo. Nice hat." "The figure most central to the story would have to be her, the murdered, not the murderer, the one who lost everything and had no say in any of it" (xviii). Here Beloved is not an aggressor but someone killed. Though dreadful, Beloved stands for the highest love, the greatest beauty, the truest identity. Even as a living victim, she is the deepest self of the others because that self has been locked up and abused by white authority. It is through the suppressed, abused part of themselves that they have glimpses of the erased vision of the homeland—just as ideal sexual love can only be reached through shame. She first appears when Sethe and Paul D. get together because she embodies the passions that are emerging in them. She provides crucial help for Paul, Sethe, and Denver in developing themselves toward both freedom and family. The perfect fusion that Beloved offers—"You are my face; I am you" (*B* 256)—is the union with the lost African spirit that could make identity whole.[9] This is the Real, and one can never reach it, but one can never stop aiming at it. One benefits by looping through its field, but to head directly into it is to leave language behind and die. While the absolute indulgence in Beloved that Sethe pursues toward the end is perilous, the characters cannot be helped or saved without passing through this spirit.

They emphasize Beloved's demonism because European contexts bring out negative aspects of African manifestations. As both victim and spirit, she is what they have been forced to deny and cannot forgive themselves for denying. In such a situation, the black community of Cincinnati consistently rejects Beloved, just as most black Chicagoans seem to reject Bigger Thomas. The community fails to warn Sethe in 1856 because they do not think that Negroes should have as much happiness as Baby Suggs's party reveals: "Maybe they just wanted to know if Baby really was special, blessed in some way they were not" (*B* 185)—and this makes the murder possible. They show the influence of racism by denying to black people the margin of extreme happiness (or manna) that Beloved alive represents. Then they make up for this and protect Sethe in 1874 by chasing Beloved away. In both cases, they reject Beloved, whether it is because she represents an excess of joy or an excess of resentment.

Yet they all depend on her, for their Europeanized perceptions need to be cleansed by her sub-Saharan ones to increase their capacity for love and truth. With Beloved, Sethe and Denver talk about crucial experiences they could not talk about before; and for Sethe and Paul D, Beloved unlocks the tin boxes that had long enclosed their deep feelings. Paul locks up his feelings in a "tobacco tin lodged in his chest" after being on the chain gang in Georgia: "nothing in this world could pry it open" (*B* 133). When he makes love to Beloved, who is not in this world, "flakes of rust" fall away "from the seams," and when "the lid" gives, he repeats what he has recovered: "Red heart, Red heart" (138). Valerie Smith recognizes this scene as "a bodily cure" for Paul D (348). Likewise, when Sethe realizes that Beloved is singing a song she sang to her baby, a "casket of jewels" that has been "hidden" approaches its miraculous opening up (*B* 207). Though she separates Sethe and Paul D, Beloved prepares them to reunite on a more real level by bringing them in touch with their most profound feelings, which she incarnates. In a 1998 interview, Morrison speaks of the role of "the beloved" in her trilogy (*Beloved, Jazz, and Paradise*): "This, she says, is the corner of our soul 'that is reliable, that never betrays us, that is cherished by us, that we tend to cover up and hide and make into a personality'" (Streitfeld). It is not clear that this refers to Beloved herself, but it suggests that she embodies a level deep within everyone.

The time that Sethe and Denver spend isolated in 124 with Beloved allows Sethe to work through her obsession and perceive that her dream of reclaiming her child cannot be realized. No one but Beloved could modify Sethe's desperate, pitiful conviction that she was absolutely right to kill Beloved. Sethe may not avoid noticing what grows obvious to Denver, that Sethe does not really want to be understood: she wants to be denied forgiveness (*B* 297). This is how she reaches the reality of Beloved, not just her fantasy; but this is a kind of Real that is uninhabitable, beyond subjectivity. In the overall economy of the book, the African aspect of Beloved is invaluable as a corrective to Western values, but turns out to be a dead end if it is pursued for itself. *Beloved* may therefore include an allegory on a phase of Afrocentric thinking that was growing during the 1960s, but that may have begun to become aware of its limitations by the 1980s.

The retreat with Beloved also has a powerful positive impact on Denver, most obviously because it forces her to go out into the world as starvation looms. Like Sethe, she moves through and beyond her attachment to Beloved by seeing its implications acted out—a parallel to Wright's idea that the emotions of nationalism must be gone through. The image of Denver drinking Beloved's blood with her milk (*B* 179, 242) indicates not only that they are bound together, but that they have opposite fates. Oppression can pit people against each other, and the extremity of hardship may dictate that one sibling has to do badly so that another can do well—whether what is in short supply is physical or mental. If Beloved were not killed, Denver would become a slave. As racism forces Denver to drink her sister's blood, it has forced many impoverished people to sacrifice in some measure those beloved to them. The hothouse period also promotes Denver's progress in a more subtle way. She begins the retreat convinced that she must protect Beloved from her mother, whom Denver has unconsciously imagined decapitating her (243). But during the retreat, Denver realizes that it is Sethe who needs protection from Beloved (see Rushdy 50–51). So she sees how vulnerable her mother is, how it was love that caused the murder. This is a step toward Denver's maturity and her ability to love.

The productive effects that Beloved has on Sethe, Denver, and Paul D amount to the basis of their regeneration. Beloved could not have these effects if she were not in the position of a dead person. To have conversation or intercourse with a revenant allows one to communicate something vastly different from what one can address to the living, who are attached to interests and defenses from which the projection of the nonliving frees one. Many Africans, as Mbiti observes, find visits from the living dead to be helpful: people "experience a sense of psychological relief when they pour out their hearts' troubles before their seniors who have a foot in both worlds" (82).

The figure of Beloved allows Morrison to present a series of levels and operations that are not accessible as long as the impulses of the mind are conceived of as abstract categories in isolated individuals. As a person, she can, for examples, be alive or dead, have different relations with people, and be filled with contradictions. Moreover, she materializes a field of forces between Paul D, Sethe, and Denver. It may be that human impulses never exist except as involved in life, interaction with others, and contradictions. So rational Western systems of psychology may be seen as crude and limited in comparison to the workings of the spirit that Beloved enacts.

Ancient Roman families had household deities, and many Africans make similar use of ancestral spirits. Even in our society, it is not unusual for people to commune with deceased relatives. Perhaps every family has an active spirit, a personified ego-ideal with which members interact on different levels. The interplay between family members may indeed only be conceivable as operating through the spirit. Beloved is the spirit of the family in 124, and they could not be represented—or exist—without her. The spirits in Morrison's novels reveal the operation of African psychological insights and forces in American life. Her Afrocentric aspect, however, is balanced in *Beloved* by the way in which the ghost ends up sending Denver into the outside world.

Denver's outward move requires a conversation with the ancestral spirit of Baby Suggs, who tells her not to let pessimism stop her. It also involves as main obstacle the risk of contact with whites: "Suppose they . . . grabbed her" (*B* 288). Denver does it, and her connection with Nelson Lord suggests that she may be the first woman in the family to have children she can hold in America; moreover, the Bodwins plan to send her to college (314). And Sethe and Paul D seem ready at the end to follow her lead into "some kind of tomorrow" (*B* 322), which is black slang for a really fine tomorrow.[10] This auspicious aspect of *Beloved* implies through its plot of spirit visitation that by developing their own vision, African Americans can enable themselves to dialogue with European Americans rather than being culturally deficient.

AMERICAN AFRICAN POSTMODERNISM IN LANGUAGE

What Morrison presents in *Beloved* is not African culture, but American African—a culture formed by the interaction of African and American components, altered by each other. Such a mix, with input from other sources, such as Native Americans and Europeans, is the basis of both African American and modern American culture in different proportions. In this interaction, elements of African culture tend to speak for the Real, which breaks down comprehensible order. As Karla F. C. Holloway puts it, Beloved disrupts the narrative structures of Sethe and Denver's thinking (520). Every signifying instance of Beloved works to express a revolutionary new American African understanding that gains its meaning by interacting disruptively with the European American Symbolic system. White discourse here provides a framework that serves to reveal the expansive possibilities of the projected African discourse that plays on it. Neither one is creative without looping into the other.

The strangeness of Beloved's words and actions contribute to what Morrison as an artist is most concerned with, the creation of language. For "the words to say it" (*PD* xiii) speak to bring mental possibilities and realities into consciousness, play, and use. Beloved the potential person embodies the imperative of the *differend* as the need to be heard. In this role, she herself, like the novel, transforms language through the interaction of black and white discourses. Consider one of Morrison's most striking innovations, a violation of the rules of punctuation that becomes the key description of Sethe's living infant Beloved: "the crawling already? girl" (*B* 110, 111, 178, 187). The question mark between the modifier and its noun expresses better than correct punctuation could Sethe's amazement that Beloved is so advanced. We are later told that under the hardships of slavery, babies were given inadequate care, and developed slowly (187). Sethe sees the infant as a prodigy, and her intense adoration of Beloved compels her to kill her first when slavery looms—an extreme reversal of values by racism. Insofar as Sethe's excitement violates the rules of Standard English, Beloved's vitality is opposed to the racist framework.[11] Sethe's language expresses Baby Suggs's preachment that we have to love our flesh because they hate it. At the same time, this question mark is a fine example of literary experimentation insofar as no previous fiction writer had used such punctuation. It is modernist in expressing Sethe's amazement exactly, yet postmodern in dis-integrating the ability of the English language to express what is perceived.

Morrison says, "Modern life begins with slavery. . . . black women had to deal with post-modern problems in the nineteenth century and earlier" (Gilroy, *Black* 221). Beloved projects multiple, fragmented points of view that make up modern consciousness: her African core, which is inherently traditional, becomes the leading edge of modernism through its decentered interaction with the European discourse it sees through. The experimental, disjointed writing of Beloved's monologues, in which words are not tied to recognizable actions or causal sequences (*B* 248–52), resembles the disordered discourse of disturbed figures in Faulkner and Woolf—such as Benjy Compson in *The Sound and the Fury* and Septimus Warren Smith in

Mrs. Dalloway—who express the leading edge of technical advance. Morrison wrote her master's thesis on Woolf and Faulkner in 1955;[12] her technique here implies that twentieth-century modes of perception were employed by nineteenth-century African Americans because the decentered, polyvalent outlook of modernism was forced on such exploited Americans long before white bourgeois writers had access to it. When Morrison uses elements similar to Faulkner's, however, it should be remembered that because she has her own genius and is black, these elements have different contexts that give them different meanings and techniques. The idea that history never stops being present has one meaning in *Absalom*, where history is more of an entrapment, and another in *Beloved*, where it is more of a deliverance. When Benjy says, "I tried to get it off of my face, but the bright shapes were going again" (*S&F* 34), he may sound like Beloved—"The man on my face is dead   his face is not mine" (*B* 248)—but the substance is different. His infantile disorientation relates primarily to his family, and is addressed to himself. But Beloved's interior speech is addressed to others: Sethe, Denver, and an audience that must be told about historical injustice. He is framed more psychologically, while she is a historical spirit. Her vision reflects another world, an African perspective with different modes of language, logic, and philosophy. And these multiplying worldviews deploy the basis of postmodernism.

Morrison sees Black English or Ebonics as linked to modernism. *Playing in the Dark* says that critics should attend to the way "Africanist idiom is used . . . to signal modernity," and that "black idiom and the sensibilities it has come to imply are appropriated for the associative value they lend to modernism—to being hip, sophisticated, ultra-urbane" (52). Here Morrison anticipates North's argument that modernism develops in America through the use of black dialect (North 59–99). Her use of language to link American African discourse and modernism can be explored so as to lead toward postmodernism through two of *Beloved*'s major figures of speech, animism and pseudo-anachronism.[13] I have addressed animism, perhaps the main trope in the novel. It appears in the first sentence, "124 was spiteful," to establish that the presence that undermines conventional usage is Beloved. She signifies in the African accent of every sentence. When the corn or the antelope or the spores are infused with spirit, they speak for the African attainment of desire that Beloved embodies. In animism the natural creature or object shows it is extra-alive by stepping out of its ordinary role, so animation always carries the modernist impulse of defamiliarization. The question mark after "crawling already" causes the phrase to jump out of its containment by Standard English, like a mirror image that suddenly moves itself.

As Sethe starts to withdraw from the world with Beloved, the universe becomes animated by joy during the ice-skating: "The live oak and soughing pine on the banks enclosed them and absorbed their laughter"; and "Winter stars, close enough to lick, had come out before sunset. For a moment, looking up, Sethe entered the perfect peace they offered" (*B* 205–6). Denver's boxwood bower also represents Beloved—the branches "stretching toward each other" with "murmuring leaves" (34)—for it is a place where Denver's imagination expands. The image of the child whose fancy lives by talking with a spirit runs from *Winnie-the-Pooh* to *Calvin and Hobbes*. In projecting imagination on the world, animism expands one's life by seeing the beloved-self in objects. Reason, the denial of animism, encases that beloved in the inanimate.

The pseudo-anachronisms of *Beloved* develop its two postmodern temporal aspects. If Beloved is both a woman and a spirit, likewise Morrison may often realize the language of *Beloved* to be the language both of the former slaves of 1873 and of her own period. When Sethe yearns for a wedding in the 1850s, for example, she wants "A preacher, some dancing, a party, a something" (*B* 31). Sethe's use of "a something" may be historically accurate—vernacular idioms are hard to trace—but it sounds like it also comes from 1987, as it does.

Later on this page, Sethe and Halle are "Scrunched down" in the corn. *Scrunch,* though it is an Anglo-Saxon word, seems innovative in its peculiarity. It may well have been used characteristically by African Americans in the nineteenth century, for it appears in *Huckleberry Finn* (2). Twain announces at the start of his 1885 novel that it uses seven dialects, which he must have attuned to the antebellum setting. The dialect he lists first is "Missouri negro" (xxi), and Shelley Fisher Fishkin has demonstrated in *Was Huck Black?* that Huck's narrative is permeated with African American dialect. Fishkin says, "The voice we . . . accept as the vernacular voice in American literature—the voice with which Twain captured our national imagination in *Huckleberry Finn* and that empowered Hemingway, Faulkner, and countless other writers . . . is in large measure a voice that is "black" (4).

In the linguistic channel that Twain piloted, African American speech was to convey many active idioms and terms into later modern and "hip" language, often in reference to music. Smitherman provides African sources for several terms associated with modern attitudes: *dig, jazz, hip,* and *cool* (*Talkin* 45, 53). Many African words were allowed to pass into English, rather than being forbidden, because they sounded like English words. For example, the word *dig* is from the Wolof *dega,* "to understand" (45). I speculate that the phrase "dig it" sounded enough like "get a shovel in it" so that it was allowed to mean "understand it." That African words had to sound English to survive indicates how restrictive and obliterating the suppression was, and how what was permitted was shaped by the template of European culture.

Whether or not phrases in *Beloved* are anachronistic—and I generally think that they are not—they tend to *sound* anachronistic. For example, we are told that as Sethe grew more attracted to Paul D, the notion of life with him "was beginning to stroke her mind" (*B* 51). This bothers Denver, and soon she "flat-out asked Paul D" how long he would stay (52). "Stroke" and "flat-out" seem more like words from the 1970s than from the 1870s. Later Sethe feels that Paul D expresses "upfront love" (190), and Stamp Paid recalls that Sethe "split to the woodshed" (186). The use of "split" to mean "go away" seems to be hipster lingo, but it turns out that Jim uses it in the manuscript pages that were recently added to *Huckleberry Finn* (55). In emphasizing possible anachronisms, Morrison suggests that we cannot find the right words for the lost language of the oppressed.

Characters in *Beloved* often use "sixties" thinking, as Stanley Crouch pointed out in his famous negative review of the book ("Aunt Medea," Solomon 66–68). For example, in courting Sethe, Paul D says this: "Tell her [Denver] it's not about choosing somebody over her—it's making space for somebody along with her. . . . There's no way I'm going to hurt her. . . ." "Go as far inside as you need to. . . . We can make a life, girl" (*B* 55). It may be that African Americans had such language and such conceptions: slavery gave them acute senses of freedom, of suffering, of personal space, and these might later have passed into the general American culture through the 1920s and the 1960s. Morrison says in her foreword that her aim was to relate "history to contemporary issues about freedom, responsibility and women's 'place'" (xvii). Perhaps no less radical a sense of linguistic experimentation could capture the cauldron of transition out of which so much that was modern was generated. As Baker points out, the word *vernacular* originally meant "pertaining to slaves" in Latin (*Blues* 2).

As for Paul D, having criticized African American males strongly in previous novels (as she would in later ones), Morrison here pays tribute to them. She recognizes the millions of black men who have had to endure unbearable conditions, but yet remained gentle and understanding, who learned from brutality the value of kindness. For political reasons, the conciliatory black person has often had to be denounced as an Uncle Tom; but there may be value in celebrating the strength of African Americans who are generous to those who deserve it. It is true that Paul D does resent Sethe's independence from the start (B 11–12), but he does a remarkable pseudo-anachronistic job of learning and growing to understand her.

When Sethe finally gets to nurse Beloved in freedom in 1855, the text says, "They hit home together" (B 110). This is probably not an anachronism, but the use of the phrase "hit home" to describe nursing seems to look forward to a freewheeling modern sensibility. The strange multiplicity of these words indicates the marginal creativity of the African Americans' language. Caught between worlds, they recombined words in new ways that vitalized expression. The oppressed speak for what cannot be said and what needs to be said— the *differend*—so their words fall a little aside from what they aim at. This displacement expresses freedom through feelings that can scarcely be known because the established sociolinguistic order excludes them. Mother and daughter "hit home" so vigorously because of the system that holds them apart, and when Sethe longs for "a something," it is a dignity that is more real because she can scarcely conceive it. Here is a basis for the "wrong words" ($V.$ 144) of postmodernism that depart from what they describe.

The creative potential of Black English for negative truth rests on the fact that its words do not fit into clearly defined frames. Because there is no highly developed dictionary for Ebonics, which overlaps with Standard English, it is partly outside the Symbolic order, which may be equated with the order of determinate words embodied by a dictionary.[14] It is connected to the feelings of the in-between that are dynamic, so meanings change readily. Black words are highly charged with the pattern that Freud describes in his essay "The Antithetical Meaning of Primal Words" (SE 11: 153–62). That is, the ambivalence of unconscious thinking—which is embodied by the extremes of Beloved's positive and negative feelings for Sethe—has not yet been artificially separated into supposedly isolated components. Therefore, for example, *uptight* has a negative meaning if applied to a repressed person, but it is positive for James Brown; and the n-word may be the worst thing to call an African American or—for a rapper—the best. Such ambivalence often reflects what Smitherman calls the "push-pull" syndrome, in which one pushes toward white America while simultaneously pulling away from it (*Talkin* 10–11). She says that when white words are given black interpretations, "*their range of referents increases*" (*Talkin* 59; italics in original).

In *Beloved*, as in all of the books that I treat, every detail should be seen from a black point of view and a white one. This may be inferred from Karla F. C. Holloway's description of the two levels of language in *Beloved* that she calls "orate" and "literate" (518). In the case of the anachronisms, the Afrocentric view is that they show the power of black language to reach beyond its time. The Eurocentric view emphasizes the postmodern ideas that language can never quite fit its subject and that we can only see history from our viewpoint: a twentieth-century writer can never really match nineteenth-century language. But, in fact, the two viewpoints intertwine, as they often do. For the sense that language is searching for "a something" that it can never quite recover often adds to the poignancy of the book. So the European theory makes the African poetry more beautiful—more beautiful because we know that it cannot fully exist in the sense of claiming a solid framework, beautiful in spirit.

THE CODA: DISREMEMBERED

At the end, Beloved disintegrates, feeling herself deserted by Sethe "Again" (*B* 309). Sethe's attempt to solve the terrible rememory by killing the white man in the hat instead of her daughter turns out to be a delusion. Stamp and Paul agree that it would have been "the worst thing in the world for" the black community if Sethe had killed Bodwin (312). It would show that she could not distinguish the best European American from the worst. The ultimate lesson that Beloved implants in Sethe may be that revenge is impossible because the person you attack is not the person who was guilty, and the demonstration of the impossibility of revenge may be one reason that the ghost disappears.

Beloved goes back underwater, and as Grewal points out (117), she is locked up. In fact, she goes back into the metal boxes in the breasts of Sethe and Paul D to the tune of exquisite syncopation: "a latch latched and lichen attached its apple-green bloom to the metal" (324). As the metal box closes, it is suddenly covered again with the lichen that had slowly grown on it earlier. The hearts of Sethe, Paul, Denver, and the others go back to being closed and encrusted with convention. At this point in history, the African dream must be buried so as to live in the ordinary world that demonizes it. When Morrison speaks in "Rootedness" of the "strong place" of black knowledge in her work, she says, "the press toward upward social mobility would mean to get as far away from that kind of knowledge as possible" (342).

In the gorgeous two-page coda, Beloved as the deepest inner reality is equated with loneliness, what one feels when one is not engaged with someone else. Of the two kinds, the "loneliness that can be rocked," the "inside kind" (B 323), is Beloved as immanent spirit, hidden in the house or under the surface. The "loneliness that roams," that "is alive, on its own," is Beloved as a person, but also transcendent because she is always on the brink of disappearing: "No rocking can hold it down." The coda's elegant language suggests that as African Americans rise into the middle class, the horror of their past, which is the source of their poetry, has to appear to them as poeticized, a form of sublime concealment.[15]

When Beloved disappears for the last time in the book, she repeats the sense she had the first time she died, that Sethe was deserting her: "leaving Beloved behind. Alone. Again" (B 309). The most powerful division in experience for the infant may be between the presence of the mother and her absence. Melanie Klein suggests that the rhythm of alternating happiness and sadness in most people's lives (particularly those who are bipolar) may be based on the rhythm of being at the mother's breast and being away from it, for the infant does not know that the mother will return (cited in Caramagno 134–36). It seems that what Beloved felt more than having her throat cut was her separation from her mother, a perceptive presentation of infant mentality, and a womanly one. In *Beloved*, separation from loved ones is the worst abuse of slavery.

Beloved's certainty that Sethe has deserted her corresponds to a real sense in which Sethe denied Beloved independent existence by killing her. Sethe was constrained into an excessive love that appropriated or internalized its object—constrained by a white power system that mutilated her ability to love. Like Othello, she "loved not wisely, but too well" (*Othello* 5.2.398). She thrust the object of desire out of reality into fantasy. Sethe's description of her immediate motivation for killing Beloved suggests that in taking Beloved to the afterworld, she meant to take her to the lost haven of Africa: "Collected every bit of life she had made, all the parts of her that were precious . . . , and carried, pushed, dragged them through the veil, out, away, over there where no one could hurt them. Over there. Outside this place, where they would be safe" (*B* 192). It is logical for Sethe to equate the afterlife with the realm of the ancestors. She tried to cross the Jordan into freedom when she crossed the Ohio, but it was not enough. Now crossing the Jordan will have to mean for her what it means for diaspora Jews, death as a return to the motherland. But in sending Beloved "over there," she dispatches her into a construction of Sethe's mind, one in which the beloved, the inner truth, must always be doomed to exile.

Placing Beloved in this realm makes her unattainable, unable to be expressed in known language. Beloved as the object of desire cannot be contained in any term, so she is dispersed through the linguistic field incomprehensibly as she goes back to Africa: "In the place where long grass opens, the girl who waited to love and cry shame erupts into her separate parts, to make it easy for the chewing laughter to swallow her all away" (*B* 323). The place of the long grass seems to be Africa (perhaps the veld), which Beloved described in her second monologue as "the place before the crouching" (before the Passage) where Sethe picked flowers (253).

As Beloved is finally turned away from the mirror of the (M)Other, she falls apart, as she feared she would (*B* 157), into fragments of meaning that can't be put together. This dispersed Beloved is the possible connections of words that are excluded by the existing language. Like the unconscious, she is the source of creativity, but she seems so ridiculous that one laughs at her.

Language becomes sensible by excluding certain links between phrases, just as society creates values by excluding what is improper. Beloved, as the excluded links, is the object of Lyotard's definition of modernism, which tries "to present the fact that the unpresentable exists" (*PM* 78). Postmodernism, he says, "puts forward the unpresentable in presentation itself," denying itself "the solace of good forms" (81). As the object of both movements, Beloved appears most directly in her monologues as a radically incoherent discourse composed of phrases that are shockingly lacking in comprehensible linkages (*B* 248–52). Only in this avant-garde form can she embody the trauma of the Middle Passage.

Actually, she appears most purely in her first monologue. In the last one

(B 253–56), she joins the other two women in a fusion outside the white/ male world of control. As Jean Wyatt points out (481), the triple repetition of "You are mine" (256) shows the three women reflecting each other as mirrors. This fusion is crucial to the psychic survival of Sethe and Denver, but it is irrational and dangerous.

Afterward, "They forgot her like a bad dream" (B 323). People cannot remember a thing Beloved said (323) because nothing that she said made any sense in ordinary terms. In 1874, as the country moves from dreams of Reconstruction toward racist conservatism, all of the characters try to deny the African spirit and to explain its manifestations in empirical terms, insisting that nature is dead: "Not the breath of the disremembered and unaccounted for, but wind in the eaves, or spring ice thawing too quickly. Just weather. Certainly no clamor for a kiss" (324). In her talk on "Home," Morrison says that the final "kiss" was originally another word more related to history (Quashie, Lausch, and Miller 788–89). I suggested above that the kiss of Beloved could signify recovering the lost African identity. But from the point of view of Beloved's "clamor," it could be a longing for union with those who have to some extent joined America. Beloved need not dream of joining Africa, for she is Africa, in it wherever she goes. So if Beloved could be recovered, the wound of "race" could be healed, but at this stage, it seems impossible.

The word *spirit* originally meant "breath," and "the breath of the disremembered and unaccounted for" is a strong definition of spirit. The wind tended to be personified until modern times. The most famous poem on a wind, Shelley's "Ode to the West Wind" (1820), sees it as the spirit of revolution. At the end of *Beloved*, people are obliged to see wind as inanimate, but the animation that they deny is not really gone. This corresponds to the rationalized age that Lyotard sees as calling forth the opposition of postmodernism (*PM* xxv, 4ff.). In this age, alternative knowledges are denied, and the only kind that is recognized is cognitive knowledge tied to efficiency tied to greed. But the animism that is denied is not really gone; it is only suppressed. This ending also corresponds to the end of *Mumbo Jumbo*. In Reed's novel, a plague called Jes Grew sweeps the United States in 1921. The symptoms are that people start feeling loose and dancing, and Reed conceives the Jazz Age of the 1920s as a visitation of Jes Grew as an African spirit. The Atonists fear the end of "Civilization As We Know It" (*MJ* 4), so the government stops Jes Grew by arranging a Depression, which forces everyone to quit having fun and concentrate on economic necessity (*MJ* 155). In the parallel in *Beloved,* there was in fact a major economic depression in America from 1873 to 1875 (S. Morison 732). In both novels, the African spirit is submerged by hard times, but is still alive under the surface. Morrison insists in the last paragraph that Beloved is still there at the bottom of the creek: "By and by all trace is gone, and what is forgotten is not only the footprints but the water too and what it is down there" (*B* 324). This is one of the lines that will be missed by readers who are not aware of Beloved's primary identity as a water spirit.

Beloved remains as a hidden level that may be defined as the spirits of things behind objective experience: "Occasionally, however, the rustle of a skirt hushes when they wake, and the knuckles brushing a cheek in sleep seem to belong to the sleeper" (*B* 324). Beloved's margin is evoked by subtle sensations that straddle the border between sleep and waking, between subject and object. This is the margin between the language we know and the language we do not know, which suggests the Real beyond language. Denver, to whom Beloved was a familiar spirit before she appeared, remembers similar feelings in her monologue: "sometimes in the day I couldn't tell if it was me breathing or somebody next to me" (244). The marginal status of the residence where Beloved spends most of her time is suggested by her reference to it as a bridge (140, 251). She is between water and land, like the turtles she is fascinated by (124), just as she is between unconscious and conscious.

The bridge, which is the bridge of a ship as well as a land bridge, is glossed in the interview with Darling when Morrison says, "The gap between Africa and Afro-America and the gap between the living and the dead and the gap between the past and the present does not exist. It's bridged for us by our assuming responsibility for people no one's ever assumed responsibility for. They are those that died en route" (Taylor-Guthrie 247). This implies that if we can extend ourselves toward the lost ones of history, we will find Beloved on the bridge because she will be the bridge. As the *differend* in the sense of the desired impossible linguistic configuration that will join the opposed systems of language, she is the poetic principle of blackness, the poetic activity of connecting discourses that cannot be reconciled. Roman Jacobson says, "The poetic function projects the principle of equivalence from the axis of selection to the axis of combination" (cited in Eagleton, *Literary* 86). But though Beloved is the source of their poetry, people avoid thinking about her because they need to be practical. The coda emphasizes the unlikelihood that we will sustain our extension toward these lost ones soon.

Gilles Deleuze says, "each time that desire is conceived as a bridge between a subject and an object: the subject of desire cannot but be split, and the object lost in advance" (*Dialogues* 89). Beloved as the lost object is the self as twin, so she is the deeper level behind the desirable image: "Sometimes the photograph of a close friend or relative—looked at too long—shifts, and something more familiar than the dear face itself moves there. They can touch it if they like, but don't, because they know things will never be the same if they do" (*B* 324). The transformation that would be caused by hearing the lost language, seeing the spirit of Beloved in what is loved, would alienate them from the ordinary reality in which they have to negotiate their lives—a reality of racism in which the best way to advance is to imitate whites.

Beloved is a revolutionary force in that contact with her wrenches one from what has been established. Morrison represents blackness in similar terms in her previous two novels. At the end of *Song of Solomon*, Milkman Dead is either going to leave the principles of the ordinary world behind and shift into an African reality by flying, or he is not going to survive. The last line of the novel is, "If you surrendered to the air, you could *ride* it." At the end of *Tar Baby*, Son Green is going to have to find a future to answer his idealism among the spirits who live in the jungle of Isle des Chevaliers. These books, like *Beloved*, develop an argument that African Americans need to confront African spiritism in order to regenerate themselves, and the grip Morrison has on white readers suggests that they too may have to confront these spirits. *Beloved* says explicitly that every African American house has its ghosts (6). A similar pattern may be traced in *Paradise* (1997), which balances the black Christians of the male-dominated town of Ruby against the pagan spirit-worshipping women in the Convent. This is no contest, for the men, who kill the women, are quite unpleasant, while the women turn out to be enchanting. As free women, they are excluded from the Symbolic order, so it is logical that they turn out to be ghosts, and one of the most successful parts of the book, the end, focuses on the ambiguity of the supernatural (*Paradise* 309–18).

Yet none of the African spiritism in any of these books can be sustained or institutionalized. In every case, blackness cannot be held in the terms of existing reality. Its value lies not in anything that it could conceivably be, but in its drive beyond the knowable. In this respect, it is the soul of modernism, or the soul that leads modernism forward toward postmodernism through American Africanism. Of course, as the black aspect of American English expands, African Americans will have a greater share of the Symbolic, or a greater Symbolic of their own; but I suspect that this clarified language will be encumbered with propriety, and that the creative margin of Black English will maintain an ongoing elusiveness. The distinction is another reminder that these language levels cannot be identified with particular people. At the end of *Beloved,* 124 is freed of the spirit with which the novel began. It will now be inhabitable, a place to raise children decently. Earlier, before 1856, the neighbors resented the fact that Baby Suggs and Sethe had "a house with *two* floors *and* a well" (*B* 162; italics in original). Compare *Native Son,* in which Bigger's family of four slept in one bedroom and he was amazed at the private spaces of the Daltons. The inhabitants of 124, with its elegant staircase, will be middle-class, as the image of meditating on the photo of the dear one tends to confirm.

Near the end of the novel, Stamp Paid tells Paul D that the Bodwins' plan to sell 124, and Paul says that he doubts that anyone with the money to buy the place will want to live in the neighborhood (*B* 311). If the house is sold, it will probably be to a rising black family like the one to be formed by Denver and Nelson Lord. Each book of *Beloved* begins with the number 124, so the novel seems to be attached to the house, and it may be taken to imply the future development of a black middle class that follows from the novel's framework. Morrison focused on the alienation of the middle class from black culture with Geraldine (81–87) and Soaphead Church (164–73) in *The Bluest Eye,* and particularly through the Dead family in *Song of Solomon.* The propriety of all of these characters is stifling: they tend to be portrayed as brainwashed (Soaphead) and inanimate (Dead). *Beloved* lays the basis for a possible earned reconciliation to middle-class values, but it does not want to forget the alignment of the middle class with racism or the great beauty of what has been lost, the beloved as one's own soul.

Yet the book is more than just an elegy: a century after it ends, it tells abstrusely the story that cannot be passed on openly. Beloved can only survive in the form of undercurrents of language because of the structure in which she is caught. Through the wavering forms of this submerged narrative, the black middle class may be enabled to pass beyond stifling imitation and to claim a beauty and a knowledge of its own, and Americans will be enriched by this recovery. Moreover, the concealed Beloved, as a victim of racism, also evokes the need for attention to the forgotten ones from whom the middle class has cut itself off. The difficulty of making their hidden suffering manifest impels Morrison to focus on their occultation and their terrible fascination. The possibility of building a bridge to them must be maintained despite the extremity of its challenge if the soul is to be reclaimed. This will not be an easy excavation to dig, but in all of the novels I cover, the knowledge is there for us to advance into.

To the New World

FOUR STEPS FORWARD

The four novels that I examine contribute to the building of an American African field of opposition in fiction and culture, and each answers a challenge posed by its predecessor. Faulkner was responding to an inchoate voice of oppression that, while it was filtered through his fantasies, also had African American sources. *Native Son* filled in the realization of the dark mystery of human violation toward which Faulkner drove, a violation with two racial sides. Wright made it morally and intellectually necessary to attack the center, and Pynchon unfolded from his side the systematic ramifications of the fundamental opposition that Wright probed. Morrison carried on Pynchon's quest for ways to present the unpresentable as the lost object of American desire, and his repulsion from the Western inanimate toward the inspiration for change in the fantasy of the non-Western animate.

All of them were concerned with turning the victims of racism and imperialism from notations into agents of resistance by unfolding the motivations behind Bon's letter, Bigger's crime, Sarah's fate, Sidney Stencil's writings, and an imaginative extension of Margaret Garner and her child. In American racial contexts, each went further toward realizing that the path to advancement led through reversing the denial of Africa. Faulkner moves toward Charles Bon with little sense of any positive implications Bon's action might have. Wright extends Bon's counteraction in its worst implications (killing Mary as a grim parody of marrying Judith) and develops the multiple meanings behind it. Pynchon searches the world and finds the center of the problem in Africa, which provided one foundation for the nationalism Wright struggled to control. Morrison acts out the African dream turned to nightmare by racism and explores its potentials and limits. They all seek ways to speak for black people rather than imposing European systems on them.

This conclusion discusses the problematic importance in contemporary American fiction of African-based ideas that center on spiritism or animism. The active role of such ideas expanded in America during the period I cover. These ideas may be criticized for promoting escapist mythologies, but the cultural nationalism of those who are situated as minorities is the most immediate voice of the downtrodden, so the means of bringing it into the service of progress need to be examined. And in rational contexts, spirits can be powerful tools of inquiry. I hold that the discoveries made possible by these projected spirits outweigh the dangers of their delusory aspect, that the Africanist visions of both races can serve for communication as well as defense.

Of course, I am selecting a sequence, and many fine novels of this period moved in other directions that may be defined as more important. The truth of African American literature must be seen in the power of its own unfolding; and the strengths and weaknesses of European American literature should be seen in themselves. The limitations of Marxism must be examined in order to support it; and the limitations of the categories of black and white need to be considered, for like any social group, they can neither be isolated from other ethnic and cultural categories nor ascertained as facts. Moreover, it would be misleading to focus on a few of the most enlightened works or impulses of European American culture as a way of denying the vast undercurrent of racism that runs through most of it. But there are advantages to seeing the interaction of the two sides, for they take their dynamism by shaping each other.

Because both European American and African American writers are driven by visions of African culture that are transformed by American influences, they may both be seen to participate in developing an American African tradition. Black writers play the leading roles in this transmission of African culture into America. Yet figures like Faulkner and Pynchon add active perceptions of minority thinking to the tradition and contribute to its growth through the century; Faulkner portrays not only white guilt, but black defiance, and Pynchon, not only the strains of integrated hipness, but the horrors of African genocide.

The American African tradition in the twentieth century may be divided into two historical shifts.[1] The first resulted from the 1920s, in which a wave of rural black culture was infused into American society by the northward migrations and the popularization of the blues in the Jazz Age. It helped produce a modernist fiction that, like most earlier American literary narrative, was predominantly tragic and concerned primarily with the problems of sons (though there are lost daughters in Faulkner's works, such as Caddy in *The Sound and the Fury*). In relation to modernism, Morrison's treatment of Hemingway in *Playing* (69–90) suggests how important Africanism was to his work, both as a threat and an ideal. The second shift made itself manifest in the 1960s, though it began during the 1950s, when Pynchon and Morrison both attended Cornell. In this transition a wave of urban black culture was infused into American society through civil rights and the transformation of blues into rock and modern jazz (both parodies of the blues). This produced a shift toward the postmodern and work in which the excluded child was female and the form was ironic and cyclical. The growing role of women is important to postmodern decentering. In this context, Hurston's *Their Eyes Were Watching God* (1937) appears as a late modern work that anticipates postmodernism by its focus on the feminine and the cyclical. Insofar as these works are comic like *V.* or have happy endings like *Beloved*, they imply that the "race" problem can be solved, if only problematically.

Questions may arise about Morrison as a postmodernist and about Pynchon's treatment of women. I see *Beloved* as combining modern and postmodern elements, but the idea that it is postmodern has become standard.[2] Fuston-White indicates why *Beloved* must use postmodern techniques to escape Western frames: the penetrating account of slavery that it thus renders may be the basis of a new African American concept of subjectivity. As for Pynchon, like many male novelists, he has trouble representing women empathetically, but I develop the active roles of V., Paola, and Sarah at the heart of *V.*, in which Rachel Owlglass presents a strong, serious defense of women (*V.* 410–11, 426). After *V.*, *The Crying of Lot 49* (1966) unfolds the cultural crises of the 1960s as a series of conflicts engaged searchingly by a brilliant and adventurous woman protagonist, Oedipa Maas.

The alienation of the daughter seems more readily reconcilable than father-son conflict—especially her alienation from her mother, which is at the center of *Beloved,* for the great intimacy of mother and daughter provides a basis for return. Therefore the later works indicate more hope, but this hope is problematic. The possibility of recovery through the Maijstrals in *V.* is faintly figured against the background of a chilling cosmic void. And the reconciliation at the end of *Beloved* (not of Beloved, but of Sethe, Paul D, and Denver) is seldom found in the ends of Morrison's other works. Indeed, the ending of *Beloved* is moving because it is so improbable, against the odds. Paul D's seduction by Beloved has taught him to doubt the male authority that made him condemn Sethe, while her experience with Beloved has been the only way for her to see the extent to which she was not right. They may be prepared to forgive each other, though each still has the lost one locked within. To reach the tragicomic situation of the daughter, the tragic situation of the son had to be passed through, just as Morrison had to write *Song of Solomon* before *Beloved.*[3]

Let us return to the generation shift within my four novels. In the modernist *Absalom,* and *Native Son,* the lost children are sons, Bon and Bigger, and sonship stands for a transmission of African culture that seeks a dominant position and is doomed from the start, but passes on a message of rebellious spirit. The consolidation of the family that could validate the son's position is riven, constitutively split by racism. The loss of the son who sought to combine blackness with proper identity is unbearable and tragic, so that the earlier works deliver a more powerful protest than the later pair. In the postmodern *V.* and *Beloved,* the lost daughter returns as someone else: V. returns as Paola (who may also stand for Sarah), and Beloved is carried on by Denver, who drank her blood and was monstrously close to her. Transmission from Africa (where V. first appeared in Egypt) is possible, but only by being mixed. Paola, who passes as a Negro, can be any race; and Denver, who owes her life to Amy Denver, lives with the Bodwins at the end (*B* 314). Daughtership stands for a passing on of diaspora Africanism that is mixed and recessive—capable of working, if only indirectly, and finally comic. The family was the unattainable truth in the earlier works, but in the later pair, family and truth are fantasy constructs in the future. Like family and truth, African culture cannot be recovered directly, but it operates effectively in combinations, as dissonance, under the surface, as potential. Such partial presence is well enacted by spirits, a feature of African lore that is active in all of my novelists and across contemporary American fiction.

SPIRITS IN QUESTION

> Then away out in the woods I heard that kind of a sound that a ghost
> makes when it wants to tell about something that's on its mind and can't
> make itself understood, and so can't rest easy in its grave.
> MARK TWAIN, *Huckleberry Finn*

If one tries to follow the stages I have outlined into their next phase, one question is what Morrison brings to the development of American literature as perhaps our greatest novelist of the last quarter century (another possibility is Don DeLillo). Her woman's version of black culture supplements and modifies the idea of black power that Gayle derives from Wright (xviii, 167), with its emphasis on conflict. She holds out a vision of self-acceptance that can free all Americans by facing terrible memories, releasing us from the compulsion of violence forced on black people by white ones, on the exploited by the exploiters. In so doing, she finds it necessary to use spirits to express the depth of the injustice and the potential for hope and reconciliation.

Morrison's emphasis on African and Native American spirits matches a widespread trend in contemporary American literature by virtually all ethnic groups. Certainly black writers, led by Baraka, Reed, John Edgar Wideman, Alice Walker, Gayle Jones, Randall Kenan, Edward P. Jones, and Colson Whitehead, have followed Hurston in examining the belief in spirits. Samuel R. Delany and Octavia E. Butler derive black spiritual manifestations from science fiction. Spirit lore is intense in Caribbean Americans like Derek Walcott and Jamaica Kincaid. Kincaid is especially preoccupied with the Mammy Wata; and Xuela Richardson, the protagonist of *The Autobiography of My Mother* (1996), sees such a water spirit vividly (38–39). Kincaid's *At the Bottom of the River* (1983) ends with a rapt vision of a woman who lives underwater (74–80), and this may well have influenced *Beloved*. Outstanding examples of novels by writers from other ethnic minorities in which spirits are active are Maxine Hong Kingston's *The Woman Warrior: Memoirs of a Girlhood among Ghosts* (1976) and *Tracks* (1988), Louise Erdrich's account of the holocaust visited on the Ojibway tribe. More surprisingly, spirits play powerful roles in some of the best novels by European Americans in the last third of the century.

In Marilynne Robinson's *Housekeeping* (1980), they take the form of dream children in the wilderness who lead the protagonist, Ruth Stone, to give up her property: "Now there was neither threshold nor sill between me and these cold, solitary children who almost breathed against my cheek and almost touched my hair" (154). Similarly, in Faulkner's "The Bear," a forest spirit in the form of a bear (often a totem among Native Americans) forces Ike McCaslin to give up his property, starting with the white man's tools of gun, compass, and watch (*Go* 207–8). But though Ike is convinced that the bear is supernatural, the spirits are more clearly spirits in *Housekeeping* because non-Western sensibilities become more audible in the forty years between Faulkner and Robinson. Yet at the climax of "The Old People," the story that precedes "The Bear," in *Go Down, Moses,* Ike is ritually presented by Sam Fathers with an ancestral spirit in the form of an uncanny stag. Sam, the son of a Chickasaw chief hails this buck as "Chief . . . . Grandfather" (184).

North of the border, such forest spirits surface in Margaret Atwood's *Surfacing* (1972), in which the nameless protagonist gives herself over to them completely at the end in order to become a new kind of woman. Don DeLillo often seems to be a more rational, realistic version of Pynchon, yet he often invokes spirits, especially through technology. Early in *White Noise* (1985), the protagonist, Jack Gladney, wonders, "Is there a level of energy composed solely of the dead? . . . Perhaps we are what they dream" (98). At the end of the novel, as at the end of *Underworld* (1997), the level of the dead is located behind the computer screen: "This is the language of waves and radiation, or how the dead speak to the living" (326).

Pynchon's *Gravity's Rainbow* contains perhaps the greatest assemblage of spirits to be found in any novel. Pynchon says, "Check out Ishmael Reed. He knows more about it than you'll ever find here" (*GR* 588). In reference to "where those Masonic Mysteries came from," this is an endorsement of Reed's theory that monotheism was a great blight on human history because it corrupted the original African polytheism (*Mumbo* 161–88). *Gravity's Rainbow* approaches spirits through the scientific notion of wave frequencies outside the range of our perceptions. It suggests that the entire planet earth is a living being (*GR* 590), and it presents a host of sentient objects—such as Byron the Bulb, who tries to organize the other electric bulbs to rebel against human control (647–55). One character, Felipe, communicates with rocks. He emphasizes that rocks think at a very slow frequency (612).[4] Yet these spirits may be taken seriously: Kabalistic spirits loom over the end of the novel (747–50) because, like *V.,* it is deeply concerned with the Jewish Holocaust.

One of the climaxes of *Gravity's Rainbow* is the appearance, to a witch named Gelli Tripping, of the European landscape as it would look before linguistic interpretation: "This is the World just before men. Too violently pitched alive in constant flow ever to be seen by men directly. They are meant only to look at it dead, in still strata" (*GR* 720). The Real world before it is reduced to inanimate categories is filled with spirits: "In harsh-edged echo, Titans stir far below. They are all the presences we are not supposed to be seeing—wind gods, hilltop gods, sunset gods—that we train ourselves away from to keep from looking further even though enough of us do . . ." (720). The ultimate revelation here is Pan, the god of pantheism, "its face too beautiful to bear" (720). *Pan* means "all," the Real totality that we reduce to formulate our worlds. These spirits—who are frightening partly because they are attractive—represent the free flow of linkages that we cut down into the restricted paths of perception that direct us. This is a key intellectual area that America delegates to minorities by denying their views.

In Pynchon's *Mason & Dixon* (1997), spirits in the wilderness are among the most effective elements. The movement into the unknown that constitutes America is a movement toward a spiritual power that consists entirely of pure indeterminacy. In Christian terms, Rev. Wicks Cherrycoke writes, "The ascent to Christ is a struggle . . . into an interior unmapp'd, a Realm of Doubt. . . . the America of the Soul. . . . The final pure Christ is pure uncertainty" (*Mason* 511). Yet the spirit presences in this novel are ultimately not Christian. As Mason and Dixon proceed into the wilderness in the 1760s, they sense "some Energy unknown . . . . out there ahead someplace" (650). They "both dream of going on" to attain fantastic powers that the natives know: "Rays of light appear from behind Clouds, the faces of the Bison . . . grow more human, unbearably so, as if just about to speak" (677).

As Pynchon's historical framework suggests, spirits in the wilderness have always been submerged in American literature. The epigraph at the beginning of this section shows how they are audible in *Huckleberry Finn,* which may be called the first book to describe the American landscape in a style that is truly American rather than imitating European models—a style rich in African American dialect: "if a breeze fans along and quivers the leaves, it makes you feel mournful, because you feel like it's spirits whispering—spirits that's been dead ever so many years—and you always think they're talking about *you*" (*HF* 246–47). Huck's spirits have African origins because he is instructed in spirit lore by Jim, who "knowed all kinds of signs" (47). Such spirits are cognate with American African spirits developed more actively by Pynchon and Morrison. These writers move further along the axis from realism toward modernism and postmodernism by exploring the otherness that Huck touches on. So spirits have literary, political, and intellectual powers worth investigating.

While spirits have retrograde implications in traditional contexts, or may allow escapism, they can serve as radical instruments of inquiry when experimental writers use them to undermine conventional European standards of reality. As Cathy Davidson puts it, "By testing the definition of 'reality' and putting to a critical test the assumptions of realism, Gothic novels raise rational human questions about the possible nature of the irrational and the superhuman" (22). The American Gothic is especially racial. To recognize or consider spirits is to perceive grievances and to add a dimension of communication with what is outside the rule of the Enlightenment. Spirits constitute an intermediate area between those who say something is there and those who say it is not; the uncertainty they enact is indicated in African philosophy by Esu as the figure of indeterminacy (Gates, *Signifying* 11).

The lost women V. and Beloved are surrounded by elaborate superstructures of uncertainty that cannot be resolved. Whether they exist objectively as transhistorical, supernatural forces or are largely projections cannot be determined, and their quasi-ontological status is extensively linked to weighty historical and political issues. They cannot be clarified because they change continually in relation to a large number of other agents. Whatever their factual status, all of the spirits I discuss tend (as apparitions often do) to be spirits of the land, of the people, and of history. In effect, they operate as what Jameson calls the "absent cause" of history, the real or ultimate cause that would result from combining all factors, and that can never be determined (*Political* 34). Shawn Smith sees that this absent cause corresponds to V. (9), and the fact that it can take such a very different form as Beloved is a fine indication of how this cause must vary from different perspectives.

One of the most effective images of this ineffable cause is the ghost, as in the opening of *The Communist Manifesto* of Marx and Engels (1848): "A specter is haunting Europe" (335). The idea of the specter carries with it a strong sense of injustice, and the most famous ghost in literature, Hamlet's father, is a revolutionary who urges Hamlet to overthrow the existing government. The *Manifesto* speaks of capitalism as a "sorcerer, who is no longer able to control the powers of the nether world whom he has called up by his spells" (340). Here the material realities that communism supports operate most effectively as spirits. It may be said that just as capitalism was troubled by the alienated workers it created, so America has been troubled by the angry black people it created, as well as by its workers.

In *Specters of Marx* (1993), Derrida sees Marx's specter as descended from Hamlet's, and sees the principles of Marxism as related to the spectral state, a state of potentiality to which it has been returned by its political eclipse. I would say that the decline of Marxism has been parallel to the decline of black liberation, the submerging of Beloved. There is a danger that cultural nationalism can deflect energy from Marxism, but among African Americans, or progressive Americans, they usually tend to go together as motivators of protest against oppression. Doreatha Drummond Mbalia, for example, in *Toni Morrison's Developing Class Consciousness* (2004), sees Morrison's works as having both African and Marxist sides. Mbalia insists that the desperate situation of black people makes it imperative to see socialism as the real issue (20–21), but this does not stop her from making Africa central (178).

For Derrida, the attempt to know something always leads to mourning, for one can only define the object by repetition, so all that one can see is the ghost of the object, and "hauntology" replaces knowledge of being (*Specters* 9–11). In *Hamlet,* Horatio cannot talk to the ghost because "A traditional scholar does not believe in ghosts—nor in . . . the virtual space of spectrality." The scholar holds to the "sharp distinction between the real and the unreal . . . the living and the non-living" (11). But the specter, like Beloved or Marxism, is "a paradoxical incorporation, the becoming-body . . . of the spirit" (6). Neither one nor the other, it is a notion that cannot be expressed in established language, "the specter as possibility" (12).

V., as a ghost in 1955, represents the absent cause of history for European Americans, the European dream that can fulfill desire and explain history. Beloved is such a cause for African Americans, an African dream that can fulfill desire and restore what has been lost. Both of the two women (de)constructed by history are like its absent cause: they stand for crucial networks of connection in which desire is involved that are too complex to be formulated

202 TEARS OF RAGE

in conventional language. These apparitions of what has been silenced speak for the language systems that have been excluded to make up the systems we use. Spiritual manifestations arise when the language of ordinary perception is violated by something outside of its ken, so spirits speak for levels on which the complexity of the existing system proves inadequate.

The idea that ghosts stand for an intellectual area beyond what is known is expressed by Hamlet in famous lines after he speaks with the ghost: "There are more things in heaven and earth, Horatio, / Than are dreamt of in your philosophy" (1.5.165–66). Carl Plasa, discussing *Beloved,* says that the distinction between supernatural and natural needs "to be seen as symptomatic of a Western epistemological schema, culturally determined rather than absolute and pregiven" (58). In terms I've cited, the uncertainty of V. and Beloved, combined with their cultural charge, speaks for the *differend* that leads to the Real—what cannot be expressed without vanishing. Jameson equates the absent cause with Lacan's Real as what "resists symbolization absolutely" (*Political* 35). Just as a ghost vanishes when one tries to hold it, so the *differend* and the Real stop being what they are when they are clearly expressed; then it becomes necessary to look for a further outside level.

Lyotard says that every linkage is a victory over others that "remain . . . repressed possibilities" (*D* 136). Spirit manifests these outside possibilities as a showing forth without a conceptual frame to contain it. The violation of the Symbolic order by a phrase without a regimen in the system displaces the subject from self-containment to self-division, and this division is exchanged with the object. Spirits are always on the verge of disappearing into otherness, and that vanishing represents the interchange between self and other, the overlap between subject and object. For Bhabha, the doubleness of postcolonial discourse disturbs the Westerner's need to separate his subject from the colonial object (162), so whatever confuses this distancing tends to be apparitional.

If these spirits represent the Real and its political gateway, the *differend,* and if these functions are bound by American history to the denied groups of women and minorities, then the activity of spirits circulates along the borders of these groups. Ghosts usually manifest inexpressible wrongs that generate them, and so spirits are also present in the first two novels. As Rosa runs through Sutpen's mansion, she hears an echo "*of the lost irrevocable might-have-been which haunts all houses*" (*AA* 109), and Sutpen's children are the denied spirits of youth, color, and gender that haunt the book, including Sutpen's own youthful might-have-been. At the start of *Absalom*, Sutpen is introduced as a ghost that haunts the voice of Rosa, who is also a "ghost," and the South is "peopled with . . . ghosts," so that although Quentin does not want to be a ghost, he has to (*AA* 4). He is "a barracks filled with . . . backlooking ghosts" (7). The most poignant of these wraiths is Charles Bon, the black man killed for combining love and freedom.

As for Bigger, haunted by the women he has killed, he is himself on one eerie level a ghost. Racists have called black people "spooks," and African Americans have sometimes made ironic use of the ugly term. Gladys Damon, the wife of the protagonist of Wright's *The Outsider* (1953), says of a party, "I'm afraid I'll be the only spook there" (65).[5] The forest that Bigger haunts consists of blocks of empty buildings abandoned by white flight, for he sees them as havens into which he can disappear (*NS* 173). He has the ghostly qualities of a photographic negative because his existence itself is defined as a crime: every manifestation of his actuality appears as a disturbing reversal of what is accepted. He embodies the Real beyond expression that is oppugnant to the reality constituted by ordinary language. His final choice of alienation means that the life of the black future to which he belongs has to be opposed to the life of the existing world in which he is trapped. In the future, when he will finally be able to exist, he will be a ghost. His ghostly qualities are shared by many tragic heroes who are opposed to present reality: they assert the alienated values that they stand for by destroying themselves as revolutionaries who die for the future.

All of the novels I treat are concerned with assembling and conveying ghosts. The main phantoms I develop—Charles Bon, Bigger Thomas, V., and Beloved—are doomed from their earliest appearance to lead lives of self-destruction, so they are already ghosts when they are alive. The idea of being doomed from the start echoes Puritanism; and while these figures do not *seem* to be doomed by a God who judges them individually, but by social categories, yet the God is the maker of the categories. The cultural identities that weigh the scales against them are supposed to make them personally evil, and are heavily racial in every case. When these abstractions were originally developed—over several centuries, including the twentieth—the black "race" was seen as subject to righteous indignation because God had condemned it to be the color of sin.

V. seems to be an exception to this racial influence, but her sexual conflicts are conditioned by "race" through Anglo-Saxon ideas of female purity that she violates. Her reaction against being a victim (as most of the other women in *V.* are, especially Sarah) is to turn dominant, and this dominance leads her to white supremacy, a racism that hurts her almost as much as it hurts others. The pattern is parallel to Sutpen's choice of power. Morrison focuses in *Playing in the Dark* on how racism injures racists, and V. derives the racial aspect of her doom from being Anglo-Saxon, or purely white. *Absalom* indicates through Sutpen's children that to approach pure whiteness can be extremely destructive. So the distinct "races" are not characterizations of living people, but virtual abstractions that destroy people, turning them into specters. Yet insofar as spirits are excluded on everyone's black side, they represent possibilities denied. Because their fate is racially determined, these ghostly characters survive in our literature as specters of protest against racism, speaking for spirits that have been eradicated. To hear these spirits, we must disassemble the linguistic technology that conceals them while speaking for them. Therefore, my speculation will explore the conceptual borders of knowable, technologically processed reality in order to reveal the American African spirit behind these novels.

THE NEW WORLD OF LANGUAGE

> What is crucial to such a vision of the future is the belief that we must not merely change the *narratives* of our histories, but transform our sense of what it means to live, to be, in other times and different spaces, both human and historical.
>
> HOMI K. BHABHA, *The Location of Culture*

Spirits as potentialities evoke the most radical transformation of reality and its basic principles. To sense the other world is to turn the photo to a negative, to reverse the sound, to make up down, soft hard, and cold hot. As a negative is developed, so the construction of Western perception must be turned inside out to speak for what is inaccessible to whites in black discourse. What I am saying is the opposite of essentialism, for I argue that existing realities that seem natural are artificial constructions of language that need to be opened up. My intention is not to make the Other incomprehensible, but to make it comprehensible, for the difference in African American thinking can be clarified by tracing it back to African patterns.

The novels that I focus on follow a progression of the American English language away from Standard English toward Black English, moving from Faulkner's Latinate baroque (with southern touches that often parallel Ebonics) to *Beloved*, which is written in the blackest English ever to occupy such a prominent literary position. In between, Pynchon's freewheeling hipster pastiche is in many ways less like Standard English than is Wright's black combination of naturalism and modernism. Pynchon's "wrong words" are continually signifying on Standard English. If there has been a literary or cultural shift toward Black English, what principles of reality are involved? Any attempt to describe such principles will have to be inadequate, but some approximate sense of them could be valuable. I will approach these principles in a limited way by focusing on one fundamental European word that operates differently in many West African languages, the verb of being.[6] Smitherman says that in Ebonics, *be* refers to habitual action and is not used for a single occurrence. Therefore, "He be tired" means "he is tired all the time," whereas "He tired" means "he is tired at present" (*Talkin* 19). The verb of being is reserved for something that acts out continuity, that be's over and over, but it is not accorded to a present action. This pattern seems to come from African languages in which the verb of being is omitted, as reflected in pidgin formulas (hybrids of African and English) like "he God" (*Talkin* 5). In "he tired" and "he God," the nouns take on verbal characteristics. Another way of activating a state or position in Ebonics is the use of *go* instead of *is* after *here* and *there,* as in "There go my brother in the first row" (Smitherman, *Talkin* 30). William E. Welmers, in *African Language Structures,* says that it is very common in Niger-Congo that the predication expressed by the verbs *be* and *have* in English is nonverbal (309). The English word for a verb of being, the *copula,* also means the connection between the subject and the predicate. It is fundamental to the construction of Western language and logic as the link that holds a proposition together.

Lacan identifies the copula with the phallus as the power to signify or to have authority (*Écrits* 277), and he condemns the copulative as authoritarian. In *Encore,* book 20 of his seminars, Lacan refers to "to be" as "a verb that is not even, in the complete field of the diversity of languages, employed in a way we could qualify as universal—to produce it as such is a highly risky enterprise" (31). He says here that since the idea of being is not found in every language, its claims to be fundamental, or even true, are suspect. He then proposes "to exorcise it" (as demonic) by pointing out that "In this use of the copula, we would see nothing .... whatsoever if a discourse, the discourse of the master, *m'être*, didn't emphasize the verb 'to be' (*être*)." He puns on the French *maître*, "master," which sounds like *m'etre*, "to be myself," for to claim one's identity is to assume the position of master or Mister. Lacan concludes that he can "situate from whence this discourse on being is produced—it's quite simply being at someone's heel, being at someone's beck and call—what would have been if you had understood what I ordered you to do" (31). He adds that "every dimension of being ... is, first and foremost, imperative" (32). So when I say that one thing equals another, I am ordering them to be equal, though they never are, except as abstractions.

Moreover, by binding the subject to the predicate, the copula requires them to be equivalent. Yet they never can be, for subject and predicate, in Lyotard's terms, are different kinds of phrases with different regimens that cannot be commensurate. The assumption that they match endorses the power of Western civilization to reduce everything to mathematical terms. In subordinating the predicate to the subject, the copula insists that they can only be linked in one way, with the subject as master and the predicate obeying. But other modes of connection are possible. Welmers speaks of a variety of different kinds of predication corresponding to being in African languages (309ff.), and these may be related to the wide range of figurative displacements that Gates lists for Signifying (*Signifying* 87). In fact, Gates calls Esu, the mediator of Signification, "the ultimate copula," linking text with interpretation and subject with predicate (*Signifying* 6). The identification of the verb of being with this trickster means that this link runs through a proliferation of tropes—modes of predication more complex and variable than Western ones. Yet these alternative connections of the subject and its action or object include some that are more direct than any in English.

The main concentration of constructions without the verb of being in *Beloved* appears early in Sethe's monologue, where, in combination with the omission of the helping verb *has,* they reiterate sextuply the urgency of Sethe's insistence that she is united with Beloved, absolutely inseparable from her: "Beloved, she my daughter. She mine. See. She come back to me of her own free will and I don't have to explain a thing. ... She my daughter. ... And my girl come home. . . . Beloved. Because you mine" (236–37). Two levels of this passage are strongly differentiated. On the white level, the dialect represents ignorance, a series of mistakes that indicate Black English is mumbo jumbo, so lacking in clear definitions and connections that it could not express valuable thought. Yet insofar as the African knowledge built into these words through their Signifying can be recovered, they express a transcendental beauty, bespeaking valuable ideas not to be comprehended in Western language. Morrison creates a context of artistic exaltation in which the aesthetic and intellectual qualities of this language can appear.

The fusion with Beloved expressed by and in this African dialect is Sethe's natural identity as the archaic language of inner desire. It represents the deepest level of Sethe that is closest to the African language she spoke as a child, for this was the only language she spoke with her mother (*B* 74). Moreover, Sethe has protected herself—and the spirits of her mother, Beloved, and Baby Suggs—by withdrawing from the outside world so that she would be less subject to the control of more Europeanized English, less often required to *explain things*. The African tongue is the primal language of inner reality for Sethe. Therefore her monologue, which is unconscious to a considerable extent, approaches African language, and Africa operates as her mother. Jean Wyatt argues that in *Beloved* maternal language takes on powers usually reserved for the paternal, constituting a "maternal Symbolic" (482–84); and these powers of feminine language may draw on African sources. Sindiwe Magona stated in a lecture that African women, who traditionally have often worked in the fields (as they did on American plantations), frequently present more stereotypically masculine strengths than are found in feminized European women. In Sethe's American African inner language, the English verb of being tends to disappear in extreme moments, an effect that Morrison strengthens and renders voluntary by using it rarely.

If the noun becomes partly a verb without the verb of being, then Beloved may be said "to mine" and "to daughter," to fill her belonging position as action. This African construction enables the image of Beloved to belong to Sethe in a more immediate way than in Standard English, without the intervention of "is"; and in a more real way, for the event of belonging to someone can occur quite beautifully, but the state of belonging to someone, as a permanent object, is a dangerous delusion. The familiar formula "she is mine" makes her chattel, a slave. It must be granted that due to the destructive situation in which Sethe is trapped, her African belief in spirits contributes to her mistake in killing Beloved. But outside the unnatural position that she is forced into by schoolteacher, her language encodes deep truths that are not framable by traditional Western structures, so they introduce new realities.

Wisdom and beauty may be elicited from Black English, yet Americans of both races are taught to regard it as a series of errors. If it were analyzed as thoughtfully as Standard English, it could support a revealing critique of the abstraction and objectification that afflict postmodern America. One thing it can help us to see is that the verb of being is not harmless because, pace Hamlet, to be is not to be. Contemporary critical theory is inclined to see the verb of being as delusory, extending Hegel's idea that something can exist only in a state of interchange (Hegel 12). In V., Fausto Maijstral calls the word *memory* "meaningless, based as it is on the false assumption that identity is single, soul continuous. A man has no more right to set forth any self-memory as truth than to say 'Maratt is a sour-mouthed University cynic' or 'Dnubietna is a liberal and madman.'" Then he adds, "Already you see: the 'is'—unconsciously we've drifted into the past" (336). When he uses *is,* even to describe the apparent natures of his best friends, he is always already claiming permanence for what used to be. This is preposterous not only because they change, but because he does.

To illustrate the fact that every object is an action, consider the example of a fist, which, like any thing, only seems to be an object as long as it is made (we see this because we make it). In fact, the Latin root for *object* refers to an action, *ob-iecto* meaning "in front-thrown." A rock is certainly an event, though this event may take thousands of years, and there are important objects that we see as events, such as a couple kissing. The distinction between objects and actions is an arbitrary language convention. African paradigms are truer insofar as they are free of the phantasm of object-ivity, the belief that one can connect with something permanently autonomous. Because the European system is in control, it is practical for teachers to tell students that they are wrong to say, "He tired," but not to correct them for saying, "He is tired." Yet the anomalous role of the verb of being is manifest in equating a person with a state. People do not notice that equating things with adjectives undercuts the pretense of sub-stance involved in verbs of being.

Another construction in which Europeans tend to have faith, linear causality, is overturned insistently in V. and *Beloved,* where the main actions are performed by the title characters and virtually nothing is really known about their motivations. Where do they come from? And where does Beloved go to? Herbert Stencil's quest for V. is a series of aleatory parodies of linear causality; and the cause of Sethe's murder of Beloved is not only obscure, but suspended between the opposed views of mother and daughter. Such erasure of the expected linkage is shocking, but there are advantages to loosening the chains of causality. Godwin S. Sogolo, in "The Concept of Cause in African Thought," says that if one wants to explain how a fire started, any number of explanations are possible. An opponent of smoking may claim that the fire started because cigarettes are legal. A physicist might speak of combustion. Someone who wanted to cast blame might say that a particular boy lit a match; yet his friend might have forced him to. A psychologist might speak of the boy's parents, a sociologist, of the historical or political situation, and so forth. Because "the explanations are of different sorts, the question of the superiority of one over the other is misplaced" (C&R 180). The assumption that one cause is the "real" one is conventional and arbitrary. Sogolo adds that Nigerian access to nonmechanistic as well as mechanistic causality constitutes an advantage over the West. Lyotard would refer to Sogolo's concept as one of multiple phrase linkages. Of course, the doctrines of linear causality are generally designed to blame outsiders who cannot see the "real" cause.

The historical plot of *V.* consists of a series of events that may or may not be connected through a possible woman called V. This fragmented novel appears in the position of the real or causative plot behind the otherwise pointless (yoyo) wanderings of the plot set in 1955–56. V. and her novel are introduced in the Egyptian chapter with an extremely discoordinated narrative that, confronting us with the chaos of the world, jolts us with the need to put identity and continuity together by conjecture. To be sure, a similar emphasis on reconstructing connections fills *Absalom,* where the motivations behind the events of the Sutpen story, and even many of the "facts," have to be inferred. The gaps in the narrative that make it necessary to imagine connections in both novels are the most active features of the texts' organizations: the plots are built around what is not known. These gaps speak for hidden causes of "race," class and gender construction that mediate external events through internalized codes, so they can only be detected by violating ordinary logic.

Similar aporias of causality are to be found at the sites of the motive for Bigger's crime and the origin of Beloved. Insofar as his motive or her origin are explained, they are dislodged from the powerful positions that they occupy. Those positions take their force by being located beyond what could be expressed by any comprehensible language. For these arrangements are designed to express the coming into being of something outside known language. In effect, one crucial action of the plots of all four of these novels consists in *the revealing of a concealed level of their motivation, a level connected to Africa.* This is where Bon, Bigger, V., and Beloved are coming from; and this level leads beyond prejudice by realizing the intellectual importance of the dark continent and how it has been obliterated.

This African level gets more active from *Absalom,* where it is muffled, to *Native Son,* where it is stronger, but neither the protagonist nor the author is much aware of it as African. Africa plays a greater role in *V.,* which contains the novelette "Mondaugen's Story." *Beloved's* characters cling to rememories (memories of memories) of Africa that are strong enough to play the most creative role in shaping their world. And this makes explicit a new world that has been swelling up beneath the surface in the previous novels. It is a world in which causality is not black and white and the division of people into categories is an illusion; but its fundamentality as the Real is incommensurate with existing linkages, so it is manifested by gaps of information in the official reality. The Real that stands for what has been denied is reflected in the indeterminacy of every subject that keeps it from being classifiable. It may be long before the world in which people can free themselves from such injustices of hierarchy as "race," class, and gender can exist, but American literature cannot stop aiming at it, or denying it. Most Americans get satisfaction from imagining it, and in doing so, we advance toward the goal of justice at the same time that this *differend* retreats. History has caused this path toward the future to lead through the denied image of Africa. This new world is opposed to the actual world in which Sutpen as patriarchy is in control, Bigger as the oppressed is doomed, Paola as the free woman has to settle for an alcoholic, and Beloved as resistance is submerged and forgotten. Through the *differend* that needs to be spoken, the imaginary world of Africanism gives us the greatest possible awareness of how slavery still exists. It does so by allowing us to see the gaping conceptual wounds of the people who have been excluded, and to see our sentences as life sentences. These damages grow visible against a background beyond known language, for such language (like *dig*) is shaped by these injuries.

The idea that modernism reveals an unknown language with incomprehensible principles of reality behind it has a long history. One of the earliest uses of the term *modern* dates from the Middle Ages, when it was used to distinguish from Latin and Greek the modern or vernacular or slave languages in which literature began to appear. Jameson, in *A Singular Modernity* (2002), speaking of the development of modern literature in Europe during the nineteenth century, says that it was built on the interaction of different languages of nations, classes, and institutions, "but also, beyond all of those, a kind of empty Utopian domain of language as non-existent and yet as demonstrable and conjectural as non-Euclidean geometry." This realm of language, like non-Euclidean geometry, goes against basic assumptions of logic to develop "the invisible outlines of whole new language structures never before seen on earth and heaven" (147). This is the Real as the source of originality, and it has formed the creative heart of American literature through the interaction of African language and European interpretation.

In book 17 of his seminars, *The Other Side of Psychoanalysis,* which just reached me, Lacan says that all real knowledge comes from slaves because they practice the techniques of craftsmen. I will add that they have the power to be original because they are excluded from the symbolic system. Academic learning is a system to transmute this knowledge so that it appears to belong to those in charge: "What does philosophy designate over its entire evolution? It's this—theft, abduction, stealing slavery of its knowledge, through the maneuvers of the master" (21). Modernism, in presenting the unpresentable, is reversing this procedure to reveal the real source of knowledge, and postmodernism advances us toward understanding this knowledge by expressing it in its own language of misdirection. In the terms we have to use, the real source can appear only as a hiatus.

OBJECTIONS

My argument may be criticized by saying that my abstractions leave politics behind, that such an elaborate construction is hardly necessary to see that people are oppressed. But most Americans are aware of the evils of racism, yet they do little about it, or they see it as a problem that has been solved. To re-cognize the seriousness of the problem, they may have to realize the force of the cultural obliteration and historical trauma that are manifested as gaps in our texts. They should know the facts about government policies that favor the rich, but they should also know that poverty is not caused by self-indulgence, that it is an expropriation of mental life; so they need to see the subjective world of the culturally despoiled. And to describe this alienated world may require new means of expression because conventional language defines itself by excluding this world. I may also be accused of rendering African American culture inaccessible; but it was history, or the Middle Passage, that rendered its roots inaccessible. I am trying to bring these roots into discourse, to see them as rational and human rather than occluding them behind the empirical construction of white supremacy—and branding them as mumbo jumbo by condemning the expression of difference.

The 1960s projected the hope that different oppressed groups could work together, unite their interests in opposition to imperialism, and stay progressive because they were all victims of injustice. Since the 1980s, we have grown aware that the interests of these groups clashed and that their commitment to socialism was often eclipsed by selfish and authoritarian tendencies. So many now see the belief in multiculturalism as mistakenly optimistic, and the astute Dubey emphasizes the problems of middle-class writers speaking for lower-class people and of recovering African culture. The growth of Islamic terrorism has underlined the danger that those who speak for the underprivileged may be reactionary and destructive. But this does not mean that we should give up the effort to speak for the downtrodden. Rather we should distinguish the validity voiced in their situation.

Skepticism about the movement toward freedom that I trace is often logical. Noel Polk says that the notion that Charles Bon is black is an illusion invented by Shreve and Quentin (137–40). Polk discounts Faulkner's entry in *Absalom*'s "Chronology"—"Sutpen learns his wife has negro blood" (305)—by saying that this is not part of the novel. Others will feel that Bigger Thomas's last decision to stand behind his murder shows the faulty basis of black revolution. Likewise, many will hold that *V.*'s lack of coherence keeps it from having political impact; yet Gerald Howard reveals in "Rocket Redux" that Pynchon considered calling the novel "The Republican Party Is a Machine" (36). Finally, many will believe that Beloved is merely a demon and deserves to remain buried. This might imply that while completing the novel,

Morrison shifted away from the affirmation of Blackness in "Rootedness."
The drive toward black liberation in these novels is conflicted and easy to as-
sail, but perhaps liberation requires a factor that is not realistic and defensible
because it is outside the existing world, because it does something new.

Dubey calls "Rootedness" "incoherent" because it mixes genres. Morrison first says that novels will *replace* the bygone folk culture of the southern
community, but she then calls her novels "political" because they *reproduce*
the black oral community (Dubey 236). But this contradiction may be justified, for Morrison portrays city life in her novels (*Bluest Eye, Beloved,* and
Jazz) as preserving black folk culture through neighborhoods. Does Dubey
want city dwellers to give up such supportive ambience? She also sees Morrison as wrong to concentrate on features of the "lost" black tradition such as
the auditory, "ancestral presences," communal sharing, and the "supernatural"
of a "black 'cosmology'" (Dubey 236). These features derive from Africa.
Dubey cannot understand why Morrison would want to convey this tradition by building intimate connections with black people who are not literary,
though Dubey admits that Morrison's work has been "immensely productive"
(235–37). Dubey feels that this "esthetic tribalism" blocks integration—yet it
is popular among whites. If Morrison—like Dickens, Joyce, and Faulkner—
can successfully transmit oral culture through the novel, why should Dubey
feel that it necessary to deprive African Americans of their heritage?

The attitudes of the 1960s that now look naïve actually brought improvement for African Americans both economically and culturally. Now that the
tendency is to see each group as out for its own interests, the drive toward reform seems to be stalled. I believe that we should revive the effort to reach
across the boundaries that separate people, and that the novels I examine develop perspectives that show how such cultural interchange can be effectu-
ated. Lyotard, developing ideas of Kant's, says that the disinterested enthusiasm people feel for great changes in history like the French Revolution is
a positive sign of progress toward human betterment. The differing interests
of various groups make it impossible to put this hope in a particular, definite
form that all can accept; but they can share it in indefinite form as enthusiasm,
a strong sense of the sublime, which Lyotard defines as the imagination going
beyond itself (*D* 165–66). The object of enthusiasm, like a spirit, is there and
not there, an event of delivering itself (*D* 164). This is one level of Lyotard's

thinking on which conflict leads toward resolution. Yet in my conception, the sublime object combines black and white sides, and this keeps it from being ideologically resolved, keeps it moving forward.

THE AMERICAN AFRICAN DISCOVERY OF AMERICA

In delivering these American African spirits, these writers are reaching outward through language into the racial *differend* of modern American civilization. So there are purposes of understanding and justice behind the expansion of the African presence in American literature that is accomplished by all of these novels. White writers share it insofar as both groups participate in the revolutionary spirit of America, which Sundquist describes as starting early and recurring perennially (*To Wake* 30–91, 495–96). Writers of both races share a vision of new principles of reality that combine versions of African culture with the avant-garde. The founding doctrine that all men are equal has never included all human beings, but it aims in that direction, and its potential is shown most powerfully by the cause of black liberation.

The revolutionary spirit of these artists may seem at odds with their imaginative expansion, but my argument is that the revolutionary and the imagination are at their best when they work together, combining their differing agendas in a poetry that is bound to freedom by the injustices of history. James Williams says that in Lyotard, "the sense of 'avant-garde' is fully political in art," while "the sense of 'political' is revolutionized by avant-garde art. The deepest sense of the political comes with the avant-garde, as it disturbs established knowledge and laws" (6). Crucial to progressive politics is action that drives toward the future, a common thrust of art and revolution, a movement of change as release from containment. Oppression is a denial of vision, and central to the revolution on which America is built is the hope of mixing cultures to multiply insight by exchange, so America discovers and creates itself in striving for equality.

The points at which these novels pass outside of understanding as they grapple with moral and political issues involved in "race" are the points at which they are most beautiful and also the points at which they are charged with the greatest progressive political force. The incomprehensible motives of Sutpen on the white side and Thomas on the black, the uncertain existences of the white V. and the black Beloved—these questionings lift the suffering of these characters and others into exaltation insofar as the questions cannot be answered. And, at the same time, the questions constitute the *differend* that points most accurately to the gaping of injustice. Here the political is needed to keep the avant-garde in focus. Advanced art can gravitate toward change that is reactionary, as it did in the case of Pound; but the struggle for black liberation tends to concentrate on the economic needs of the deprived, and the challenge of brotherhood repays any level of difficulty. The progressive and the avant-garde can share their sense that cultural identity must remain unsettled. In the last century, African-influenced models for this sense of division have worked powerfully to drive the American novel forward.

NOTES

INTRODUCTION

1. Other such studies include those of Chase, Baumbach, Tanner, Karl, Bradbury, Hilfer, Werner, and Minter. The liberal Fiedler in 1960 gives only a page to African American writers (456); and Baumbach praises Ellison in 1965 for being a European or universal writer (68). Among the few studies that put literary developments on the black and white sides in a balanced frame are Sundquist's *To Wake*, Weinstein's *What Else*, the Spillers collections, Gilroy's *Black Atlantic*, and McKee's *Producing Races*.

2. There are studies of African American fiction by Bone, Gayle, Gates, Baker, Bell, Callahan, Joyce, Tate, Dubey, and Kemayo. Bell sees a "dialectic in American society between black and white cultures" (12).

3. The idea that Americans can be purely white or black has grown obsolete. Gates's essay " 'Authenticity,' or the Lesson of Little Tree" provides an amazing list of white writers and musicians who have passed for authentic minorities—and of black ones who have passed for white. Nevertheless, it is usually valid to distinguish most discourse as being mainly one or the other. Borderline cases may switch their predominant orientations often.

4. There are of course many other cultural and literary traditions that feed the development of the novel, from advertising to Zen. Ethnic American traditions such as those of Native Americans, Hispanic Americans, Asian Americans, and Jewish Americans are particularly germane to the area I discuss because they shape the role of minority literature. Unfortunately, I have space to concentrate only upon the two main racial groups.

5. Morrison takes this phrase from Boileau through Marie Cardinal (*PD* v).

6. Similar definitions of the Real appear in Ragland-Sullivan 188, Lemaire 52, and Alan Sheridan's "translator's note" to his edition of the *Écrits* (Sheridan x). In *The Four Fundamental Concepts*, Lacan says that the Real is "what lies behind the fantasy" (54). There are many differences between Lyotard and Lacan, yet both see the subject as an activity of language formed by linguistic structures that represent cultural formations. Both focus on particular words (Lacan's

signifier and Lyotard's phrase) and valorize points at which words break out of their containment by determined structures. Such moments lead to the unconscious for the analyst Lacan and to the *differend* for the social philosopher Lyotard. Fredric Jameson sees Lacan's Real as a social construct (*Political* 35), and I argue that Lyotard's *differend* corresponds to Lacan's Real. I have tried to align concepts of theirs that are parallel so as to illuminate the four novels. Good introductions to the ideas of Lacan and Lyotard respectively may be found in Fink and Reading.

7. The term *essentialism* may be used conservatively. Jonah Goldberg condemns proponents of civil rights and feminism as essentialist because they hold that black people and women have definite attitudes of their own.

8. "[B]etween 1994 and 1998, the gap in household access to the internet between blacks and whites grew 39 percent" (Horn and Woodall).

9. Morrison explains in "The Site of Memory" how she set out to fill in the inner life that was excluded from slave narratives, partly because they aimed to demonstrate rationality to white audiences.

10. The tendency toward multiple points of view was always marked in America. Minter notes that both George Santayana and W.E.B. Du Bois saw at the turn of the century a moral and aesthetic authority deriving from "a sense of marginality" (*Cultural History* 4). He adds that T. S. Eliot and Fitzgerald "claimed the experience of being excluded because they thought it charged with creative potential," but their aesthetic version of exclusion did not provide the same experience as that of someone who really was excluded (125). Wright's demonstration of the division in America made exclusion irrevocable, at least for fifty years.

11. It may well be argued that *Invisible Man* is a valuable advance on *Native Son*. Gates presents this argument strongly in *The Signifying Monkey* when he speaks of Ellison Signifying on or critiquing Wright (105–7). Here Gates says that Wright's protagonist is voiceless, whereas Ellison's is articulate. The opposing argument that I favor is that Bigger Thomas makes progress toward articulating himself at the end of *Son*, whereas *Man* rejects social activism to lead to a final submerged position in which action is impossible.

12. *PD* 69–90. Morrison does not treat Hemingway's *Green Hills of Africa*. She says of him that although he is liberal and sees black people sympathetically, he is subject to racist codes and fantasies that cause the positions of his black characters to be servile. This argument is sound, but she may overstate it. Her most shocking point about Hemingway involves a scene in *To Have* in which Harry Morgan's wife, Marie, asks him in tough lingo what it was like to do it with a "nigger wench." Harry says it was "Like nurse shark" (113). Morrison is appalled that the black woman is compared to something so "brutal" (*PD* 85). Yet a student from Florida pointed out that a nurse shark is one that will not hurt you. So Harry's remark, though crude, may mean, "She looks tough, but she's harmless." The Florida Museum of Natural History, however, reports on its Web site that, while nurse sharks may seem relatively docile, they sometimes commit "unprovoked attacks on swimmers and divers."

13. Late in the first part of Fitzgerald's *Tender*, a dead black man appears in the hotel bed of a white character. The whites do not know how he got there, but they get rid of the body so they won't be questioned. A defense of Fitzgerald would argue that their avoiding of social reality leads to later disasters for them; and the racism of Tom Buchanan in *The Great Gatsby* (12–13)

decidedly marks him as a villain. Yet the section in *Tender*—which speaks of "simple races" (298)—seems insensitive.

14. Reeves, who defends Wolfe, grants that his work showed prejudice; but says that Wolfe struggled against racism and made progress (137–38).

15. Patell cites an influential study, *Habits of the Heart: Individualism and Commitment in American Life*, by Robert N. Bellah et al. (1985). The authors find that each American generally uses more than one cultural discourse, each discourse implying a different set of values.

16. Between 1985 and 1995, the fraction of young African American males in prison, on parole, or on probation went from one-quarter to one-third (Currie 13). Angela Y. Davis says in 2002 that in thirty years the overall prison population increased 800 percent and is now 70 percent nonwhite (54).

1. *ABSALOM, ABSALOM!* AND THE TRAGEDY OF "RACE"

1. A good account of the composition of *Absalom* appears in Muhlenfeld's introduction to her casebook on *Absalom*. Apparently, as of January 1934, Faulkner still thought that his next novel would be either "Requiem for a Nun" (continuing *Sanctuary*) or a novel about the Snopeses, but by 11 February, he realized that it would be the Sutpen story (xviii). In focusing on Sutpen, he returned not only to "Evangeline," but to "Wash," the story about Wash Jones that he wrote in 1933. He was also returning to the idea of the "Dark House," which was the original title for both *Light in August* and *Absalom* (see Polk 24–98). Singal (189–92) adds details on the stages leading to *Absalom*. He feels that after publishing *Light* in February 1932, Faulkner wrote nothing "of real literary weight" through 1933. I suspect that the prospect of carrying his grim critique of racism further was so stressful that he stalled, yet wrote "Wash."

2. Sundquist demonstrates that in the nineteenth-century South, miscegenation was equated with incest (*Faulkner* 111). Irwin shows how the images of shadows that Quentin is obsessed with are associated with African Americans, and shows how Quentin projects Charles Bon as a shadow self (36–37).

3. Joyce here cites Sewall, *The Vision of Tragedy* 5. This book examines eight great tragedies from the Book of Job to *Absalom*.

4. Singal describes the narrative of *Absalom* as cubist and credits Pamela Reid Broughton with developing the observation (205, 318n.). The word *cubistic* appears in *As I Lay Dying* (219).

5. It is relevant that West Virginia became a state by separating from Virginia in order to support the Union in 1861 (Catton and McPherson 68).

6. There are discussions of racist stereotypes of the Scots in Pynchon's *Mason & Dixon* 276–77, 280, 572. W. J. Cash refers to the Virginia Scots of this period as "ragged throat-slitting Highlanders" (9).

7. Faulkner describes such resentment in "The Big Shot," a story written during the 1920s that was a source for *Absalom* (Muhlenfeld xvii). When Dal Martin, the story's protagonist, is turned away from a landowner's door, he is upset by a black servant who stands behind the boss grinning. Faulkner's narrator, Don Reeves, sees in Martin an attitude typical of poor whites: "the antipathy between them and negroes was an immediate and definite affair, being

at once biblical, political, and economic: the three compulsions—the harsh unflagging land broken into sparse intervals by spells of demagoguery and religio-neurotic hysteria—which shaped and coerced their gaunt lives. A mystical justification of the need to feel superior" (*Uncollected* 508). This suggests that Faulkner's focus on racism in the 1930s only accented what he was aware of earlier.

8. This pattern is illustrated by the architect who eludes Sutpen by using architecture, falling back "upon what he knows best in a crisis" (*AA* 193).

9. Cited in John Edward Philips, "The African Heritage of White America," in Joseph E. Holloway 230.

10. Polk suggests that Bon may not be black, that the reason Sutpen leaves Eulalia is that he finds that she was not a virgin when they married (140). While there is an aspect of the book that puts Bon's blackness in question, the evidence for his African blood is very strong. The "Chronology" that Faulkner appended says that he married her in 1827 and left her in 1831, and it would be unlikely that it would take him four years to figure out that she was not a virgin. Faulkner's entry for 1831 is explicit: "Sutpen learns his wife has negro blood, repudiates her and child" (*AA* 305). Within the novel, Sutpen says that Eulalia could not fit his plan "through no fault of her own" (194), implying that her "race," not her transgression, was the problem. Sutpen also refers to "a fact which I did not learn until after my son was born" (212). The infant's body was more likely to provide evidence of his racial makeup than of his mother's lack of virginity four years earlier. Moreover, a narrator refers to Eulalia as "the woman who Sutpen's first father-in-law had told him was a Spaniard" (268), meaning she was not. Further arguments that Bon is black appear in a long note in Singal 201–2.

Faulkner makes the scene in which Bon says, "I'm the nigger that's going to sleep with your sister" (286) the most powerful climax of the book. To claim that this scene is only imagined by Quentin and Shreve is to overlook the pattern whereby everything that the characters imagine about Sutpen is part of the truth. *This truth is not a matter of fact, but of a black historical vision that shapes lives.*

11. Patell, citing Joyce Appleby, argues that the phrase "the pursuit of happiness" in the Declaration of Independence assumes that the pursuit of property in America serves a higher cause, an ideal freedom that justifies itself as universal when it only applies to white males (20–22).

12. John T. Irwin argues that Henry uses Bon as a dark double to fulfill his unconscious wish to seduce his sister (31ff.), but more can be explained.

13. Please see note 10 above.

14. *Totem* appears in volume 13 of the *Standard Edition* of Freud, so this passage is cited conventionally as SE 13: 138–40.

15. See Brivic, *Joyce between* 206–11, for an examination of the role of *Totem* in the *Wake*.

16. The most admirable white Christians in Faulkner's fiction may be Byron Bunch and Rev. Gail Hightower of *Light in August*. Bunch has considerable moral beauty, but his extreme inhibition makes him pitifully incapable of action, an embarrassingly stunted figure. He is pulled along by forces he cannot control emanating from Lena Grove, who is touchingly innocent although she is a fallen woman who was seduced and abandoned. Hightower, Bunch's spiritual advisor, says that his own life "ceased before it began," mainly because he is fixated on the he-

roic death of his grandfather in the Civil War. For him, Christianity is essentially a quiet space to worship the spirit of his ancestor (*LiA* 478), as Africans do. The story of Hightower's grandfather's death was given to him by a black woman, Cinthy (*LiA* 477). Hightower thinks of this story: "It's too fine, too simple, ever to have been invented by white thinking. A negro might have invented it. And if Cinthy did, I still believe. Because even fact cannot stand with it" (*LiA* 484). In framing the object of his worship, the sacred nature and visionary power of the sacrificed people far outweighs any concern for the truth of the facts.

17. Faulkner's images of contact and isolation are extended and transformed in one of the greatest novels of the Third World, Gabriel Garcia Marquez's *One Hundred Years of Solitude* (1966). Garcia Marquez is devoted to Faulkner, and this Colombian version of *Absalom* also deals with the rise and fall of a family led by a colonel whose members are divided from each other by invisible barriers. The word *solitude* echoes through *Absalom* (*AA* 82, 116, 161, 195, 250, 254). Colonel Aureliano Buendia, who goes to fight in a civil war, has a "metallic hardness" that resembles Sutpen's look of pottery (*AA* 24); and Buendia also looks "like a man capable of anything" (*Solitude* 151). He customarily draws a ten-foot chalk circle around himself and forbids anyone to enter (159).

18. Werner Sollors traces the history of the curse of Ham and how it became attached to racism in *Neither Black* 79–111.

19. Kristeva's original definition of the abject as a disturbing infantile breakdown of the boundary between self and other appears in *Powers of Horror: An Essay on Abjection* 2–5.

20. Garcia Marquez's Colombian Rosa, Amaranta Buendia, seems so hard that she drives men to suicide; but just before she dies in a flourish of virginity, we learn that she actually had the tenderest feelings in the book (*Solitude* 234). It was because she was so sensitive that she could never give in, and there is a similar element of sensitivity behind Rosa's bitter pride—yet Rosa only has one poisoned chance.

21. Comparison of the four narrators to Evangelists is made by Virginia V. Hlavsa 70. It also applies to the four sections of *The Sound and the Fury*. Hlavsa also points out that the most penetrating accounts of the Sutpen family come from Quentin and Shreve, the narrators who are furthest from it. Quentin's says, "*If I had been there I could not have seen it this plain*" (*AA* 155).

22. The rebellious quality of Luster in *The Sound and the Fury* is splendid. Yet even though he calls Luster a "man" (*S&F* 215), Faulkner may find it easier to make Luster forceful and assertive because he is fourteen and powerless.

2. *NATIVE SON*

1. To be sure, naturalism was more prominent in Wright, and modernism, in Faulkner, yet Faulkner includes a good deal of naturalism, especially when treating poor people, even in a modernist masterpiece like *Light in August*. For a reading of *Native Son* as modernist, see Brivic, "Conflict."

2. Drake and Cayton were friends of Wright's, and Carla Cappetti, in "Sociology of an Existence: Richard Wright and the Chicago School" (Robert J. Butler 81–94), argues that he was influenced by the Chicago School of Sociology.

3. The racist journalism here is based on articles in the *Chicago Tribune* during the trial of

Robert Nixon in 1938. Some of this material is quoted in Keneth Kinnamon's "How *Native Son* Was Born" in Gates and Appiah 113–14.

4. This scene is included in the video *Richard Wright: Black Boy*. Instructions for getting this video are on the back of the title page of the edition of *Native Son* that I use.

5. Greenblatt analyzes some early examples of this pattern (226–28).

6. See Mitchell's introduction to Lacan and the École Freudienne's *Feminine Sexuality*, 4–5, for an explanation of why the center is empty—because the subject is made up of other people's language.

7. The first critic to see *Native Son* as a version of *Crime and Punishment* was Kenneth T. Reed. Brivic describes some parallels between the two novels in "Conflict" 232, and Magistrale presents a substantial discussion of the connection. As Gates explains in *Signifying* 118–20, Wright tended unfairly to regard all black fiction writers before himself as compromised, so he believed that the strongest models for revolutionary writing were European. See the opening page of "Blueprint for Negro Writing" (1937) (*Reader* 40).

8. The story of how Wright came to revise the novel is told in *NS* 486. Rampersad's Library of America edition of 1991, which is reprinted in the paperback I use, restores Wright's original version and includes his considerable revisions of 1940 in the notes. Both the 1940 text and the restored one have their advantages. See James W. Tuttleton, "The Problematic Texts of Richard Wright," and Keneth Kinnamon, "The Library of America Edition of *Native Son*," both in Robert J. Butler's collection 67–76.

9. There is, however, a danger that Wright can be misinterpreted, as Susan Bordo indicates while mainly defending Wright in "Material Girl." She censures a rapper who justifies what she calls a gleeful description of gang rape by comparing himself to Wright: "The fact that Richard Wright embedded his depiction of Bigger Thomas within a critique of the racist culture that shaped him, and that *Native Son* was meant to be a tragedy, was not, apparently, noticed" (Rivkin and Ryan 1114).

10. On Wright's friendship with Sartre, see Fabre 299, 304, 321–22, 327, 375.

11. Similarly, Ellison's Invisible Man starts out with an ability to stir up his people over their oppression through a sense of group solidarity (chap. 13). But after this, he has to be taught what socialism is, and it remains rather abstract for him even when he provisionally follows it.

12. A number of perceptive black critics have condemned Bigger as a harmful stereotype, including Bell (157–65) and David Bradley. Yet both tragedy and modernism present powerful critiques by focusing on negative examples. If Bigger were less desperate, the protest that caused this book to spur the civil rights movement would be vitiated. I see the need to focus on positive examples as a limitation.

13. The collection on Wright edited by Richard Macksey and Frank E. Moorer includes a set of eight essays on his existentialism (129–220), but the definitive statement on this aspect is JanMohamed, *Death-Bound*.

14. Visual imagery in *Native Son* is discussed by Joyce, *Richard* 86–90, and by James Nagel, "Images of 'Vision' in *Native Son*," in Kinnamon 86–93. Neither of them deals with the pattern I examine.

15. See "The Pitfalls of National Consciousness," *Wretched* 148–205. Fanon sees that nation-

alism in power among Africans can easily work as a continuation of colonialism (160, 173). Yet in the following chapter, "On National Culture," Fanon insists on the vital importance of the phase of national culture (247). Fanon corresponded with Wright and met him in Paris. Walker says that they were friendly for seven years (8).

Even Tommie Shelby, in his formidable critique of black nationalism in *We Who are Dark* (2005), grants that nationalism runs "so deep" among so many African Americans that it cannot be rejected; we must rather try to build on its valuable elements (25). Shelby's views thus parallel Wright's: both aim for practical reasons to privilege the European side of black American thinking. For Shelby this leads toward the hope for a nationalism without ethnicity.

16. Lyotard's general term for the kinds of knowledge that are not legitimated as knowledge in the West is *narrative knowledge,* and it includes ethics, aesthetics, and social interaction (PM 18–22).

3. OPPOSING TRAJECTORIES IN *V.*

1. A reference to Wallace Stevens's poem "Thirteen Ways of Looking at a Blackbird," in which none of the thirteen diverse images is the true one.

2. Postmodern history emphasizes that the past and the present cannot exist without continuously reshaping each other. Shawn Smith discusses Pynchon's postmodern theory of history cogently in *Pynchon and History,* deriving from Hayden White the idea that the cataclysmic events of modern history have to be represented through conflicting narratives in order to confront their terrifying incomprehensibility (6–7). Smith maintains that Pynchon has a serious ethical purpose in exploring the confused background of contemporary alienation, and therefore is not subject to Jameson's charge that postmodernism is irresponsible (8–9).

3. To explain how she can pass for black without makeup, Paola says, "nobody knows what a Maltese is. The Maltese think they're a pure race and the Europeans think they're Semitic, Hamitic, crossbred with North Africans, Turks and God knows what all" (*V.* 388). Malta is south of Algiers and Tunis and slightly east of Tripoli. Pynchon emphasizes the eastern aspect by having Sidney Stencil approach Malta in a xebec with Mehemet, who sees the island from an Islamic perspective (*V.* 507–17). Grant points out that the Maltese language is based on Arabic (150).

4. Lacan holds that the subject forms itself by looping through the Other so that the message it sends returns in reverse. See *Four Fundamental Concepts* 178, 183.

5. In his later years, Lewis became a famous bluesman, and he influenced hipsters in Pynchon's circle. Pynchon's friend Richard Fariña, a folksinger who died young, wrote a novel called *Been Down So Long It Looks Like Up to Me* (1966). The title is a quote from Lewis's 1928 version of "I Will Turn Your Money Green."

6. The use of *Second World* has not clearly been determined. Stephen Slemon's article "Unsettling the Empire: Resistance Theory for the Second World," in the Ashcroft, Griffiths, and Tiffin collection (104–10), refers to Australia, New Zealand, Canada, and South Africa. The United States is analogous, but its power puts this in doubt. *Second World* is also applied to Eastern Europe.

7. Žižek says, "So what about the ghosts which are not to be simply dismissed as fantasmatic, since they haunt us on account of their very excessive, unbearable *reality*, like the Holocaust?" (*Fragile* 69).

8. In a talk at Temple University in 1987 called "On Not Knowing," Donald Barthelme said that the best model for his activity as a writer was the jazz improviser. Barthelme and Pynchon are two of the best postmodern writers.

9. Robert Edenbaum, a colleague of mine, had for years a sign in his office window saying, "Keep Cool But Care." David Witzling, in "The Sensibility of Postmodern Whiteness in *V.*" (2006), claims that the slogan has a conservative force indicated by "Keep cool" (381), but Edenbaum was very active in the civil rights and antiwar movements. Witzling makes sharp points about the tension and guilt involved in the way whites related to blacks in the 1950s and 1960s, but he overlooks how both races often worked together productively and happily for civil rights, politics, and jazz. *V.* listens to the ironies of racial exchanges in order to improve on them.

10. A famous fictional treatment of the clash between northern and southern European cultures is Forster's first novel, *Where Angels Fear to Tread* (1905), and the theme recurs in his third, *A Room with a View* (1908).

11. Grant cites seven Pynchon critics who think that V. either is or may be Herbert Stencil's mother (28–29), and none who disagree.

12. Monk recorded during the 1950s for Riverside Records, which seems to be the label on which Winsome's Outlandish Records is based. Winsome's apartment is on Riverside Drive (*V.* 129), and his company also records automobile sounds (129), as did Riverside. In 1960, Fred Hauptmann came to my high school wearing a pin that said "All the Way with Ornette!" David Yaffe parodies Woolf to express the impact of Coleman's debut at the Five Spot: "On or about November 17, 1959, human character changed . . ."

4. AMERICAN AFRICAN POSTMODERNISM IN *BELOVED*

1. The only exceptions I know of are the nameless protagonists of Flann O'Brien's *The Third Policeman* (1939) and Samuel Beckett's *The Unnamable* (1954).

2. Margaret Garner attempted to kill her children and succeeded in killing one when slavers caught her in Cincinnati in January 1856, and the same date seems to be used for Sethe. The Garner case is covered by Frances Ellen Watkins Harper's 1857 poem and in pieces by Samuel L. May and by Ashraf H. A. Rushdy in the Andrews and McKay *Casebook* 21–46.

Kentucky was divided during the war, for it was a slave state, but its legislature voted not to secede. This need not have been a liberal move, for secession would be taking a chance on a cause likely to lose. In 1861, Kentucky voted to support the Union, and Rebel attempts to take Kentucky did not get far. Sweet Home is in the northern part of the state, which was on the Union side all through the War ("Kentucky," *Encyclopedia Britannica*). While Kentucky slaves might take hope from being in the Union from 1861, and from the Emancipation Proclamation of January 1863, they were not actually freed until after the end of the war in 1865 (S. E. Morison 654).

3. Reed refers to the blues as a loa, the Haitian word for an African spirit (128, 151–52).

4. Kubik seems to observe that blues are spirits here, but he does not say so, being more interested in their psychological functions. Since Reed's reference is general, I may be the first critic to say that the term *blues* refers to African spirits, a strong indication of the suppression of Africana. Another uncanny connection for the blues appears when Kubik sees a parallel between Robert Johnson's famous claim that he sold his soul to the devil for musical powers and a widespread African belief that one cannot develop great musical skills without "a secret liaison with the supernatural" (24). Kubik cites a recording by the Nigerian Sir Victor Uwaifo, "Guitar Boy and Mamywater," which implies that he gained amazing abilities from a water goddess who speaks through his guitar (24–25). In addition to the examples from Johnson, Smith, and Leadbelly, all giants, there is massive evidence that the blues are about spirits in their continual references to African lore. Gates lists eight blues artists who have recorded titles that mention Signifying (*Signifying* 51), but he does not get to songs that focus on signifying though it is not in the title, such as "Don't Start Me Talking" (1955), by Rice "Sonny Boy Williamson" Miller. Cripple Clarence Lofton refers to "goopher dust," a powder that bears a spell; and many bards—including Blind Willie McTell, Sam "Lightning" Hopkins, and McKinley "Muddy Waters" Morganfield—refer to a *mojo*, a magic object. Walter Page's Blue Devils was an important jazz band that broke up in 1931 (Wynn 509).

5. Larson (468) indicates that these lines are spoken by the title character of a story, "Sarzan," who attempts to destroy his village's sacred idols, but ends up being possessed by spirits and losing his mind. Despite the disturbing context, both Jahn and Larson see the lines as suggesting typical views.

6. The pushme-pullyou is an imaginary quadruped with a head at both ends in the children's classic *The Story of Doctor Dolittle* by Hugh Lofting.

7. Samuel Eliot Morison says, "Altogether, the thirty years from 1890 to 1920 were the darkest for the dark people of America," and notes that from 1889 to 1918, 2,522 African Americans were lynched (793). This is a conservative figure. Williamson claims at least 2,000 lynchings in the South alone in the shorter period of 1889–1909, and there were many in other parts of the country (161). Moreover, African Americans who returned from World War I and objected to humiliation set off massacres around the country from 1919 through the 1920s. Two bad ones were the destruction of Rosewood, Florida, in 1923 and the riot in Tulsa in 1921 in which some 300 African Americans were slaughtered (Staples).

8. In "Daughters Signifyin(g) History," Ashraf H. A. Rushdy sees that in slavery, "you have to kill what you love most" (Andrews and McKay 46).

9. This idea was given to me by two black undergraduate students, Kemie King and Raquel Morrison, in a 1997 class.

10. The usage appears in "Some Kind of Wonderful," a song by Carole King recorded by Buddy Guy.

11. North shows that the idea of Standard English was developed late in the nineteenth century to protect pure Anglo-Saxon language from pollution by the dialects of racially inferior groups (13–18).

12. "Virginia Woolf's and William Faulkner's Treatment of the Alienated," master's thesis, Cornell University, 1955.

13. Yvonne Atkinson analyzes the use of Ebonics in "The Black English Oral Tradition in

Beloved: 'listen to the spaces,'" in Solomon 247–60. She focuses on rhetorical devices—Call/ Response, Signifyin [the correct spelling?], and Witness/Testify—that help Morrison to convey what is unspeakable in black experience so as to resist racism.

14. The best dictionary of Black English that I know of is Clarence Major's *Juba to Jive: A Dictionary of African American Slang* (1994). It is over four hundred pages long, but still rather spotty compared to a good Standard English dictionary. It has little in the way of derivations, yet is a good step toward expanding the Black Symbolic. Also valuable, though shorter, is Smitherman's *Black Talk,* revised in 2000.

15. The poetic position of Beloved in the first paragraph of the coda reminds me of the first stanza of Rainer Maria Rilke's "Die Einsamkeit" ("Loneliness," 1906), which personifies loneliness as the spirit of water, who goes through a cycle of rising and falling:

> Loneliness is like the rain
> She rises from the sea toward the evening
> And from the far-off plain ascends again
> To heaven, who has her always.

I have modified the translation of "Die Einsamkeit" by Kate Flores in the Angel Flores anthology 387: "Die Einsamkeit ist wie ein Regen. / Sie steigt vom Meer den Abenden entgegen; / von Ebenen, die fern sind und entlegen, / geht sie zum Himmel, der sie immer hat."

CONCLUSION

1. The two shifts may have been promoted by the two World Wars, both of which worked in somewhat different ways to break down segregation.

2. Bhabha (15–18) and Gilroy (217–22) both treat *Beloved* as postmodern because of its cultural multiplicity. An argument that *Beloved* is postmodern is developed by Rafael Perez Torres in "Between Presence and Absence: *Beloved,* Postmodernism, and Blackness," in Andrews and McKay 179–201. Patell sees Pynchon and Morrison as postmodern because they attack the apolitical stance of modernism (xvii).

3. Two prominent versions of the idea that tragedy precedes comedy appear in Karl Marx and Northrop Frye. Marx says at the start of "The Eighteenth *Brumaire* of Louis Bonaparte" that all great events of history occur twice, "the first time as tragedy, the second as farce" (Marx–Engels 436). Frye, in *Anatomy of Criticism,* presents a sequence of fictional modes in which the tragic is historically followed by the comic (33–48).

4. Jim Holt argues in "Mind of a Rock: Is Everything Conscious?" that in 2007 panpsychism "is enjoying something of a vogue" among philosophers and scientists.

5. Compositions by leading saxophonists of the free jazz movement show a tendency for the avant-garde black sensibility to identify with apparitions: "Spooks," by Archie Shepp, recorded by Marion Brown; "I Talk with the Spirits," by Rahsaan Roland Kirk; "Ghosts," by Albert Ayler; "Spirits in the Field," by Arthur Blythe; and "Spirits Before," by Charles Gayle.

6. I planned to include here a more systematic account of how non-Western languages overturn Western metaphysical assumptions, but left it out because it was too lengthy and complicated. A version of some of this argument appears in my "Borges's *Orbis Tertius.*"

WORKS CITED

Aaron, Daniel. "The South in American History." *The South and Faulkner's Yoknapa-tawpha.* Ed. Evans Harrington and Ann J. Abadie. Jackson: U of Mississippi P, 1977.

Agee, James. *A Death in the Family.* New York: Bantam, 1969.

Andrews, William L., and Nellie Y. McKay, eds. *Toni Morrison's* Beloved: *A Casebook.* New York: Oxford UP, 1999.

Appiah, Kwame Anthony. "Race." *Critical Terms for Literary Study.* 2nd ed. Ed. Frank Lentricchia and Thomas McLaughlin. Chicago: U of Chicago P, 1995. 274–87.

Appiah, Kwame Anthony, and Henry Louis Gates, eds. *The Dictionary of Global Culture.* New York: Knopf, 1997.

Asante, Molefi Kete. *The Afrocentric Idea.* Rev. ed. Philadelphia: Temple U Press, 1998.

Ashcroft, Bill, Gareth Griffiths, and Helen Tiffin, eds. *The Post-Colonial Studies Reader.* New York: Routledge, 1995.

Atkins, Ronald, ed. *All That Jazz: The Illustrated History of Jazz Music.* London: Carlton, 1996.

Atwood, Margaret. *Surfacing.* New York: Ballantine, 1987.

Ayler, Albert. *Spiritual Unity.* ESP Disk LP 1002, 1965.

Baker, Houston A., Jr. *Blues, Ideology, and Afro-American Literature: A Vernacular Theory.* Chicago: U of Chicago P, 1984.

———. *Workings of the Spirit: The Poetics of Afro-American Women's Writing.* Chicago: U of Chicago P, 1991.

Bakhtin, Mikhail M. *The Dialogic Imagination: Four Essays.* Ed. Michael Holquist. Trans. Caryl Emerson and Holquist. Austin: Texas UP, 1981.

—————. *Problems of Dostoevsky's Poetics.* Trans. Caryl Emerson. Minneapolis: U of Minnesota P, 1984.

Baldwin, James. *Notes of a Native Son.* Boston: Beacon Press, 1955.

Baraka, Amiri [Leroi Jones]. Dutchman *and* The Slave: *Two Plays.* New York: Morrow, 1964.

Baraka, Amiri [Leroi Jones], and Fundi [Billy Abernathy]. *In Our Terribleness.* Indianapolis: Bobbs-Merrill, 1970.

Barnett, Pamela E. "Figurations of Rape and the Supernatural in *Beloved.*" *PMLA* 112 (1997): 418–27.

Barthes, Roland. *The Pleasure of the Text.* Trans. Richard Miller. New York: Hill and Wang, 1975.

Baumbach, Jonathan. *The Landscape of Nightmare: Studies in the Contemporary American Novel.* New York: New York UP, 1965.

Behn, Aphra. *Oroonoko, The Rover, and Other Works.* Ed. Janet Todd. London: Penguin, 1992.

Bell, Bernard W. *The Afro-American Novel and Its Tradition.* Amherst: U of Massachusetts P, 1987.

Bellow, Saul. *Henderson the Rain King.* New York: Viking, 1959.

Bennett, Lerone, Jr. *Before the Mayflower: A History of Black America.* 6th ed. Chicago: Johnson, 1987.

Berger, James. "Ghosts of Liberalism: Morrison's *Beloved* and the Moynihan Report." *PMLA* 111 (1996): 408–20.

Bernal, Martin. *Black Athena: The Afroasiatic Roots of Classical Civilization.* 2 vols. London: Free Association Books, 1987, 1991.

Berressem, Hanjo. *Pynchon's Poetics: Interfacing Theory and Text.* Urbana: U of Illinois P, 1993.

Bhabha, Homi K. *The Location of Culture.* New York: Routledge, 1994.

Blake, William. *The Complete Poetry and Prose of William Blake.* Rev. ed. Ed. David V. Erdman. New York: Doubleday, 1988.

Blotner, Joseph. *Faulkner: A Biography.* 2 vols. New York: Random House, 1974.

Blythe, Arthur. "Spirits in the Field." *The Grip.* India Navigation LP 1029, 1977.

Boheemen-Saaf, Christine van. *Joyce, Derrida, Lacan, and the Trauma of History: Reading, Narrative, and Postcolonialism.* Cambridge: Cambridge UP, 1999.

Bone, Robert A. *The Negro Novel in America.* New Haven: Yale UP, 1958.

Bonnet, Michele. " 'To take the sin out of slicing trees': The Law of the Tree in *Beloved.*" *African American Review* 31 (Spring 1997): 41-54.

Borges, Jorge Luis. *Labyrinths: Selected Stories and Other Writings.* Ed. Donald A. Yates and James E. Irby. New York: New Directions, 1964.

Bowie, Malcolm. *Lacan.* Cambridge: Harvard UP, 1991.

Bradbury, Malcolm. 1983. *The Modern American Novel.* New York: Oxford, 1993.

Bradley, David. "On Rereading *Native Son.*" *New York Times Magazine* 7 Dec. 1986: 68–79.

Brignano, Russell Carl. *Richard Wright: An Introduction to the Man and His Works.* Pittsburgh: U of Pittsburgh P, 1970.

Brivic, Sheldon. "Borges' *Orbis Tertius,*" *Massachusetts Review* 16 (Spring 1975): 387–99.

———. "Conflict of Values: Richard Wright's *Native Son.*" *Novel* 7 (Spring 1974): 231–45.

———. *Joyce between Freud and Jung.* Port Washington: Kennikat, 1980.

———. *Joyce's Waking Women: An Introduction to* Finnegans Wake. Madison: U of Wisconsin P, 1995.

Brooks, Cleanth. *William Faulkner: The Yoknapatawpha Country.* New Haven: Yale UP, 1966.

Butler, Judith. *Bodies That Matter: On the Discursive Limits of "Sex."* New York: Routledge, 1993.

———. *Gender Trouble: Feminism and the Subversion of Identity.* New York: Routledge, 1990.

———. *The Psychic Life of Power: Theories in Subjection.* Stanford: Stanford UP, 1997.

Butler, Octavia E. *Kindred.* Boston: Beacon, 1988.

Butler, Robert J., ed. *The Critical Response to Richard Wright.* Westport, CT: Greenwood P, 1995.

Callahan, John F. *In the African-American Grain: The Pursuit of Voice in Twentieth-Century Black Fiction.* Urbana: U of Illinois P, 1988.

Caramagno, Thomas C. *The Flight of the Mind: Virginia Woolf's Art and Manic-Depressive Illness.* Berkeley and Los Angeles: U of California P, 1992.

Carney, Judith A. *Black Rice: The African Origins of Rice Cultivation in the Americas.* Cambridge: Harvard UP, 2005.

Cash, Wilbur J. *The Mind of the South.* New York: Knopf, 1941.

Catton, Bruce. *The American Heritage New History of the Civil War.* Ed. James M. McPherson. New York: Viking, 1996.

Cervantes, Miguel de. *Don Quixote.* Norton Critical Edition. Trans. John Ormsby. Ed. Joseph R. Jones and Kenneth Douglas. New York: Norton, 1981.

Chase, Richard. *The American Novel and Its Tradition.* Garden City, NY: Doubleday Anchor, 1957.

Chesnutt, Charles W. *The Collected Stories of Charles W. Chesnutt.* Ed. William L. Andrews. New York: Mentor, 1992.

Christian, Barbara. "Fixing Methodologies: *Beloved.*" *Cultural Critique* 24 (1993): 5–15.

Cleaver, Eldridge. *Soul on Ice.* New York: Dell Delta, 1969.

Coetzee, Pieter H., and Abraham P. J. Roux, eds. *The African Philosophy Reader.* London: Routledge, 1998.

Cooley, Ronald W. "The Hothouse or the Street: Imperialism and Narrative in Pynchon's *V.*" *Modern Fiction Studies* 39 (1993): 307–25.

Cooper, James Fenimore. *The Last of the Mohicans.* New York: Bantam, 1989.

Crenshaw, Kimberle, Neil Gotanda, Gary Peller, and Kendall Thomas, eds. *Critical Race Theory: The Key Writings That Formed the Movement.* New York: New Press, 1995.

Currie, Elliott. *Crime and Punishment in America.* New York: Holt, 1998.

Davidson, Cathy N. *Revolution and the Word: The Rise of the Novel in America.* New York: Oxford, 1986.

Davis, Angela Y. "Masked Racism: Reflections on the Prison Industrial Complex." In *Race and Resistance: African Americans in the 21st Century.* Ed. Herb Boyd. Cambridge, MA: South End Press, 2002.

Davis, Thadious M. *Faulkner's "Negro": Art and the Southern Context.* Baton Rouge: Louisiana State UP, 1983.

Day, Martin S. *History of English Literature: 1660–1837.* Garden City, NY: Doubleday, 1963.

Deleuze, Gilles, and Felix Guattari. *Kafka: Toward a Minor Literature.* Minneapolis: U of Minnesota P, 1986.

Deleuze, Gilles, and C. Parnet. *Dialogues.* New York: Columbia UP, 1987.

DeLillo, Don. *Underworld.* New York: Simon and Schuster, 1997.

———. *White Noise: Text and Criticism.* Ed. Mark Osteen. New York: Penguin, 1998.

Derrida, Jacques. *Specters of Marx: The State of the Debt, the Work of Mourning, and the New International.* Trans. Peggy Kamuf. New York: Routledge, 1994.

———. "Structure, Sign, and Play in the Discourse of the Human Sciences." *Writing and Difference.* Trans. Alan Bass. Chicago: U of Chicago P, 1978. 278–93.

Dostoyevsky, Fyodor. *Crime and Punishment.* Trans. Constance Garnett. New York: Random House Modern Library, 1950.

Douglass, Frederick. *Narrative of the Life of Frederick Douglass, An American Slave. Slave Narratives.* Ed. William L. Andrews and Henry Louis Gates Jr. New York: New American Library, 2000. 267–423.

Doyle, Don H. *Faulkner's County: The Historical Roots of Yoknapatawpha.* Chapel Hill: U of North Carolina P, 2001.

Drake, St. Clair, and Horace R. Cayton. *Black Metropolis: A Study of Negro Life in a Northern City.* 1945. 2 vols. New York: Harper and Row, 1962.

Dreiser, Theodore. *Short Stories.* New York: Dover, 1994.

Du Bois, William E. B. *The Souls of Black Folk. Three Negro Classics.* Ed. John Hope Franklin. New York: Avon, 1965.

Dubey, Madhu. *Signs and Cities: Black Literary Postmodernism.* Chicago: U of Chicago P, 2003.

Dunaway, Philip, and Mel Evans, eds. *A Treasury of the World's Great Diaries*. Garden City, NY: Doubleday, 1957.

Dylan, Bob. "Chimes of Freedom." *Another Side of Bob Dylan*. Columbia LP 2193, 1964.

Eagleton, Terry. *Literary Theory: An Introduction*. 2nd ed. Minneapolis: Minnesota UP, 1996.

———. *Sweet Violence: The Idea of the Tragic*. Oxford: Blackwell, 2003.

Eliot, Thomas Stearns. "The Metaphysical Poets." *Selected Prose of T. S. Eliot*. Ed. Frank Kermode. New York: Harcourt Brace Jovanovich, 1975. 59–67.

Ellison, Ralph. *Invisible Man*. New York: Vintage, 1972.

Ellmann, Richard. *James Joyce*. Rev. ed.. New York: Oxford UP, 1982.

Equiano, Olaudah. *The Interesting Narrative of the Life of Olaudah Equiano, Written by Himself*. Ed. Robert J. Allison. Boston: Bedford Books, 1995.

Erdrich, Louise. *Tracks*. New York: Holt, 1988.

Fabre, Michel. *The Unfinished Quest of Richard Wright*. 2nd ed. Trans. Isabel Barzun. Urbana: U of Illinois P, 1993.

Fanon, Frantz. *Black Skin, White Masks*. Trans. Charles Lam Markmann. New York: Grove Weidenfield, 1967.

———. *The Wretched of the Earth*. Trans. Constance Farrington. New York: Grove Press, 1968.

Faulkner, William. *Absalom, Absalom!: The Corrected Text*. Ed. Noel Polk. New York: Vintage, 1990.

———. *As I Lay Dying: The Corrected Text*. Ed. Noel Polk. New York: Vintage, 1990.

———. *Faulkner in the University* See Gwynn, Frederick L.

———. *Go Down, Moses*. New York: Vintage, 1973.

———. *Intruder in the Dust*. New York: Signet, 1949.

———. *Light in August: The Corrected Text*. Ed. Noel Polk. New York: Vintage, 1990.

———. *Requiem for a Nun*. New York: Vintage, 1975.

———. *Selected Letters of William Faulkner*. Ed. Joseph Blotner. New York: Vintage, 1978.

———. *The Sound and the Fury*. Ed. David Minter. Norton Critical Edition. 2nd ed. New York: Norton, 1994.

———. *Uncollected Stories of William Faulkner*. Ed. Joseph Blotner. New York: Vintage, 1981.

Fiedler, Leslie A. *Love and Death in the American Novel*. 1960. London: Paladin, 1970.

Fink, Bruce. *The Lacanian Subject: Between Language and Jouissance*. Princeton: Princeton UP, 1995.

Fisher, Dorothy Canfield. Introduction. *Native Son*. By Richard Wright. New York: Modern Library, 1940. ix–xi.

Fishkin, Shelley Fisher. *Was Huck Black? Mark Twain and American Voices.* New York: Oxford UP, 1993.

Fitzgerald, F. Scott. *The Portable F. Scott Fitzgerald.* Ed. Dorothy Parker. New York: Viking, 1945.

Flores, Angel, ed. *An Anthology of German Poetry from Hölderlin to Rilke in English Translation.* Garden City, NY: Doubleday Anchor, 1960.

Forster, Edward Morgan. *Where Angels Fear to Tread.* 1905. New York: Harcourt, Brace, 1958.

Foucault, Michel. *Discipline and Punish: The Birth of the Prison.* Trans. Alan Sheridan. New York: Vintage, 1979.

Fowler, Doreen. *Faulkner: The Return of the Repressed.* Charlottesville: UP of Virginia, 1997.

Fox-Genovese, Elizabeth. *Within the Plantation Household.* Chapel Hill: U of North Carolina P, 1988.

Freud, Sigmund. *The Standard Edition of the Complete Psychological Works of Sigmund Freud.* Ed. and trans. James Strachey et al. 24 vols. London: Hogarth, 1953–74.

Frye, Northrop. *Anatomy of Criticism: Four Essays.* New York: Atheneum, 1966.

Fuller, Jesse. "Stranger Blues." *Brother Lowdown.* Fantasy LP 24704, n.d. (ca. 1968).

Furman, Jan. *Toni Morrison's Fiction.* Columbia: U of South Carolina P, 1996.

Fuston-White Jeanna. " 'From the Seen to the Told': The Construction of Subjectivity in Toni Morrison's *Beloved.*" *African American Review* 36 (Fall 2002): 461–73.

Garcia-Marquez, Gabriel. *One Hundred Years of Solitude.* Trans. Gregory Rabassa. New York: Avon, 1971.

Gates, Henry Louis. " 'Authenticity,' or the Lesson of Little Tree." *New York Times Book Review* 24 Nov. 1991, sec. 7: 1, 26–30.

———, ed. *"Race," Writing, and Difference.* Chicago: U of Chicago P, 1986.

———, ed. *Reading Black, Reading Feminist: A Critical Anthology.* New York: New American Library, 1990.

———. *The Signifying Monkey: A Theory of Afro-American Literary Criticism.* New York: Oxford UP, 1988.

Gates, Henry Louis, and Kwame Anthony Appiah, eds. *Richard Wright: Critical Perspectives, Past and Present.* New York: Amistad, 1993.

Gayle, Addison, Jr. *The Way of the New World: The Black Novel in America.* Garden City, NY: Doubleday Anchor, 1975.

Gayle, Charles. *Charles Gayle Trio: Spirits Before.* Silkheart CD 117, 1988.

Genovese, Eugene D. *Roll, Jordan, Roll: The World the Slaves Made.* New York: Vintage, 1976.

Gilroy, Paul. *Against Race: Imagining Political Culture beyond the Color Line.* Cambridge: Harvard UP, 2000.

———. *The Black Atlantic: Modernity and Double Consciousness*. Cambridge: Harvard UP, 1993.

Girard, René. *Violence and the Sacred*. Trans. Patrick Gregory. Baltimore: Johns Hopkins UP, 1979.

Glissant, Edouard. *Faulkner, Mississippi*. Trans. Barbara Lewis and Thomas C. Spear. Chicago: U of Chicago P, 1999.

Goldberg, Jonah. "A Stand That Lacks Moral Authority." *Philadelphia Inquirer* 18 Aug. 2005: A15.

Grant, J. Kerry. *A Companion to* V. Athens: U of Georgia P, 2001.

Greenblatt, Stephen. *Renaissance Self-Fashioning: From More to Shakespeare*. Chicago: U of Chicago P, 1980.

Grewal, Gurleen. *Circles of Sorrow, Lines of Struggle: The Novels of Toni Morrison*. Baton Rouge: Louisiana State UP, 1998.

Guy, Buddy. "Some Kind of Wonderful." *Feels Like Rain*. Silvertone CD, 1993.

Gwynn, Frederick L., and Joseph Blotner, eds. *Faulkner in the University: Class Conferences at the University of Virginia, 1957–1958*. New York: Vintage, 1959.

Harris, Trudier. *Fiction and Folklore: The Novels of Toni Morrison*. Knoxville: U of Tennessee P, 1991.

Hegel, Georg W. F. *Phenomenology of Spirit*. Trans. A. V. Miller. Oxford: Oxford UP, 1977.

Heinze, Denise. *The Dilemma of "Double Consciousness": Toni Morrison's Novels*. Athens: U of Georgia P, 1995.

Hemingway, Ernest. "The Battler." *In Our Time*. 1925. New York: Scribner's, 1970.

———. *The Garden of Eden*. New York: Collier, 1987.

———. *Green Hills of Africa*. New York: Scribner's, 1935.

———. *To Have and Have Not*. New York: Scribner's, 1937.

Higgins, Therese E. *Religiosity, Cosmology, and Folklore: The African Influence in the Novels of Toni Morrison*. New York: Routledge, 2001.

Hilfer, Tony. *American Fiction since 1940*. London: Longman, 1992.

Hlavsa, Virginia V. "The Vision of the Advocate in *Absalom, Absalom!*" *Novel* 8 (Fall 1974): 51–70.

Hobson, Fred, ed. *William Faulkner's* Absalom, Absalom!: *A Casebook*. New York: Oxford UP, 2003.

Holloway, Joseph E., ed. *Africanisms in American Culture*. Bloomington: Indiana UP, 1991.

Holloway, Karla F. C. "*Beloved:* A Spiritual." *Callaloo* 13 (1990): 516–25.

Holt, Jim. "Mind of a Rock: Is Everything Conscious?" *New York Times Magazine*, 18 November 2007: 19–20.

Holton, Robert. "In the Rathouse of History with Thomas Pynchon: Rereading *V.*" *Textual Practice* 2 (1988): 324–44.

Horkheimer, Max, and Theodor W. Adorno. *Dialectic of Enlightenment*. 1944. Trans. John Cumming. New York: Continuum, 1990.

Horn, Patricia, and Martha Woodall. "Report Identifies Growing Technological Underclass." *Philadelphia Inquirer* 9 July 1999: A1+

Horvitz, Deborah. "Nameless Ghosts: Possession and Dispossession in *Beloved*." *Studies in American Fiction* 17 (1989): 157–67.

House, Eddie James "Son." "Louise McGee." *The Legendary Son House: Father of Folk Blues*. Columbia LP CS 9217, n.d. (ca. 1966).

House, Elizabeth B. "Toni Morrison's Ghost: The Beloved Who Is Not Beloved." *Studies in American Fiction*. 18 (1990): 17–26.

Howard, Gerald. "Rocket Redux." *Bookforum* 12.2 (Summer 2005): 29–40.

Hurston, Zora Neale. *The Sanctified Church*. New York: Marlowe, 1981.

———. *Their Eyes Were Watching God*. New York: Harper Perennial, 1990.

Hyman, Stanley Edgar. "The Goddess and the Schlemihl." *On Contemporary Literature*. Ed. Richard Kostelanetz. New York: Avon, 1964. 506–10.

Irwin, John T. *Doubling and Incest/ Repetition and Revenge: A Speculative Reading of Faulkner*. Baltimore: Johns Hopkins UP, 1975.

Jacobs, Harriet. *Incidents in the Life of a Slave Girl. Slave Narratives*. Ed. William L. Andrews and Henry Louis Gates Jr. New York: Library of America, 2000. 743–947.

Jahn, Janheinz. *Muntu: An Outline of the New African Culture*. Trans. Marjorie Grene. New York: Grove Press, 1961.

James, William. *Pragmatism (Selections)*. Chicago: Henry Regnery, 1953.

Jameson, Fredric. *The Political Unconscious: Narrative as a Socially Symbolic Act*. Ithaca: Cornell UP, 1981.

———. *A Singular Modernity: Essay on the Ontology of the Present*. London: Verso, 2002.

JanMohamed, Abdul R. *The Death-Bound Subject: Richard Wright's Archaeology of Death*. Durham: Duke UP, 2005.

———. "Negating the Negation as a Form of Affirmation in Minority Discourse." *Cultural Critique* 7 (Fall 1987): 245–66.

Jenkins, Lee. *Faulkner and Black-White Relations: A Psychoanalytic Approach*. New York: Columbia UP, 1981.

Johnson, Robert. "Hellhound on My Trail." *The Complete Collection*. Prism Leisure CD PLATCD 278, n.d. (ca. 2000).

Joshi, Priya. *In Another Country: Colonialism, Culture, and the English Novel in India*. New York: Columbia UP, 2003.

Joyce, James. *A Portrait of the Artist as a Young Man*. 1915. New York: Viking, 1964.

———. *Ulysses: The Corrected Text*. Ed. Hans Walter Gabler. New York: Random House, 1986.

Joyce, Joyce Ann. *Richard Wright's Art of Tragedy*. Iowa City: U of Iowa P, 1986.

Kaplan, Amy, and Donald E. Pease, eds. *Cultures of United States Imperialism.* Durham: Duke UP, 1993.

Karl, Frederick R. *American Fictions, 1940–1980: A Comprehensive History and Critical Evaluation.* New York: Harper and Row, 1983.

Kawin, Bruce F. *Faulkner and Film.* New York: Ungar, 1977.

Kazin, Alfred. *Bright Book of Life: American Novelists and Storytellers from Hemingway to Mailer.* New York: Delta, 1974.

Kelley, Robin D. G. *Freedom Dreams: The Black Radical Imagination.* Boston: Beacon, 2002.

Kemayo, Kamau. *Emerging Afrikan Survivals: An Afrocentric Critical Theory.* New York: Routledge, 2003.

Kincaid, Jamaica. *At the Bottom of the River.* New York: Farrar, Straus and Giroux, 1983.

———. *The Autobiography of My Mother.* New York: Plume, 1997.

Kingston, Maxine Hong. *The Woman Warrior: Memoirs of a Girlhood among Ghosts.* 1976. New York: Vintage, 1989.

Kinnamon, Keneth, ed. *Critical Writings on Richard Wright's* Native Son. New York: Twayne, 1997.

Kinnamon, Keneth, and Michel Fabre, eds. *Conversations with Richard Wright.* Jackson: UP of Mississippi, 1993

Kinney, Arthur F., ed. *Critical Essays on William Faulkner: The Sutpen Family.* New York: Hall, 1996.

Kirk, Roland. *I Talk with the Spirits.* Limelight LP LM 82008, 1965.

Kristeva, Julia. *Powers of Horror: An Essay on Abjection.* Trans. Leon Roudiez. New York: Columbia UP, 1982.

Kubik, Gerhard. *Africa and the Blues.* Jackson: U of Mississippi P, 1999.

Kuyk, Dirk, Jr. *Sutpen's Design: Interpreting Faulkner's* Absalom, Absalom! Charlottesville: UP of Virginia, 1990.

Lacan, Jacques. *Anxiety, 1962–1963: The Seminar of Jacques Lacan, Book 10.* Trans. Cormac Gallagher from unedited manuscripts. For private use only. Unofficially published in Ireland around 1997.

———. *Écrits: A Selection.* Trans. Bruce Fink, in collaboration with Heloise Fink and Russell Grigg. New York: Norton, 2002.

———. *Encore.* See *On Feminine Sexuality.*

———. *The Ethics of Psychoanalysis, 1959–1960: The Seminar of Jacques Lacan, Book 7.* Ed. Jacques-Alain Miller. Trans. Dennis Porter. New York: Norton, 1992.

———. *The Four Fundamental Concepts of Psycho-Analysis* [The Seminar of Jacques Lacan, Book 11]. Ed. Jacques-Alain Miller. Trans. Alan Sheridan. New York: Norton, 1981.

———. *On Feminine Sexuality, The Limits of Love and Knowledge, 1972–1973: The Semi-*

nar of Jacques Lacan, Book 20 (*Encore*). Ed. Jacques-Alain Miller. Trans. Bruce Fink. New York: Norton, 1998.

———. *The Other Side of Psychoanalysis: The Seminar of Jacques Lacan, Book 17*. Ed. Jacques-Alain Miller. Trans. Russell Grigg. New York: Norton, 2007.

Lacan, Jacques, and the École Freudienne. *Feminine Sexuality*. Ed. Juliet Mitchell and Jacqueline Rose. New York: Norton, 1985.

Larson, Charles R. "Heroic Ethnocentrism: The Idea of Universality in Literature." *American Scholar* 42 (1973): 463–75.

Leadbelly [Huddy Ledbetter]. "Good Morning Blues." *Lead Belly: Where Did You Sleep Last Night?* Smithsonian Folkways CD SFCD 40044, n.d. (ca. 1998).

Lemaire, Anika. *Jacques Lacan*. Trans. David Macey. London: Routledge and Kegan Paul, 1977.

Levine, George, and David Leverenz, eds. *Mindful Pleasures: Essays on Thomas Pynchon*. Boston: Little, Brown, 1976.

Lewis, Richard W. B. *The American Adam: Innocence, Tragedy and Tradition in the Nineteenth Century*. Chicago: U of Chicago P, 1955.

Lewis, Walter "Furry." "I Will Turn Your Money Green." *Done Changed My Mind*. Prestige Bluesville BV 1037. LP, n.d. (ca. 1961).

———. "Kassie Jones, Part Two." *Furry Lewis in His Prime, 1927–28*. Arhoolie LP, n.d. (ca. 1970).

Lind, Michael. *The Next American Nation: The New Nationalism and the Fourth American Revolution*. New York: Free Press, 1995.

Lyotard, Jean-Francois. *The Differend: Phrases in Dispute*. Trans. Georges Van Den Abbeele. Minneapolis: U of Minnesota P, 1988.

———. *The Postmodern Condition: A Report on Knowledge*. Trans. Geoff Bennington and Brian Massumi. Minneapolis: U of Minnesota P, 1984.

Macksey, Richard, and Frank E. Moorer, eds. *Richard Wright; A Collection of Critical Essays*. Englewood Cliffs: Prentice-Hall, 1984.

Madsen, Deborah L. *The Postmodern Allegories of Thomas Pynchon*. New York: St. Martin's Press, 1991.

Magistrale, Tony. "From St. Petersburg to Chicago: Wright's *Crime and Punishment*." *Comparative Literature Studies* 23 (Spring 1986): 59–70.

Magona, Sindiwe. "My Role as a South African Woman Writer." Lecture, Temple University. October 1998.

Mailer, Norman. "The White Negro: Superficial Reflections on the Hipster." *Advertisements for Myself*. New York: Signet, 1959. 302–22.

Major, Clarence. *Juba to Jive: A Dictionary of African-American Slang*. New York: Penguin, 1994.

Marx, Karl, and Friedrich Engels. *The Marx–Engels Reader*. Ed. Robert C. Tucker. New York: Norton, 1972.

Mattesich, Stefan. *Lines of Flight: Discursive Time and Countercultural Desire in the Works of Thomas Pynchon.* Durham: Duke UP, 2002.

Matus, Jill. *Toni Morrison.* Manchester: Manchester UP, 1998.

Mbalia, Doreatha Drummond. *Toni Morrison's Developing Class Consciousness.* 2nd ed. Selinsgrove: Susquehanna UP, 2004.

Mbiti, John S. *African Religions and Philosophy.* 2nd ed. Oxford: Heinemann, 1990.

McBride, Dwight A. "Speaking the Unspeakable: On Toni Morrison, African American Intellectuals, and the Uses of Essentialist Rhetoric." *Toni Morrison: Critical and Theoretical Approaches.* Ed. Nancy J. Peterson. Baltimore: Johns Hopkins UP, 1997. 131–52.

McGee, Patrick. *Telling the Other: The Question of Value in Modern and Postcolonial Writing.* Ithaca: Cornell UP, 1992.

McKee, Patricia. *Producing American Races: Henry James, William Faulkner, Toni Morrison.* Durham: Duke UP, 1999

McKnight, Reginald. "Confessions of a Wannabe Negro." *Lure and Loathing: Essays on Race, Identity and the Ambivalence of Assimilation.* Ed. Gerald Early. New York: Allen Lane/Penguin, 1993. 95–111.

McTell, Blind Willie. *Blind Willie McTell: 1940.* Melodeon LP MLP 7372, 1961.

Mezzacappa, Dale. "Study: Pa. Schooling Is Highly Segregated." *Philadelphia Inquirer* 20 July 2001: B1, 5.

Michaels. Walter Benn. *Our America: Nativism, Modernism, and Pluralism.* Durham: Duke UP, 1995.

Miller, Eugene E. *Voice of a Native Son: The Poetics of Richard Wright.* Jackson: U of Mississippi P, 1990.

Minter, David. *A Cultural History of the American Novel: Henry James to William Faulkner* Cambridge: Cambridge UP, 1994.

———. *Faulkner's Questioning Narratives: Fiction of His Major Phase, 1929–42.* Urbana: U of Illinois P, 2001.

Mishkin, Tracy. *The Harlem and Irish Renaissances: Language, Identity, and Representation.* Gainesville: UP of Florida, 1998.

Mobley, Marilyn Sanders. "A Different Remembering: Memory, History and Meaning in Toni Morrison's *Beloved.*" *Toni Morrison.* Ed. Harold Bloom. New York: Chelsea House, 1990. 189–99.

Moglen, Helene. "Redeeming History." *Cultural Critique* 24 (Spring 1993): 17–39.

Mohanty, Satya P. "The Epistemic Status of Cultural Identity: On *Beloved* and the Postcolonial Condition." *Cultural Critique* 24 (Spring 1993): 41–66.

Morison, Samuel Eliot. *The Oxford History of the American People.* New York: Oxford UP, 1965.

Morrison, Toni. *Beloved.* New York: Vintage, 2004.

———. *The Bluest Eye.* New York: Plume, 1994.

————. *Conversations with Toni Morrison.* See Taylor-Guthrie.

————. "Home." *New Bones: Contemporary Black Writers in America.* Ed. Kevin Everod Quashie, Joyce Lausch, and Keith D. Miller. Upper Saddle River, NJ: Prentice Hall, 2001.

————. Interview with Wendy Steiner. Free Library of Philadelphia. 7 Nov. 1996.

————. *Love.* New York: Knopf, 2003.

————. *Paradise.* New York: Knopf, 1997.

————. *Playing in the Dark: Whiteness and the Literary Imagination.* New York: Vintage, 1993.

————. "Rootedness: The Ancestor as Foundation." *Black Women Writers, 1950–1980: A Critical Evaluation.* Ed. Mari Evans. New York: Doubleday, 1984. 339–45.

————. "The Site of Memory." *Inventing the Truth: The Art and Craft of Memoir.* Ed. William Zinsser. Boston: Houghton Mifflin, 1987. 103–24.

————. *Song of Solomon.* New York: Signet, 1978.

————. *Tar Baby.* New York: Signet, 1983.

————. "Unspeakable Things Unspoken: The Afro-American Presence in American Literature." *Michigan Quarterly Review* 28 (Winter 1989): 1–34.

Muhlenfeld, Elisabeth. *William Faulkner's* Absalom, Absalom!*: A Critical Casebook.* New York: Garland, 1984.

Newman, Robert D. *Understanding Thomas Pynchon.* Columbia: U of South Carolina P, 1986.

Nida, Eugene A., and William A. Smalley. *Introducing Animism.* New York: Friendship Press, 1959.

Nietzsche, Friedrich. *The Birth of Tragedy* and *The Genealogy of Morals.* Trans. Francis Golffing. New York: Doubleday Anchor, 1956.

North, Michael. *The Dialect of Modernism; Race, Language, and Twentieth-Century Literature.* New York: Oxford UP, 1994.

Oates, Joyce Carol. *Because It Is Bitter and Because It Is My Heart.* New York: Plume, 1991.

Olupona, Jacob K., ed. *African Spirituality: Forms, Meanings, and Expressions.* New York: Crossroad, 2000.

Otten, Terry. *The Crime of Innocence in the Fiction of Toni Morrison.* Columbia: U of Missouri P, 1989.

Parker, Robert Dale. *Absalom, Absalom!: The Questioning of Fictions.* Boston: Hall, 1991.

Parrinder, Geoffrey. *African Mythology.* London: Paul Hamlyn, 1967.

Patell, Cyrus R. K. *Negative Liberties: Morrison, Pynchon, and the Problem of Liberal Ideology.* Durham: Duke UP, 2001.

Patterson, Orlando. *Slavery and Social Death: A Comparative Study.* Cambridge: Harvard UP, 1982.

Pearce, Richard. *The Politics of Narration: James Joyce, William Faulkner, and Virginia Woolf.* New Brunswick: Rutgers UP, 1991.

Peterson, Nancy J. *Toni Morrison: Critical and Theoretical Approaches.* Baltimore: Johns Hopkins UP, 1997.

Pinn, Anthony B. *Varieties of African American Religious Experience.* Minneapolis: Fortress Press, 1998.

Plant, Deborah G. *Every Tub Must Sit on Its Own Bottom: The Philosophy and Politics of Zora Neale Hurston.* Urbana: U of Illinois P, 1995.

Plasa, Carl, ed. *Toni Morrison: Beloved.* New York: Columbia UP, 1998.

Polk, Noel. *Children of the Dark House: Text and Context in Faulkner.* Jackson: UP of Mississippi, 1996.

Presberg, Charles D. *Adventures in Paradox: Don Quixote and the Western Tradition.* University Park: Pennsylvania State UP, 2001.

Prince, Mary. *"The History of Mary Prince: A West Indian Slave." Six Women's Slave Narratives.* Ed. William L. Andrews. New York: Oxford UP, 1988.

Pynchon, Thomas. *The Crying of Lot 49.* New York: Harper Perennial, 1986.

———. *Gravity's Rainbow.* New York: Viking, 1973.

———. "A Journey into the Mind of Watts." *New York Times Magazine* 12 June 1966: 34–35, 78, 80–82, 84.

———. *Mason & Dixon.* New York: Holt, 1997.

———. *Slow Learner: Early Stories.* Boston: Little, Brown, 1985.

———. *V.* New York: Harper Perennial, 2005.

Quashie, Kevin Everod, Joyce Lausch, and Keith D. Miller, eds. *New Bones: Contemporary Black Writers in America.* Upper Saddle River, NJ: Prentice Hall, 2001.

Ragan, David Paul. *William Faulkner's Absalom, Absalom! A Critical Study.* Ann Arbor: UMI Research Press, 1984.

Ragland-Sullivan, Ellie. *Jacques Lacan and the Philosophy of Psychoanalysis.* Urbana: U of Illinois P, 1986.

Readings, Bill. *Introducing Lyotard: Art and Politics.* New York: Routledge, 1991.

Reed, Ishmael. *Mumbo Jumbo.* 1972. New York: Atheneum, 1988.

Reed, Kenneth T. *"Native Son:* An American *Crime and Punishment." Studies in Black Literature* 1 (1970): 33–34.

Reeves, Paschal. *Thomas Wolfe's Albatross: Race and Nationality in America.* Athens: U of Georgia P, 1968.

Richard Wright: Black Boy. Videocassette. California Newsreel, n.d. (ca. 1992).

Rivkin, Julie, and Michael Ryan. *Literary Theory: An Anthology.* Oxford: Blackwell, 1998.

Robinson, Marilynne. *Housekeeping.* New York: Farrar, Strauss and Giroux, 1980.

Rose, Jacqueline. "The Imaginary." *The Talking Cure.* Ed. Colin McCabe. London: Macmillan, 1981.

Roth, Phillip. *The Human Stain*. Boston: Houghton Mifflin, 2000.

Rushdie, Salman. *The Ground Beneath Her Feet* New York: Holt, 1999.

Rushdy, Ashraf H. A. "Daughters Signifyin(g) History: The Example of Toni Morrison's *Beloved*." *Toni Morrison's* Beloved*: A Casebook*. Ed. William L. Andrews and Nellie Y. McKay. New York: Oxford, 1999.

Said, Edward W. *Orientalism*. New York: Vintage, 1979.

Sewall, Richard B. *The Vision of Tragedy*. New Haven: Yale UP, 1959.

Shelby, Tommie. *We Who Are Dark: The Philosophical Foundations of Black Solidarity*. Cambridge: Harvard UP, 2005.

Shepp, Archie (composer). "Spooks." *Three for Shepp*. By Marion Brown. Impulse LP A 9139, 1968.

Sheridan, Alan. "Translator's note." Jacques Lacan. *Écrits: A Selection*. Ed. Sheridan. New York: Norton, 1977. vii–xii. For the *Écrits*, see Lacan.

Singal, Daniel J. *William Faulkner: The Making of a Modernist*. Chapel Hill: U of North Carolina P, 1997.

Smith, Bessie. "The Gin House Blues." 1926. *Bessie Smith: Chattanooga Gal*. 4 CDs, Properbox 78. Beckenham, UK: Proper Records, 2004.

Smith, Shawn. *Pynchon and History: Metahistorical Rhetoric and Postmodern Narrative Form in the Novels of Thomas Pynchon*. New York: Routledge, 2005.

Smith, Valerie. "'Circling the Subject': History and Narrative in *Beloved*." *Toni Morrison: Critical Perspectives Past and Present*. Ed. Henry Louis Gates Jr. and K. A. Appiah. New York: Amistad, 1993.

Smitherman, Geneva. *Black Talk: Words and Phrases from the Hood to the Amen Corner*. Rev. ed. Boston: Houghton Mifflin, 2000.

———. *Talkin and Testifyin: The Languages of Black America*. Detroit: Wayne State UP, 1977.

Snead, James A. *Figures of Division: William Faulkner's Major Novels*. London: Methuen, 1986.

Sollors, Werner. *Neither Black Nor White Yet Both: Thematic Explorations of Interracial Literature*. New York: Oxford UP, 1997.

Solomon, Barbara H., ed. *Critical Essays on Toni Morrison's* Beloved. New York: Hall, 1998.

Somé, Malidoma Patrice. *Of Water and the Spirit: Ritual, Magic, and Initiation in the Life of an African Shaman*. New York: Penguin Compass, 1995.

Spillers, Hortense. "'All the Things You Could Be by Now, If Sigmund Freud's Wife Was Your Mother': Psychoanalysis and Race." *African American Literary Theory: A Reader*. Ed. Winston Napier. New York: New York UP, 2000. 580–601.

———. *Black, White, and in Color: Essays on American Literature and Culture*. Chicago: U of Chicago P, 2003.

———. "Mama's Baby, Papa's Maybe: An American Grammar Book." *Diacritics* 17 (Summer 1987): 65–81.

———. "Who Cuts the Border: Some Readings in 'America.'" *Comparative American Identities: Race, Sex, and Nationality in the Modern Text.* Ed. Hortense J. Spillers. New York: Routledge, 1990. 1–16.

Staples, Brent. "Unearthing a Riot." *New York Times Magazine* 19 Dec. 1999, sec. 6: 64–69.

Stein, Gertrude. *Selected Writings of Gertrude Stein.* Ed. Carl Van Vechten. New York: Vintage, 1972.

Stowe, Harriet Beecher. *Uncle Tom's Cabin.* New York: Bantam, 1981.

Streitfeld, David. "Pondering 'Paradise.'" *Philadelphia Inquirer* 19 Jan. 1998, sec. F: 1, 9.

Styron, William. *The Confessions of Nat Turner.* 1957. New York: Bantam, 1981.

Sullivan, Andrew. "This Is a Religious War." *New York Times Magazine* 7 Oct. 2001, sec. 6: 45–47.

Sundquist, Eric J. *Faulkner: The House Divided.* Baltimore: Johns Hopkins UP, 1993.

———. *To Wake the Nations: Race in the Making of American Literature.* Cambridge: Harvard UP, 1993.

Sweeney, James Johnson. *African Sculpture.* Princeton: Princeton UP, 1970.

Sweet Honey in the Rock. "Breath." *Good News.* Flying Fish LP 245, 1981.

Tanner, Tony. *City of Words: American Fiction 1950–1970.* London: Jonathan Cape, 1971.

Tate, Claudia. *Psychoanalysis and Black Novels: Desire and the Protocols of Race.* New York: Oxford UP, 1998.

Taylor-Guthrie, Danille, ed. *Conversations with Toni Morrison.* Jackson: UP of Mississippi, 1994.

Thompson, Robert Farris. *Flash of the Spirit: African and Afro-American Art and Philosophy.* New York: Vintage, 1984.

Toomer, Jean. *Cane* 1923. Ed. Darwin T. Turner. New York: Norton, 1988.

Twain, Mark. *Adventures of Huckleberry Finn.* Comprehensive ed.. New York: Ivy Books, 1996.

Valente, Joseph. *James Joyce and the Problem of Justice; Negotiating Sexual and Colonial Difference.* Cambridge: Cambridge UP, 1995.

Wadlington, Warwick. *Reading Faulknerian Tragedy.* Ithaca: Cornell UP, 1987.

Walcott, Derek. *Omeros.* New York: Farrar, Straus and Giroux, 1990.

Walker, Margaret. *Richard Wright, Daemonic Genius: A Portrait of the Man, a Critical Look at His Work.* New York: Amistad, 1993.

Warren, Robert Penn. *All the King's Men.* 1946. New York: Bantam, 1959.

Watt, Ian. *The Rise of the Novel: Studies in Defoe, Richardson, and Fielding.* Berkeley and Los Angeles: U of California P, 1965.

Weber, Max. *The Protestant Ethic and the Spirit of Capitalism.* Trans. Talcott Parsons. New York: Scribner's, 1958.

Weinstein, Philip M. *Faulkner's Subject: A Cosmos No One Owns.* Cambridge: Cambridge UP, 1992.

———. *What Else But Love?: The Ordeal of Race in Faulkner and Morrison.* New York: Columbia UP, 1996.

Welmers, William E. *African Language Structures.* Berkeley and Los Angeles: U of California P, 1971.

Werner, Craig Hansen. *Paradoxical Resolutions: American Fiction since Joyce.* Urbana: U of Illinois P, 1982.

White, Hayden. *The Content of Form: Narrative Discourse and Historical Representation.* Baltimore: Johns Hopkins UP, 1987.

Wideman, John Edgar. *The Homewood Books.* Pittsburgh: U of Pittsburgh P, 1992.

Williams, James. *Lyotard: Toward a Postmodern Philosophy.* Oxford: Polity Press, 1998.

Williams, John A. *The Most Native of Sons.* New York: Harper and Row, 1970.

Williamson, Joel. *William Faulkner and Southern History.* New York: Oxford, 1993.

Williamson, Sonny Boy II [Rice Miller]. "Don't Start Me Talking." *His Best.* MCA Chess CD CHD 9377, n.d. (ca. 1998).

Witzling, David. "The Sensibility of Postmodern Whiteness in *V.,* or Thomas Pynchon's Identity Problem." *Contemporary Literature* 47.3 (2006): 381–415.

Wolfe, Thomas. *Look Homeward, Angel.* New York: Scribner's, 1929.

Woolf, Virginia. *A Haunted House and Other Short Stories.* New York: Harcourt, Brace, 1944.

———. *Mrs. Dalloway.* San Diego: Harcourt Brace Jovanovich, 1981.

Wright, Richard. *Black Boy (American Hunger): A Record of Childhood and Youth.* New York: Harper Perennial, 1993.

———. *Black Power: A Record of Reactions in a Land of Pathos.* New York: Harper and Brothers, 1954.

———. *Conversations with Richard Wright.* See Kinnamon and Fabre.

———. *Eight Men.* New York: Pyramid, 1969.

———. Foreword. *Blues Fell This Morning: The Meaning of the Blues.* By Paul Oliver. New York: Horizon Press, 1960. vii–xii.

———. Introduction. *Black Metropolis.* By St. Clair Drake and Horace R. Cayton. xvii–xxxiv. See Drake and Cayton.

———. *Lawd Today.* Boston: Northeastern UP, 1993.

———. *Native Son.* The Restored Text. Ed. Arnold Rampersad. New York: Harper Perennial Classics, 1998.

———. *The Outsider.* New York: Harper Perennial, 1993.

———. *Richard Wright Reader.* Ed. Ellen Wright and Michel Fabre. New York: Harper and Row, 1978.

———. *Rite of Passage.* New York: HarperCollins, 1994.

———. *White Man, Listen!* New York: Anchor, 1964.

Wyatt, Jean. "Giving Body to the Word: The Maternal Symbolic in Toni Morrison's *Beloved.*" *PMLA* 108 (May 1993): 474–88.

Wynn, Ron, ed. *All Music Guide to Jazz.* San Francisco: Miller Freeman, 1994.

Yaffe, David. "The Art of the Improvisor: Ornette Coleman." *Nation* 14 May 2007: 39–44.

Žižek, Slavoj. *The Fragile Absolute or, Why Is the Christian Legacy Worth Fighting For?* London: Verso, 2000.

———. *The Metastases of Enjoyment: Six Essays on Woman and Causality.* London: Verso, 1994.

———. *The Sublime Object of Ideology.* London: Verso, 1989.

———. *The Ticklish Subject: The Absent Center of Political Ontology.* London: Verso, 1999.

Aaron, Daniel, 41

Absalom, Absalom!: The Corrected Text
(Faulkner), 6, 16–19, 26, 31–37, 39–41,
43–45, 47, 49–67, 69–71, 76, 78, 100, 107,
109, 116–17, 149, 153, 169, 181, 203–4, 209–
10, 212, 219n1, 219nn3–5, 221n17; Charles
Bon, 26, 35–36, 41–43, 45–48, 50–52,
54–59, 61–65, 67–72, 88, 95, 100, 107,
117–18, 121, 193, 196, 203, 210, 212, 219n2,
220n10, 220n12; Charles Etienne Saint-
Valery Bon, 54–55, 59, 64, 66; Eulalia Bon,
41, 64, 68, 100, 220n10; Jim Bond, 66; Rosa
Coldfield, 38, 41, 49; Quentin Compson,
31–32, 38–39, 43, 45, 54, 58, 60–62, 64–67,
203, 212, 219n2, 220n10, 221n21; Shreve
McCannon, 43, 58, 61–62, 64–69, 212,
220n10, 221n21; Clytemnestra (Clytie)
Sutpen, 49–50, 52, 59–60, 64; Henry Sutpen, 26, 35–36, 41–43, 46–52, 56–59, 61–65,
67, 70, 78, 107, 114, 121, 220n12; Judith Sutpen, 31, 36, 38, 41–42, 48, 50, 58–60, 63,
69–70, 78, 193; Col. Thomas Sutpen, 26, 31,
33–42, 46, 50, 54–55, 57–58, 61–66, 68–70,
72–73, 75–77, 118, 121, 130,167, 202–4, 210,
212, 214, 219n1, 220n8, 220n10, 221n17,
221n21. *See also* Faulkner, William

Adorno, Theodore W., 124

African art: masks, 100–101; multiple perspectives of, 100, 149. *See also* Thompson,
Robert Farris

African culture: attempted eradication of,
99, 175; recovery of, 28, 147, 196, 212; and
southern folklore, 75, 158, 162; transmission of, 4–6, 27, 100, 141, 157, 194, 196; value
of, denied, 40. *See also* Gilroy, Paul; Morrison, Toni; spirits, Afro-Atlantic tradition of

Agamemnon (Aeschylus), 43

Agee, James, 22

Althusser, Louis, 128

American Africanism: in *Beloved,* 144–92;
defined, 148; mentioned, 61; multiple perspectives of, 98–103

Anderson, Sherwood, 16

Andrews, William, 224n2, 225n8, 226n2

Appiah, Kwame Anthony, 19, 73, 96, 160, 222n3

Asante, Molefi Kete, 18

Ashcroft, Bill, 223n6

Atkins, Ronald, 99

Atkinson, Yvonne, 225n13

Atwood, Margaret, 198

Ayler, Albert, 226n5

Whitehead, Colson, 197

Wideman, John Edgar, 197

Williams, James, 214

Williams, John, 92

Williamson, Joel, 16, 34, 44, 66–67, 73, 225n7

Williamson, Sonny Boy, 225n4

Witzling, David, 224n9

Wolfe, Thomas, 22, 219n14

Woolf, Virginia, 43, 153, 180–81, 224n12, 225n12

Wright, Richard, 2, 6–7, 13, 15–16, 18, 21, 26–27, 29, 37, 60, 69–70, 72–77, 79–80, 82–83, 85, 87, 89–94, 96, 98, 100, 103–7, 109, 130, 137, 141, 164, 178, 193–94, 197, 203, 205, 218nn10–11, 221nn1–2, 222n4, 222nn7–10, 222n13, 223n15; and African culture, 72,

75, 104; and de Beauvoir, 89; and Marxism, 27, 37, 91–92, 95, 104, 106; and nationalism, 27–28, 86, 92, 103; and Sartre, 90, 98, 222n10. Works: *Black Boy (American Hunger): A Record of Childhood and Youth,* 16, 21, 26, 73, 222n4; *Black Metropolis,* 92; *Blues Fell This Morning: The Meaning of the Blues,* 100; *Eight Men,* 85; *Lawd Today,* 89; *The Outsider,* 98, 203; *White Man, Listen,* 104–5. See also *Native Son*

Wyatt, Jean, 188, 207

Yaffe, David, 224n12

Yeats, William Butler, 10, 146

Žižek, Slavoj, 14–15, 44, 62, 70, 146, 224n7